About the Author

Donald Rumbelow writes and lectures on crime and London history. He is a former Chair of the Crime Writers' Association. He is a Member of the Institute of Tourist Guiding and a London Blue Badge Guide. He is married and lives in London.

THE COMPLETE
JACK
THE
RIPPER

DONALD RUMBELOW

First published in the UK in 1975 by WH Allen

This edition published in 2013 by Virgin Books,
an imprint of Ebury Publishing

A Random House Group Company

www.randomhouse.co.uk

Addresses for companies within The Random House Group Limited can be
found at www.randomhouse.co.uk/offices.htm

The Random House Group Limited Reg. No. 954009

A CIP catalogue record for this book is available from the British Library

Penguin Random House is committed to a sustainable future for
our business, our readers and our planet. This book is made from
Forest Stewardship Council® certified paper.

Printed and bound in Great Britain by Clays Ltd, Elcograf S.p.A.

ISBN: 9780753541500

To Molly

'This is 1888 isn't it? I knew I was Jack. Hats off. I said Jack. I'm Jack, cunning Jack, quiet Jack. Jack's my name. Jack whose sword never sleeps. Hats off I'm Jack, not the Good Shepherd, not the Prince of Peace. I'm Red Jack, Springheeled Jack, Saucy Jack, Jack from Hell, trade-name Jack the Ripper!'

Peter Barnes, *The Ruling Class*

Contents

Foreword to the 2013 Edition

Among the updates for this edition I have deleted Timothy Donovan, for a long time my own suspect, who like Oscar Wilde's Bunbury has been completely exploded by new information. More controversially I have included a photograph (a detail taken from a group photograph taken at Leman Street police station when he was stationed there) of Inspector Abberline himself. This inclusion is controversial as no portrait photograph is known to exist, we have only drawings, and I have included one for comparison, but the hat, face, long side whiskers and moustache, and clean shaven chin, convinces me that we do have here a photograph, once described as the Holy Grail of Ripperology, of the man himself.

Equally controversial, I have argued that 'Long Liz' Stride was not a Ripper victim.

The letters and correspondence regarding the murders received by the City of London Police, which I deposited in the Guildhall Records Office, can now be found in the London Metropolitan Archives. A complete list can be found in Appendix 2 of *Jack the Ripper: Scotland Yard Investigates* which was written in collaboration with Stewart P. Evans.

Once more I must thank Stewart Evans for all his ever-generous help and advice. Thanks too to Rosie, his wife, who steered me through the troublesome and difficult shoals of Powerpoint. Thanks likewise to my wife Molly who gave 'gentle guidance'.

Donald Rumbelow 2013

1. Outcast London

'This street is in the East End': so begins Arthur Morrison's *Tales of Mean Streets*, which is about life at the end of the nineteenth century.

There is no need to say in the East End of what. The East End is a vast city, as famous in its way as any the hand of man has made. But who knows the East End? It is down through Cornhill and out beyond Leadenhall Street and Aldgate Pump, one will say; a shocking place, where he once went with a curate; an evil plexus of slums that hide human creeping things; where filthy men and women live on penn'orths of gin, where collars and clean shirts are decencies unknown, where every citizen wears a black eye, and none ever combs his hair. The East End is a place, says another, which is given over to the Unemployed. And the Unemployed is a race whose token is a clay pipe, and whose enemy is soap; now and again it migrates bodily to Hyde Park with banners, and furnishes adjacent police courts with disorderly drunks. Still another knows the East End only as the place whence begging letters come; there are coal and blanket funds there, all perennially insolvent, and everybody else wants a day in the country. Many and misty are people's notions of the East End; and each is commonly but the distorted shadow of a minor feature.

To the average Victorian the East End was outcast London. There was a feeling that it was separated from the rest of the metropolis geographically as well as spiritually and economically. Its people were as strange as the African pygmies and the Polynesian natives with whom they were often equated by journalists and sociologists who wished to draw attention to its problems. So little was known about them, until slumming became fashionable in the 1870s and 1880s, that an educated woman who was visiting St George's-in-the-East in the 1870s remarked with some astonishment on the fact that the people didn't sleep squatting against a wall, and that they lived in houses and not in railway carriages, as she had expected.

For the greater part of Victoria's reign, the East End was ignored by the Church. Occasional lip service was paid to the needs of the 'lapsed masses' but very little practical help was given them. An impact was beginning to be made on some of the area's major social problems by philanthropists and private charities when the Revd Samuel Barnett and his wife moved to St Jude's vicarage in 1873. The previous incumbent was still in residence and too ill to be moved, so they were forced to take temporary lodgings nearby. The landlady had some careless habits: she apologized one day for not serving Mr Barnett his usual rice pudding as a mouse had drowned in it. Many years later, there was still a rasp in Mrs Barnett's voice when she retold the story for her memoirs.

Their church, St Jude's, was an isolated and empty one. At the first Sunday service there was a congregation of six or seven old women who all expected some dole for attending. The newly hired organist played tunes on a damp-stained piano and Mrs Barnett, who could not sing a note in tune, led the hymn singing. Most of their parishioners had been lured away by the Sunday street market in Middlesex Street (Petticoat Lane), where card sharps, thimble riggers and swindlers of all sorts, as well as men seeking casual work, went in their thousands hoping to get enough money to see them through the week. Equally disgraceful to Mrs Barnett were the herds of cattle goaded through the streets of Whitechapel each week to the slaughterhouses in and around Aldgate. Sometimes the horns would catch in the spokes of moving wheels and the animals, maddened with pain and fear, would scramble onto the pavement scattering the crowds. At the slaughterhouses, which were often ordinary shops, the sheep would be dragged in backwards by their legs and the bullocks hounded in by dogs and blows, while small boys clustered excitedly round the door and passers-by stepped as best they could through the blood and urine flooding the pavement.

Mr Barnett's parish was bounded by the City on the west and Whitechapel High Street, where there were forty shopkeepers and their families, on the south. Apart from the lessees of some large warehouses in Commercial Street and several rows of well-kept cottages tenanted by Jews, the bulk of his parishioners were crowded into a network of courts and alleys, none of which was intersected by any roads. All these courts stank from the accumulated piles of rags and rubbish and a miasma of liquid sewage that flooded the cellars of the houses. At the end of each court there might be a solitary standpipe, the only source of fresh water.

Most of the rooms in these houses were let out to single families at eightpence a night. In 1883 the chairman of the London School Board reported that out of three schools with children from 1,129 families, 871 families had only one room to live in and in the majority of cases the number of people sharing with them was as many as five and sometimes as high as nine.

The broken windows were frequently stuffed with rags or covered with papers (they were rarely opened because of the smells outside, and because the wretches who lived there were badly clothed and couldn't be exposed to draughts. In Wentworth Street, a daily procession of wagons carted their uncovered piles of rubbish to the dust destructor which Mrs Barnett renamed the dust distributor because of the clouds of dust it vomited out and the way it choked the drains.) In some cases, even such inadequate window 'repairs' might be enough to justify the landlord's charging an extra threepence a week for rent. In the house at 35 Hanbury Street, typical of the parish, there were seven people in each room with adult sons and daughters sleeping on the floor. In none of the rooms was there more than one bedstead, and the only w.c. was on the ground floor. This was normally in such a filthy state that the tenants used their chamber pots which, said the Revd R. C. Billing giving evidence to a House of Commons Select Committee, were left in the rooms for a very long time before being taken down and emptied in the yard. Staircase banisters had often been removed for firewood and it was a common sight to see vermin-infested wallpaper hanging in strips from the walls. What furniture there was might consist of the broken-down remains of an old bedstead or table but was more likely to be a wooden board across some bricks, or an old hamper or box turned upside down; the bed might be a sack of flea-infested straw.

Andrew Mearns in *The Bitter Cry of Outcast London* pulled few punches:

Every room in these rotten and reeking tenements houses a family, often two. In one cellar a sanitary inspector reports finding a father, mother, three children, and four pigs! In another room a missionary found a man ill with small-pox, his wife just recovering from her eighth confinement, and the children running about half naked and covered with dirt. Here are seven people living in one underground kitchen, and a little dead child lying in the same room. Elsewhere is a poor widow, her three children, and a child who had been dead thirteen days. Her husband, who was a cabman, had shortly before committed suicide. Here lives a widow and her six children, two of them who are ill with scarlet fever. In another, nine brothers and sisters, from 29 years of age downwards, live, eat and sleep together. Here is a mother who turns her children into the street in the early evening because she lets her room for immoral purposes until long after midnight, when the poor little wretches creep back again if they have not found some miserable shelter elsewhere. Where there are beds they are simply heaps of dirty rags, shavings or straw, but for the most part these miserable beings find rest only upon the filthy boards. The tenant of this room is a widow, who herself occupies the only bed, and lets the floor to a married couple for 2s. 6d. per week. In many cases matters are made worse by the unhealthy occupations followed by those who dwell in these habitations. Here you are choked as you enter by the air laden with particles of the superfluous fur pulled from the skins of rabbits, rats, dogs and other animals in their preparation for the furrier. Here the smell of paste and of drying match-boxes, mingling with other sickly odours, overpowers you; or it may be the fragrance of stale fish or vegetables, not sold on the previous day, and kept in the room overnight. Even when it is possible to do so the people seldom open their windows, but if they did it is questionable whether much would be gained, for the external air is scarcely less heavily charged with poison than the atmosphere within.

The population of Whitechapel was about 80,000 people. For the East End as a whole the figure was about 900,000. Charles Booth, author of *Life and Labour of the People in London*, broke these figures down into several categories. At the bottom were the occasional labourers, loafers and semi-criminals. Above them were the very poor and the poor. The poor he defined as those who had a meagre but regular income of between eighteen shillings and twenty-one shillings a week, and the very poor were those whose income fell below this level. The former struggled to make both ends meet and the latter lived in a state of chronic want. The condition of the lowest class of all, which doesn't get a name, can be imagined. At a rough guess there were about 11,000 of them – about 1¼ per cent of the total population. This figure includes the 'dossers' and the homeless outcasts who slept on staircases, in doorways and even in dustbins and lavatories for warmth. Their lives, Booth said, were the lives of savages, 'with vicissitudes of extreme hardship and occasional excess'. It was not easy to say how they lived. When they could not find threepence for a night's lodging they were turned out onto the street. Booth wrote of them: 'They render no useful service, they create no wealth; more often they destroy it. They degrade whatever they touch, and as individuals are perhaps incapable of improvement.' Their children were often the ragged street arabs who might be found, separated from their parents, in pauper schools or in homes such as Dr Barnardo's.

The very poor added up to about 100,000 or 11¼ per cent of the East End's population. Three-quarters of them were women and children; children under fifteen numbered about 38,000 and young persons aged between fifteen and twenty about 9,000. This category lay between the hammer and the anvil of the outcast poor and the poor. When trade was bad the market was flooded with labour from the categories above, so the casual earnings for which they fought to exist were liable to disappear completely. The women often worked for people as poor as themselves, scrubbing floors, washing and doing needlework.

The poor numbered about 75,000, or 8 per cent of the population. This category consisted of men whose jobs were seasonal, such as builders who could work only eight or nine months in the year, or dockers, who might get only one or two days' work a week. Included too were the other victims of a competitive market, the poorer artisans, street sellers and small shopkeepers. Some of the men on casual work could earn as much as fifteen or twenty shillings a week by heaving coal, carrying grain or carting timber, but often this was done at the cost of great physical exhaustion resulting in very heavy eating and drinking and with little money left over at the end of the day to take home. Booth wrote:

The poor fellows are miserably clad, scarcely with a boot on their foot, in a most miserable state; and they cannot run, their boots would not permit them ... there are men who come on to work in our docks (and if with us, to a much greater extent elsewhere) who have come on without having a bit of food in their stomachs, perhaps since the previous day; they have worked for an hour and have earned 5d. in order that they may get food, perhaps the first food they have had for 24 hours. Many people complain about dock labourers that they will not work after four o'clock. But really, if you consider, it is natural. These poor men come on work without a farthing in their pockets; they have not anything to eat in the middle of the day; some of them will raise or have a penny, and buy a little fried fish, and by 4 p.m. their strength is utterly gone; they pay themselves off; it is absolute necessity that compels them.

The commonest work was sweatshop tailoring. For trouser finishing (sewing in linings, making button holes and stitching on the buttons) a woman might get twopence ha'penny a pair and have to buy her own thread. For making men's shorts they were paid tenpence a dozen, lawn tennis aprons threepence a dozen, and babies' hoods from 1s. 6d. to 2s. 6d. a dozen. In St George's-in-the-East women and children, some only seven years old, were employed as sackmakers and earning a farthing for each one they made. Sometimes women could earn a penny or twopence a peck by shelling peas, or twopence farthing a gross matchbox making, but out of this they would have to buy the string and the paste. None of these earnings would give them more than tenpence or a shilling a day, and might mean seventeen hours' work.

Life in such circumstances had to be lived on a day-to-day or, better still, an hourly basis. Food was bought for immediate consumption. In one family, Booth found, they would buy nothing until it was actually needed. 'They go to their shop as an ordinary housewife to her canisters; twice a day they buy tea, or three times if they make it so often; in 35 days they made 72 purchases of tea, amounting in all to 5s. 2¾d., and all most carefully noted down. The "pinch of tea" costs ¾d. [no doubt this was ½ oz. at 2s. per lb.]. Of sugar there were 77 purchases in the same time.'

Couples could struggle along on a hand-to-mouth existence until children came along. (The most common forms of contraception were syringeing, the vaginal sponge, coitus interruptus and the safe period.) Most children were physically and mentally underdeveloped – those who did not die at birth, that is. Fifty-five per cent of East End children died before they were five. One tenth of elementary school pupils were estimated later to be mentally defective or unnaturally dull. Children frequently came to school crying with hunger and fell off their seats from exhaustion. In winter they could not learn because they were too cold.

Some sort of financial relief was always expected from the Church when times were hardest. The Revd Barnett made it plain from the beginning that nothing could be expected from him. Indiscriminate charity, he argued, was one of the curses of London, and he went so far as to claim that the poor starved 'because of the alms they receive'. Demands for money were often accompanied by lies and followed by threats of violence when it was not forthcoming. Frequently the vicarage was under siege and had its windows broken with stones, and eventually a door had to be cut into the church so that the vicar could have an escape route to fetch police reinforcements. His inflexibility on this point was based on a firm belief that suffering would be reduced not by indiscriminately handing out money but only by making a realistic appraisal of each man's problems and then giving practical help to meet them. In its simplest form this was an exhortation to thrift and better money management but, as the American novelist Jack London angrily pointed out in *The People of the Abyss*, his account of several weeks spent in the East End, to be thrifty the man had 'to spend less than his income – in other words to live on less'. He went on:

This is equivalent to a lowering of the standard of living. In the competition for a chance to work, the man with a lower standard of living will underbid the man with a higher standard. And a small group of such thrifty workers in any overcrowded industry will permanently lower the wages of that industry. And the thrifty ones will no longer be thrifty, for their income will have been reduced till it balances their expenditure. In short, thrift negates thrift . . . And anyway, it is sheer bosh and nonsense to preach thrift to the 1,800,000 London workers, who are divided into families which have a total income of less than 21s. per week, one-quarter to one-half of which must be paid for rent.

A start was made on the problems of overcrowding with the passing of the Artisans Dwelling Act in 1875. This Act empowered the two governing bodies for London, the City of London Corporation (for the one square mile only) and the Metropolitan Board, to buy up slum property, demolish it and resell the land for working-class accommodation. The actual financing of the new properties was left to the commercial dwelling companies and private philanthropists. In no way was the scheme meant to impinge on the widely held belief that it was wrong for the state to finance schemes for people who, for whatever reason, hadn't practised the principles of self-help.

The next year, in Whitechapel alone, four thousand homes were condemned as uninhabitable. Demolitions did not take place for another four years and, in the meantime, until they were evicted, the tenants suffered even more than usual as their living conditions steadily deteriorated and the landlords refused to carry out repairs. Ironically, it was soon realized that the Act, instead of penalizing the slum landlords, would leave them even better off than before. Profits were so great that there was a rash of speculation in slum property which even tempted some of the reformers who had been urging for years that the properties they were now buying should be pulled down. Compensation had to take into account all the factors affecting the value. This was an open incitement to the landlords to cram even more people into their crumbling tenements and to claim even more by way of lost rents. In the Goulston Street scheme in Whitechapel, the property and land was bought for £371,600 but, because of the conditions imposed by Parliament under which it had to be sold, the auction price when it was resold was a meagre £87,600. The overall loss was catastrophic. Forty-two acres had been bought for £1,661,372. The loss, because the land was sold for homes and not for offices, was a staggering £1,100,000.

Within a very short time, both the City of London Corporation and the Metropolitan Board were urging that the terms of the Act should be changed and that they should not have to sell the land for unprofitable housing. In two years nearly two thousand people had been cleared out from the slums on the northern fringe of the City, an area so tough, it was said, that no policeman would dare enter it at night. The sites were left vacant. The City refused to sell them for housing because the commercial value was so high. In 1879 the Act was amended to allow the two authorities to rehouse those whom they had evicted from elsewhere. In reality, they only added to the overcrowding.

In October 1888, the Bell Lane area in Spitalfields was called the worst area in the whole of London. Its epicenter was Dorset Street where four of the Rippers victims – Chapman, Stride, Kelly and Eddowes – lodged at different times. This plague spot, so it was contemporaneously described, gave slum shelter to a gross overcrowding of more than 800 persons per acre. Such a figure, in the heart of the Ripper's killing ground, was horrendously disproportionate to the Whitechapel district as a whole which was of 176 persons per acre while for the metropolis as a whole it was 50 persons per acre.

In the meantime, private philanthropists such as Octavia Hill were buying up properties and finding ways of making them yield a steady 5 per cent return. There was still the same gross overcrowding in these properties but there was at least a security of tenure for the better-off artisan. But this was dependent on prompt payment of rent. Failure to pay, for any reason, meant instant eviction. Yet it was only by occasionally evading payment or going hungry that they could afford to buy clothes and necessary household items. The philanthropists viewed the problem quite differently. They thought that these ruthless methods would force the tenants to practise those principles of thrift that were always being advocated by Mr Barnett and the lady rent collectors who called each week. Unfortunately, it did not allow for the frequent periods when the men were laid off work, not through any fault of their own but through trade recession or seasonal slackness. For the better-off artisan, there was a chance that, in the long term, he would be able to move out of his one room into two, and that his children could be trained for something better. This was the only level at which this scheme might have worked. No figures are available for the number of failures and evictions, but probably they were quite high. Others who tried to work the same scheme did not have much success. One landlord complained bitterly of the dirty and destructive habits of the low strata of humanity he had been forced to accept as tenants. Lamentably, none of them had absorbed the principles of self-help.

Most of those who had been displaced by the redevelopments and clearances were dockers, costermongers, watermen and lightermen. Some were offered accommodation in the model Peabody dwellings but few of them could pay the high rent of four shillings a week. Instead they were forced to pack into already overcrowded accommodation or live on the streets and sleep, when they had the money, in the common lodging houses or seek refuge in the workhouse. In the summer months many of them slept out of doors, but between November and April the streets were generally clear. Even then, there was always a residue left, as Jack London discovered when he visited Christchurch Gardens, Spitalfields, nearly thirty years later:

A chill, raw wind was blowing, and these creatures huddled there in their rags, sleeping for the most part, or trying to sleep. Here were a dozen women, ranging in age from twenty years to seventy. Next a babe, possibly of nine months, lying asleep, flat on the hard bench, with neither pillow nor covering, nor with anyone looking after it. Next, half-a-dozen men, sleeping bolt upright or leaning against one another in their sleep. In one place a family group, a child asleep in its sleeping mother's arms, and the husband (or male mate) clumsily mending a dilapidated shoe.

On another bench a woman trimming the frayed strips of her rags with a knife, and another woman, with thread and needle, sewing up rents. Adjoining, a man holding a sleeping woman in his arms. Farther on, a man, his clothing caked with gutter mud, asleep, with head in the lap of a woman, not more than twenty-five years old, and also asleep.

The women, his guide told him, would sell themselves 'for thru'pence, or tu'pence, or a loaf of stale bread'. To illustrate the value put on these women's bodies, six eggs could be bought for 5d. or 6d., a pint of milk or beer for 2d. and a pound of cheese for 7½d. So a man would pay more for half a pound of cheese than he would for sex with one of these women.

The Lancet, in fact, had estimated that in 1857 one house in every sixty in London was a brothel and one woman in every sixteen a whore. If true, this meant that there were six thousand brothels in the capital and about eighty thousand prostitutes.

In October 1888, the Metropolitan Police estimated that there were about twelve hundred prostitutes, of a very low class, in Whitechapel. From figures supplied by the beat men they thought that there were about sixty-two brothels. Probably there was an even greater number of houses that were being used intermittently for the same purpose. Until fairly recently it had always been customary for several prostitutes to share the cost of hiring a lodging-house room to which they could take men. In 1851 a new Act made such hirings almost impossible, since its terms gave the police the right to search the common lodging houses. If exposed, the owners and keepers risked criminal charges of keeping or permitting a disorderly house. Although prostitutes continued to take customers to the lodging houses, things weren't quite so blatant as before. Generally couples just shared a double bed. They had very little privacy. The beds were in the dormitories and had screens or partitions, open at the top and bottom, pulled around them. Naturally the women preferred renting a room in a private house, if they could afford it as, quite apart from the privacy afforded, the police did not have immediate right of entry into private property. Any prosecutions had to be carried out by the local vestries, but this could be a very expensive business and few of them ever did so. The only vestry which made any attempt to suppress the brothels in its area was Mile End, where a police pensioner was hired to collect the evidence and prosecute the owners. Two streets were cleared of brothels in this way but in the long term the only result it brought was to increase sharply the number of prostitutes who harried and molested men in the streets.

The crude economic necessity that drove women to 'sail along on their bottoms' was generally glossed over with a wishy-washy sentiment that they had fallen because they had been betrayed by a wealthy seducer. A survey carried out by a prison chaplain in 1890 found that, of the sixteen thousand women he had interviewed, over eleven thousand had taken the plunge deliberately and less than seven hundred had been seduced. The age of consent was then thirteen, but prior to 1875 it had been twelve. (In Hanbury Street, Whitechapel, there was a Salvation Army refuge for young girls, many of them ten, eleven and twelve.)

Given the overcrowded homes incest was inevitable and common. Generally it was between father and daughter or brother and sister. Lord Salisbury told the story of a friend who was going down a slum court when he

saw on the pavement two children of tender years, or ten or eleven years old, endeavouring to have sexual connection on the pathway. He ran and seized the lad, and pulled him off, and the only remark of the lad was, 'Why do you take hold of me? There are a dozen of them at it down there.' You must perceive that that could not arise from sexual tendencies, and that it must have been bred by imitation of what they saw.

Not many couples bothered to get married. Often it was a question of simple economics. Much to Mr Barnett's disgust the 'Red Church', as he called it, in Bethnal Green Road was prepared to marry couples free of charge. His objection was that it was wrong to start married life with a lie, for couples had to say that they lived in the parish and this in most cases was simply not true. On a more light-hearted occasion, a lady philanthropist had finally managed to persuade a common-law husband and wife to get married, as much for their own sake as for the sake of their children, and made the arrangements for their wedding. On the day of the ceremony the couple didn't turn up and, in a towering rage, she went to their house to find out why. The woman told her that her man had been offered five shillings for a carting job and that that was much more important.

Couples, married or not, often lived for years in the lodging houses on a day-to-day basis. There were 233 common lodging houses in Whitechapel accommodating 8,500 persons. Often they were 'the resorts of thieves and vagabonds of the lowest type, and some are kept by receivers of stolen goods. In the kitchen men and women may be seen cooking their food, washing their clothes, or lolling about smoking and gambling. In the sleeping room are long rows of beds on each side, sometimes sixty or eighty in one room.' Generally these were a mixture of single and double beds for both men and women. A double bed was eightpence a night and a single bed fourpence. In some lodging houses there was the compromise of a twopenny rope lean-to; this was a rope stretched across the room for the men to lean on and on which they had to sleep as best as they could. If the women hadn't earned enough money by selling flowers, washing clothes, or scrubbing floors, and had enough money for their bread and beer but not enough for a bed, they could generally count on finding someone who would let them sleep with them in return for sex.

Each lodging house was generally visited once a week by a lodging-house police sergeant. He might just as well have stayed away. The time of his visit was always known in advance and it was always in the daytime when the dormitories were empty, never at night when they were crowded with 'dossers' and with mattresses laid out on the floors between the beds. He had to count the number of beds, see that the rooms were tidied and dusted and that the slops had been emptied. The lodging-house owners nearly always lived elsewhere in the vicinity. During the daytime they stored any extra beds and blankets in their houses. A deputy, who was generally a ticket-of-leave man (a prisoner on parole), was left in nominal charge. In spite of these inspections, the conditions inside the lodging houses were often quite grim. In one a police inspector reported that 'The place was swarming with vermin, large blocks of creeping things having been taken out from the walls and ceilings. The bedsteads and bedding were also swarming with insects, and disgusting in the extreme.'

Most dossers had casual jobs, and any work they did was generally badly done. Such money as they earned was spent on basics such as bread, margarine, tea and sugar. Meals cost on average a penny three farthings a head. In late summer, in the August slackness in the docks and many other trades, some thirty thousand Londoners went hop picking in Sussex and Kent. It was the nearest thing that most of them ever had to a holiday. Better still, the work was family work. Every child who could walk was wanted. Those over twelve could easily earn 1s. 6d. to 2s. 6d. a day for three weeks' work.

Yet even when they had any money, few of them would try to put by for the hard times that followed the next day or the next week. As well as being a brutal and rootless way of life, it was also a careless existence, with tomorrow never coming. Life as they lived it was boldly set out in a statement made by a seaman, James Thomas Sadler, when he was arrested for the murder of a prostitute, Frances Coles, in Whitechapel in 1891. As she had been ripped in the by now familiar manner, he was suspected of being not only her murderer but also Jack the Ripper.

In the statement made after his arrest, he said that he had been discharged from his ship at 7 p.m. on 11 February and, after a drink, had fixed up some lodgings. He had then gone to the Princess Alice where he saw a prostitute named Frances Coles.

He had picked her up in Whitechapel Road some eighteen months earlier, on another shore leave, and had spent the night with her at a lodging house in Thrawl Street. He asked her to have a drink but she said she would rather go on somewhere else because whenever she was flush the other Princess Alice customers expected her to spend the money with them. After an evening's drinking in other pubs in the area and buying half a pint of whisky to take home with them (Sadler later got twopence-worth of drink for returning the bottle), they finished the night in the eightpenny double, and stayed in the lodging house until almost noon the next day.

Drinking was resumed as soon as they got up. They visited several more pubs, including The Bell in Middlesex Street where they stayed for about two hours. Frances had by now wheedled out of Sadler a promise to buy her a hat. At the shop in Baker's Row he gave her half a crown and waited for her while she went inside to buy it. As some elastic had to be stitched on before the hat was ready to wear, they waited in a nearby pub and had some more drinks until it was time for Frances to return and collect it.

As this point there was some suspicion that she arranged for Sadler to be mugged later that afternoon and, in the circumstances, it seems more than likely that this was so.

When she returned with the hat Sadler made her try it on. He told her to throw her old hat away but this she wouldn't do and she pinned it instead to her dress. It was still hanging there when her body was found later that night with her throat cut and the stomach disembowelled.

By now Sadler was beginning to feel somewhat drunk. They continued drinking in the Marlborough Head in Brick Lane and afterwards he remembered that the landlady objected to Frances being there but he could not say why. It was soon afterwards, as they were walking down Thrawl Street, that he was mugged. A woman in a red shawl hit him on the head and knocked him down. As he tried to get up he was surrounded by several men who put the boot in and robbed him of his money and watch. They escaped by running into a lodging house. Sadler, when he managed to stagger to his feet, had a raging quarrel with Frances (it was this that led to his arrest) as he thought that the least she could have done was to help him when he was down.

As he was now penniless and had not got the money to pay for a bed, he went back to the docks to try and get on board his ship. He was in a foul mood and swore at the men on the dock gates and at some passing dockers who threatened to give him a good hiding if the young policeman who was standing nearby would only turn his back. He did more than that. He walked away, and after he had turned the corner one of the dockers, to whom Sadler had been particularly abusive, made a dead set at him. Sadler was knocked down and kicked and would have been badly injured if his attacker had not been forcibly restrained from doing him further injury. Sadler managed to stagger to a lodging house in East Smithfield, where he was known, and begged the night porter to let him have a bed. When he saw that pleading was useless, he hobbled back to the lodging house in Dorset Street where he'd spent the previous night with Frances, and found her in the kitchen with her head on her arms. She was fuddled with drink and, like himself, didn't have any money, not even a farthing, to pay for a bed. Sadler told her that he had £4 15s. ship money coming to him. But when he tried to persuade the lodging-house deputy to let him have a bed on the strength of it, he was thrown out, although Frances was allowed to stay.

Sadler set off for the London Hospital to have his injuries seen to. En route he was stopped by a policeman who told him that he looked a pretty pickle. Sadler grumbled that he'd had 'two doings over' that day and that he'd been cut and knocked about with a knife or bottle. Immediately he mentioned the word 'knife' the constable said, 'Oh, have you a knife about you?' and searched him in spite of Sadler's protests that he never carried one. At the hospital his head was bandaged and he was allowed to spend the rest of the night on a couch in the Accident Ward until morning when he was turned out. Once more he went to his regular lodgings and begged yet again for the loan of a few pence. Again he was unlucky. He had to wait until the shipping office was open before he could get the £4 15s. he was owed. The first thing he did was to pay for a bed. He slept and moodily drank by himself and didn't go out for the next twenty-four hours until he was arrested and accused of, but never prosecuted for, murdering Frances the night before.

Without money, anyone who was down and out had no choice but to go into the workhouse. In spite of the unpleasant regime it did offer a chance of survival. Queuing usually began early in the day and the admissions, starting in the afternoon, were taken in three at a time. Jack London's experiences in 1902, as related in *The People of the Abyss*, were of the system *after* it had been improved and not, as might easily be supposed from his account of the conditions, as they were *before*. On entering he was given a loaf of bread which, he says, felt like a brick, and was searched for knives, matches and tobacco, which casuals such as he were not permitted to have. In the cellar to which he was first sent, the light was very dim. Most of the men were wearily taking off their shoes and unwrapping the bandages from their blistered feet. For food he was given a pannikin, a small cup, three-quarters filled with skilly, a mixture of Indian corn and hot water. The sight and smell of it turned his stomach, and he gave it away. He had no better luck with his bread. It was so hard that he had to soften it with water before he could bite it. Most of the men, when they came to eat their own, dipped it into the piles of salt that were scattered about the dirty tables.

At 7 p.m. they were forced to take their baths in pairs. Twenty-two men washed in the same tub of water. London blanched when he saw that one man's back was 'a mass of blood from attacks of vermin and retaliatory scratching'. Afterwards his clothes were taken away and he was given a nightshirt and a couple of blankets to roll up in. In a long narrow dormitory lengths of canvas were stretched between two iron rails on the ground, each strip about six inches apart and eight inches off the floor. These were the beds. London tried unsuccessfully to sleep. He listened wistfully to the children playing outside in the street, and then dozed off about midnight but was woken up by a rat on his chest. His shouts woke everyone else up and he was roundly cursed by them all.

At 6 a.m. they were made to get up, and after a further meal of skilly, which London again gave away, the men were given various jobs to do. In some workhouses the work was both punitive and mindless. Stone might have to be pounded into a fine dust and sieved through a grille in the wall at the end of the room. London was included in the work party that was sent to the Whitechapel infirmary to do scavenger work.

'Don't touch it mate, the nurse sez it deadly,' warned one of the men as London held open a sack into which a garbage can was being emptied. Waste food had to be collected from the sick wards, and London had to carry the sackloads down five flights of stairs and empty them into waste bins which were immediately sprinkled with disinfectant. When the work was done they were given tea and some scraps of food that London, unable to conceal his disgust, described as

heaped high on a huge platter in an indescribable mess – pieces of bread, chunks of grease and fat pork, the burnt skin from the outside of roasted joints, bones, in short, all the leavings from the fingers and mouths of the sick ones suffering from all manners of disease. Into this mess the men plunged their hands, digging, pawing, turning over, examining, rejecting and scrambling for. It wasn't pretty. Pigs couldn't have done worse. But the poor devils were hungry, and they ate ravenously of the swill, and when they could eat no more they bundled what was left into their handkerchiefs and thrust it inside their shirts.

'Once, when I was 'ere before, wot did I find out there but a 'ole lot of pork ribs,' said Ginger to me. By 'out there' he meant the place where the corruption was dumped and sprinkled with strong disinfectant. 'They was a prime lot, no end of meat on them, and I ad'em in my arms and was out of the gate and down the street lookin' for some'un to gi'em to. Couldn't see a soul, and I was runnin' round clean crazy, the bloke runnin' after me and thinkin' I was slingin' my 'ook. But just before 'e got me I got an ole woman and poked em into 'er apron.'

London couldn't take any more. He fled to a hot bath, a decent bed and food.

In the 1870s there had been a general impression that the working class was becoming better off. It was a shock to learn that overcrowding, bad sanitation and prolonged periods of unemployment were beginning to blur uncomfortably the distinctions between the respectable working class and the thousands who were 'physically, mentally and morally unfit' to live and for whom the state could do nothing except let die by leaving them alone. There was also the growing fear that the two might combine to overwhelm the established order.

'This mighty mob of famished, diseased and filthy helots,' George Sims wrote in How the Poor Live, 'is getting dangerous, physically, morally, politically dangerous. The barriers which have kept it back are rotten and giving way, and it may do the state a mischief if it be not looked to in time. Its fevers and its filth may spread to the homes of the wealthy; its lawless armies may sally forth and give us the taste of the lesson the mob has tried to teach now and again in Paris, when long years of neglect have done their work.'

Another pamphleteer, Arnold White, wrote in The Problems of a Great City: 'How much more repugnant is it to reason and to instinct that the strong should be overwhelmed by the feeble, ailing and unfit!'

Events in 1886 and 1887 only intensified these fears. The winter of 1885–6 was the coldest for thirty years. Men and women with haggard faces and thin worn bodies crowded into the relief offices. Even the vicar's wife Mrs Barnett came near to jettisoning her principles for the sight of some temporary happiness in 'those sad faces' with the 'gift of nice bright half crowns all round' – except that Mr Barnett, 'ever wishful to redeem character stood resolute'. Mrs Barnett could still wince, many years later, as she recalled the reproaches of a broken-hearted mother who had sobbed, as she wept over her baby whose life might have been saved: 'They said it was no use a-sending to the Church, for you didn't never give nothing though you spoke kind.'

Even jobs as scavengers were beyond the physical capabilities of most of the men. A mass meeting of unemployed dockers and labourers was held in Trafalgar Square that winter, and afterwards some of the crowd marched to Hyde Park where they intended to disperse. In Pall Mall there was some provocation from clubmen and the march turned into riot. About three thousand demonstrators rampaged and looted their way through Piccadilly and Mayfair to Oxford Street where they were eventually dispersed by the police. In the aftermath, the Home Secretary appointed a committee of inquiry to look into the conduct of the police and he took the unusual step of chairing it himself . . . which meant that he presented the committee's findings to himself. The Metropolitan Police Commissioner, Colonel Sir Edmund Henderson, was made scapegoat for the debacle and he resigned.

His successor was Sir Charles Warren. The appointment of another soldier caused a few lifted eyebrows, but the feeling was that his appointment might give the force the discipline it seemed to be lacking. Already trouble was being fomented in the force from outside agitators urging them to strike, and there were genuine grievances over pay and punishments.

The next year, 1887, saw Queen Victoria's Jubilee. Trade was slack but the weather was fine and throughout the summer a great many of the destitute unemployed slept in Trafalgar Square and St James's Park. In October the weather changed, but by now camping out – in Trafalgar Square especially – had almost become a permanent way of life. Charities and well-meaning individuals had got into the habit of taking food and clothes to the square, which was described by one writer as a 'foul camp of vagrants', and by another as consisting of the 'scum of London'. Sir Charles Warren also complained that he had to employ two thousand men to shepherd workers' demonstrations through the West End, while the City police, with far fewer men and outside the scope of Home Office control, had broken up similar-sized crowds. There was one law, it seemed, for the City and one for the metropolis. Warren cleared Trafalgar Square of its ragged army of squatters but his action brought him into direct conflict with the Home Secretary, who subsequently rescinded his original order empowering him to do so. West End shopkeepers now publicly threatened to take the law into their own hands and to hire armed bands to clear the square themselves. Warren demanded additional powers to control a situation that was rapidly getting out of hand. With the Home Secretary's approval, he banned the use of the square on certain days.

His challenge was taken up, and on 13 November the battle of 'Bloody Sunday' was fought in the square. Altogether four thousand constables, three hundred mounted constables, three hundred Grenadiers and three hundred Life Guards, as well as seven thousand constables held in reserve, were used to break up the giant mob of demonstrators – many were armed with iron bars, sticks and knives – that struggled to break through to the square. More than a hundred and fifty of the crowd had to be treated for injuries and nearly three hundred more had been arrested. Some were sentenced to imprisonment with hard labour, for one, two, three or six months.

Warren's high-handed action was both censured and praised. Working-class hatred for him was perhaps epitomized by one of the many anonymous personal threats which he subsequently received: 'Beware of your life you dog. Don't venture out too far. Look out. This is yours', was followed by a crudely drawn coffin. Other threatened demonstrations against 'police rule in London' never materialized, and Warren was able to bask in the glow of official approval. The following month the Queen knighted him.

As fears of mob rule began to recede, so criticisms of the police, and of Warren in particular, began to increase. Within a year, the scorn and abuse which had been hurled at the Trafalgar Square mobs had been turned against the police who, from being the champions of liberty, had become the downtreaders of the suffering poor. George Bernard Shaw was not slow to point out how quickly attitudes had changed.

Less than a year ago the West End press was literally clamouring for the blood of the people – hounding Sir Charles Warren to thrash and muzzle the scum who dared to complain that they were starving . . . behaving, in short, as the propertied class always does behave when the workers throw it into a frenzy of terror by venturing to show their teeth.

Whilst we conventional Social Democrats were wasting our time on education, agitation and organisation, some independent genius has taken the matter in hand . . .

He was to be known as Jack the Ripper!

2. Bloody Knife

When Charles Cross walked through dark and empty Buck's Row on his way to work as a market porter at about 3.40 a.m. on the morning of Friday, 31 August 1888, the only light was a solitary gas lamp at the far end. On one side of the street was a warehouse wall, and on the other some terrace houses occupied for the most part by better-class tradesmen. He was opposite these houses when, in a gateway leading to some stables, between the houses and the board school, he saw a bundle that he at first thought was a tarpaulin. It was only when he crossed over for a closer look that he realized the bundle was in fact a woman. She was lying on her back with one hand nearly touching the stable gate and the other her black straw bonnet, which was lying close by. Her skirt was pushed up almost to her waist. His first thought was that she had been raped and was still unconscious from the attack; and his next that he might have disturbed her attacker. Normally there was a great deal of noise in the street, but at that hour of the morning it was quiet and although he listened carefully for any strange noises he could hear none. If he had disturbed the woman's attacker he must have heard his footsteps as he escaped or, supposing that the woman had been brought there in a cart and dumped, the rattle of wheels as he drove off. He was still by the body when he heard footsteps behind him.

Robert Paul, also a market porter, was likewise on his way to work when he saw Cross standing in the roadway. He stepped off the pavement to avoid him, but as he did so Cross touched him on the shoulder and said, 'Come and look at this woman.' Paul cautiously did so but when Cross, thinking she was only drunk, suggested that he should give him a hand to lift her to her feet, he refused. Instead he knelt down and felt the woman's face and hands. They were already cold and he thought she was dead. But as he straightened her clothes to make her a little more decent, he felt her heart and thought that he could detect a slight movement. The men hurried off together in search of a policeman. In the dark neither had noticed the blood, now concealed by the skirt, coagulating on the pavement.

Police Constable John Neil missed seeing them by minutes. Nearly half an hour had passed since he had last walked through Buck's Row, although his beat was a short one and could be covered at a brisk walk in twelve minutes. Shining his bull's-eye lamp into the stable gateway he saw what the two men had not been able to see, that the woman had been murdered. Blood was oozing from an ugly gash in her throat which had been cut almost from ear to ear. The windpipe and gullet had been completely severed. Her eyes were open, and though her hands and wrists were cold, her arms were still warm from the elbow up. The flashing of his lamp as he examined the body attracted the constable on an adjoining beat, and Neil called to him to run and fetch a doctor. There was a surgery close by and within a quarter of an hour a Dr Llewellyn was at the scene. He made a cursory examination of the body, watched by several policemen who obligingly shone their lamps on the body, and two or three men who, having just finished work at a nearby slaughterhouse, were on their way home.

On the left side of the neck, about an inch below the jaw, there was an incision about four inches long starting from a point immediately below the ear. On the same side, but an inch below, and beginning an inch in front of it, was a second incision which ended at a point three inches below the right jaw. This second incision, about eight inches long, had cut the throat back to the vertebrae.

The main arteries had been severed but there seemed to be very little arterial blood on the ground. Most of it, the police realized when they lifted the body on to the ambulance, had soaked into the woman's clothes as it flowed down her back from her neck to her waist. In spite of her posture and the massive loss of blood, her legs were still warm. The doctor guessed that she had been dead not more than half an hour. On his instructions the body was taken to the mortuary adjoining the local workhouse.

The body was left in the workhouse yard until two pauper inmates, one of them subject to fits, had had their breakfast and were ready to start stripping the body. The police inspector who was present jotted down a list of the clothing as they took it off – a reddish-brown ulster somewhat the worse for wear, a brown frock of coarse linsey, black ribbed wool stockings. She was wearing two petticoats, one of grey flannel and the other of wool, which had to be cut through the bands to be taken off. As the attendant tore them down with his hands, exposing the brown stays, the inspector saw in the lower part of the abdomen, two or three inches from the left side, a deep jagged incision and other mutilations. He hurriedly summoned Dr Llewellyn who came at once and made a thorough post-mortem examination of the body, which was that of a woman of about forty or forty-five. There was some bruising along the lower edge of the jaw on the right side of the face that might have been caused by a punch or thumb pressure. On the other side of the face was a circular bruise, which again might have been caused by finger pressure. Apart from the injuries to the throat and to the abdomen already mentioned, there were several other incisions running across the abdomen as well as several downward slashes on the right side of the body. The abdomen had been cut open from the centre of the bottom of the ribs along the right side, under the pelvis to the left of the stomach – there the wound was jagged; the omentum or fatty membrane which covers the front of the stomach was cut in several places and there were two small stab wounds on the vagina. From the angle of the wounds, which were from left to right, Dr Llewellyn thought that these mutilations might have been done by a left-handed person using a stout-backed knife such as a cork-cutter or a shoemaker might use with a blade about six to eight inches long.

The first problem was to identify the woman. Her only possessions were a comb, white pocket handkerchief and a broken mirror. But stencilled on the bands of her two petticoats was the mark of Lambeth Workhouse. The police hoped that the matron there might be able to identify the clothing, which could have been issued at any time in the previous two or three years. The broken mirror was a good indication that the woman had been dossing in a common lodging house where mirrors were a luxury not normally provided. As the police started to question the lodging-house keepers and news of the murder spread, first one woman and then another came forward to try to identify the body. It was soon learned that a woman answering the description of the victim had been living in a lodging house at 18 Thrawl Street, Spitalfields. Women were fetched and they identified her as Polly. She had been sleeping at the lodging house for about six weeks up until the last eight to ten days. A girl who had been sharing her bed had last seen her alive about an hour before her body was found. Earlier that same evening she had staggered back to the lodging house from the Frying Pan public house in Brick Lane but had been turned away because she had not got the 4d. doss money for a bed.

'I'll soon get my doss money,' she had laughed. 'See what a jolly bonnet I've got now.'

She had been wearing a new black straw bonnet trimmed with black velvet. She was forty-two years old, 5 ft. 2 ins. tall, with brown hair turning grey and five front teeth missing; her clothes were shabby and stained and the boots she was wearing had the uppers cut and steel tips on the heels. After she had left the lodging house she was seen about an hour later in the Whitechapel Road staggering drunkenly against a wall. Her friend had tried to persuade her to come back to the lodging house with her. Instead Polly boasted that she had had her lodging-house money three times that day but had spent it, that she was going to get some more money for her lodgings and that she would soon be back. At 3.40 a.m., about an hour and a quarter later, she was found with her throat cut not three-quarters of a mile distant from the spot where she had last been seen.

An inmate of the Lambeth Workhouse who was taken to the mortuary within a day or two of the killing identified the body as that of Mary Ann (or Polly) Nichols. According to her own statement made in the Mitcham Workhouse on 13 February 1888, Nichols had been born in August 1845 in Shoe Lane off Fleet Street. Her father, Edward Walker, was a blacksmith and her husband, William Nichols, a Fleet Street printer. She was married when she was nineteen years old, in the printer's church of St Bride's, Fleet Street on 16 January 1864. She and her husband had lived for six years (no dates) at No. 6, D Block, Peabody Buildings, Stamford Street, paying rent of 5s. 9d. per week. When they separated in 1880 after several years of marital disputes she went into Lambeth Workhouse and it was agreed that her husband should allow her 5s. every week, which he did for two years. She never had a home from the time of her separation from her husband. According to the same statement, she didn't know where her husband had been living for the past six or seven years.

William Nichols, her husband, was in fact now living in the Old Kent Road. According to him he had not seen his wife for three years. They had five children; the oldest (now twenty-one) was lodging with his grandfather and the youngest (eight or nine) was living at home. They had separated several times because of her drunken habits, but each time he took her back she got drunk again and eventually the break became final. In 1882 he learned that she was living the life of a prostitute, and he discontinued the weekly allowance. In consequence she became chargeable to the Guardians of the Parish of Lambeth who summonsed the husband to show cause why he should not contribute to her support. They dismissed the summons when they learned the grounds on which he had discontinued the allowance. Since then, after three or four years of intermittent living and quarrelling with her father, she had drabbed her way through workhouses in Edmonton, the City of London, Holborn and Lambeth. She had tried to make a new start and left the Lambeth Workhouse on 12 May for a job as a domestic servant in Wandsworth. She stuck it for two months and then absconded with clothing worth £3 10s., which she probably pawned, and since then had been living in the lodging house in Thrawl Street and a similar one in Flower and Dean Street close by.

After ten days in the Lambeth Workhouse in December 1887, Nichols was turned out. Five days later she surfaced in the Mitcham Workhouse which was run by the Holborn Board of Guardians, and where she stayed for more than three months. As she had not acquired a 'settlement' by meeting the requisite period of residence without chargeability, the Holborn Union, after giving relief, applied to the justice for an 'order of removal' transferring her back to Lambeth, where a 'settlement' had been acquired. This was effected on 16 April 1888.

There was no apparent motive for her murder. An early theory was that she was the victim of a gang allegedly terrorizing and ill-treating prostitutes who did not hand over part of their earnings to them. There was some evidence for this theory: two prostitutes had already been mutilated in a similar manner and

Mary Ann Nichols

Periods spent in Workhouses and Infirmaries. Bracketed dates indicate consecutive periods of refuge.

Lambeth Workhouse	{24.4.82–18.1.83
Lambeth Infirmary	{18–20.1.83
Lambeth Workhouse	{20.1–24.3.83
Lambeth Workhouse	21.5–2.6.83
Strand Workhouse, Edmonton	26.10–2.12.87
Lambeth Workhouse	19–29.12.87
Mitcham Workhouse (Holborn) and	
Holborn Infirmary (Archway Hospital)	{4.1–16.4.88
Lambeth Workhouse	{16.4–12.5.88
Gray's Inn Road temporary	
Workhouse (Holborn)	1–2.8.88

been murdered within three hundred yards of Polly Nichols months before the Ripper killings.

The first had been Emma Elizabeth Smith, a common prostitute of the lowest type, living in a lodging house at 18 George Street, Spitalfields. She was thought to be a widow with a son and daughter living somewhere in the neighbourhood of Finsbury Park as she was often heard to say that she thought they ought to do something for her.

She had been living in George Street for about eighteen months. Generally she left the lodging house between six and seven in the evening, returning home at all hours. When she was drunk she fought and behaved like a madwoman and it was quite a common sight to see her with a black eye and other injuries

The discovery of Polly Nichols's body

which she would explain away by saying that she had been fighting or had fallen down.

She had left the lodging house at the usual hour on 2 April and at 12.15 a.m. the next day was seen talking to a man dressed in dark clothes and a white scarf in Fairance Street, Limehouse. She was not seen again until she staggered into the house some four hours later and told the deputy that she had been assaulted and robbed in Osborn Street. Much against her will she was taken to the London Hospital by the deputy and another lodger.

She said that she had been attacked by four men but either she could not or was in no condition to describe them. Her face was bloody and her ear was cut, but the worst injuries had been internally inflicted. Something, not a knife, had been inserted into her vagina with such force that it had broken, but not cut, the partition between the front and back passage. Next day she died of peritonitis.

The police were not informed of the attack until 6 April, when the Coroner's Office told them that the inquest was to take place the next day.

After such a time lapse there was very little for the police to look into, although they went through the motions of investigating. The place where Emma Smith had been attacked was pointed out to them by the lodger who had taken her to hospital. There were no bloodstains to be seen on the pavement but an examination of her clothing showed that her woollen shoulder wrap was saturated in blood. She had apparently taken it off and put it between her legs to soak up the blood when she realized how badly she had been injured. The rest of her clothing was in such a dirty and ragged condition that it was impossible to tell if any part of it had been freshly torn.

One puzzling factor was that after the attack she must have walked nearly a quarter of a mile to the lodging house in George Street and from there half a mile to the London Hospital. In so doing she must have passed a number of police constables on duty in Brick Lane and Osborn Street itself. Since she must have been in great pain and walking with considerable difficulty, why did she not ask for help? Why was she so reluctant to go to hospital? Had the police been told earlier they might have got some answers to these questions.

The second pre-Ripper victim had been Martha Tabram whose body, with thirty-nine puncture wounds, was found at 3 a.m. on Tuesday, 7 August on the first-floor landing of George Yard Buildings. In neither case had the killer been caught. The foreman of the coroner's jury subsequently alleged class bias and said that, if a reward had been offered for the George Yard murderer, neither this nor the murder of Polly Nichols that was shortly to follow would have happened. Regulations to the contrary notwithstanding, he was convinced that a substantial reward would have been offered for the killer if the victim had been rich.

In the Nichols case the apparent ease with which the murderer had struck and then escaped was baffling. The circumstances in which the body was found proved conclusively that she had been killed where she was found. It was equally apparent that she must have met her death without a cry or shout for help, for the spot was almost under the windows of a Mrs Green, a light sleeper, and opposite the bedroom of a Mrs Purkiss, who was awake at the time. Worse from the investigating point of view was that as well as the beat policemen there were three watchmen close by, none of whom had heard any screams. It seemed astonishing that the killer could have escaped, because he must have had blood on his hands or clothes. However, there were so many slaughterhouses in the area that people would take little note of bloodstained hands and clothing, which would explain why he failed to attract attention as he disappeared into the twilight of the Whitechapel Road and lost himself in the early morning market traffic.

Not only was there no motive but there was no suspect. Robbery and jealousy as motives were out. Police inquiries in the locality, of the policemen on the adjoining beats and in every quarter where it was thought that there might be a lead, failed to throw up an atom of evidence to connect anyone with the crime. The inquiries did reveal that a man named Jack Pizer, nicknamed Leather Apron, had been ill-treating prostitutes in this and other parts of the metropolis for some time and a fruitless search was made to find him and eliminate him from the inquiry, although there was nothing to connect him with the murders. Suspicion that he was the killer, however, hardened into near certainty when a second body was discovered eight days later with a piece of leather apron close by.

This second body was found shortly after 6 a.m. on Saturday, 8 September, at the back of a lodging house at 29 Hanbury Street, less than half a mile away from Buck's Row. The house, like hundreds of others in the area, had been built for the Spitalfields weavers, but when steam power drove out the hand looms they had been taken over as cheap lodging houses. Seventeen people slept in the house, from a woman and her son in a cat's-meat shop on the ground floor to the five adults in the room in the attic. There was a yard at the back and a side hall or passage giving access to the stairs. As the house was let by rooms it was customary to leave the front and back doors of the passage open. The local prostitutes knew this and used the yard for their casual pick-ups. John Davis, whose mother ran a small business from the first floor making packing cases, subsequently told the coroner's inquest that at night he often found prostitutes and their clients in the yard and on the first-floor landing and didn't hesitate to turn them out.

The dead woman was last seen alive at 5.30 a.m. by a park keeper's wife on her way to market. She remembered seeing a man and a woman, her back to the shutters, outside a house, apparently haggling. She was certain of the time because the brewer's clock was striking the half hour. Subsequently she identified the body as that of the woman she had seen. The only description she would give of the man was that he looked like a foreigner, was apparently over forty years of age, of a shabby genteel appearance and wearing a deerstalker hat, probably brown. She had not seen his face as he had his back towards her. As she walked past them she had heard him ask 'Will you?' and the woman's reply 'Yes'. She had not looked back and, in the noise and bustle of the market carts, nobody saw them go into the passage and close the door behind them.

No attempt was made to conceal the mutilated body. The passage was about four feet above ground level and had three stone steps down to the yard. To the right of the steps there was a small recess and to the left a wooden fence about five and a half feet high. The woman was about six inches in front of the bottom step, lying parallel to the fence with her feet pointing towards a small woodshed. According to the coroner's reconstruction of what had probably happened, they had entered the yard and closed the back door.

The wretch must have then seized the deceased, perhaps with Judas-like approaches. He seized her by the chin. He pressed her throat, and while thus preventing the slightest cry, he at the same time produced insensibility and suffocation. There was no evidence of any struggle. The clothes were not torn . . . The deceased was then lowered to the ground and laid on her back; and although in doing so she may have fallen slightly against the fence, the movement was probably effected with care. Her throat was then cut in two places with savage determination, and the injuries to the abdomen commenced.

The body was found by one of the lodgers, John Davis, who had been living in the house for only two weeks. He had been awake from about three o'clock to five and then had slept for half an hour. He got up at about quarter to six and came downstairs just as the church clock was striking six. The yard door was closed, although whether it had been on the latch he couldn't say. When he pushed it open and started down the steps he saw the body. Some men from a case-maker's shop nearby had seen him stumble into the street with his trouser belt in his hands and heard him call them to come and look in the yard. Out of curiosity they had followed him through the passage but none of them would go down the steps. Nor would any of the crowd that soon began to gather outside in the street as the news of the murder began to spread. Some workmen ran off to fetch the police; one of them, after swallowing some brandy, fetched a tarpaulin to throw over the mutilated remains.

From the steps the woman's face was clearly visible. Her hands were raised with the palms upwards as though she had fought for the throat. Her hands and face were smeared with blood as though she had been struggling. Her legs were drawn up with the feet resting on the ground and the knees turned outwards. Her long black coat and skirt had been pushed up over her bloodstained stockings and she had been disembowelled. According to the staccato police report she was

lying on her back, dead, left arm resting on left breast, legs drawn up, abducted, small intestines and flap of the abdomen lying on right side above right shoulder attached by a cord with the rest of the intestines inside the body; two flaps of skin from the lower part of the abdomen lying in a large quantity of blood above the left shoulder; throat cut deeply from left and back in jagged manner right around the throat.

There was a handkerchief of some kind tied around the neck. The throat had been so savagely cut that the head was almost severed from the body. According to some newspapers the handkerchief had been tied on by the killer to stop the head from rolling away, but later evidence showed that the woman had been wearing the handkerchief as a neck scarf and that she was wearing it when she was murdered.

Inspector Joseph Chandler was on duty in Commercial Street when he saw several men running down Hanbury Street towards him and was told what had happened. He arrived at the house within a few minutes of the discovery of the body. Already a crowd (some reports say a mob) had gathered outside the house and he had to force his way through. As the crowds built up they began to threaten local Jews, abusing those they met in the streets and, according to the *East London Observer*, repeatedly asserting 'that no Englishman could have perpetrated such a horrible crime, and that it must have been done by a Jew'. As soon as reinforcements arrived Chandler cleared the passage of sightseers and refused to allow anyone into the yard until the body had been examined by the divisional surgeon who had been sent for. He hastily arranged for telegrams to be sent to Detective Inspector Frederick Abberline at Scotland Yard, who had been called in to assist in the Buck's Row murder, and to several other officers informing them of what had happened.

While he waited for the surgeon to arrive, Inspector Chandler made a preliminary search of the ground, watched by the scores of faces craning out of the back windows for a view; for some days afterwards the tenants did a brisk business charging sightseers for a look from their windows. He covered the body with some sacking. The yard had not been properly paved and it was a patchwork of stones and earth. He could detect no signs of a struggle, nor of anyone having climbed over the fence. None of the palings was broken but there were some bloodstains on the fence about fourteen inches above the ground, immediately above the blood that had flowed from the woman's throat. The only other bloodstains, varying in size from a sixpenny piece to a pinpoint, were on the back wall of the house, at the head of the body.

The police had no scientific advisers other than the divisional surgeons, whose role was much like that of today's scene-of-crime officers. Divisional surgeons like Dr George Bagster Phillips, with twenty years' practical experience to draw on, were invaluable to an investigation. After formally certifying that the woman was dead he ordered the body to be taken to the mortuary. Ironically, it was carried away in the same shell that had been used for Polly Nichols the week before.

Phillips made a thorough search of the yard, which yielded

several clues. Several items had been deliberately placed or scattered about the yard. The woman's clothing had not been torn but the pocket of her underskirt had been cut open at the front and at the side. A piece of muslin, a comb and a paper case were lying close to the body. A wedding ring and its 'keeper ring' to stop it slipping off, both brass, had been forcibly removed from a finger. Near her head was part of an envelope and a piece of paper containing two pills. On the back of the envelope was the seal of the Sussex Regiment and on the other side the letter M and a Post Office stamp, 'London, 28 Aug., 1888'.

There was also a leather apron lying saturated with water about two feet from the water tap.

One popular rumour was that the murderer had scrawled, on the wall of the yard, 'Five; fifteen more and then I give myself up.' Equally dramatic was the story told by a young woman called Lyons the following day. She claimed to have met a strange man in Flower and Dean Street close by who asked her to meet him at half past six at the Queen's Head public house and have a drink with him. Having made her promise that she would meet him he disappeared, but met her at the appointed time. As they were drinking he startled her by saying, 'You are about the same style of woman as the one that's murdered.' When she asked him what he knew about her he muttered, 'You are beginning to smell a rat. Foxes hunt geese, but they don't always find 'em.' The man then hurriedly left the bar. The young woman had followed him until they were near to Spitalfields Church when, suddenly realizing that he was being followed, the man had rushed away and was lost sight of. The woman's description was identical with the published descriptions of the elusive Leather Apron. According to *The Times* the police had already searched more than two hundred common lodging houses for him.

Shortly before 2 p.m. on the Saturday afternoon Dr Phillips went to the mortuary to make the post-mortem and was astonished to find that the body had been stripped, the blood washed off the chest and the clothes tossed into a corner of the shed except for the handkerchief which was still tied around the neck. The clerk of the guardians had ordered this to be done and detailed two nurses for the work. Later, at the inquest, Phillips protested as he had done before, at the conditions in which he was forced to work. It was incredible that so large a borough did not have its own mortuary. Bodies dragged from the river had to be packed in boxes.

It was the victim's friend Amelia Farmer who identified her. She told the coroner at the inquest when it opened on Monday, 10 September at the Working Lad's Institute, Whitechapel Road, that she lived in a common lodging house at 30 Dorset Street. She identified the body as that of Annie Chapman, nicknamed Siffey, who for the past four years had lived in common lodging houses in and about Spitalfields and Whitechapel. She was then receiving an allowance of ten shillings a week from her husband. Some eighteen months past the payments had stopped and it was then that Chapman had learned that he had died, aged forty-two, on Christmas Day 1886 after a six-month illness.

Annie's family background was military. Her father had been a guardsman and she had grown up in the military barracks in London and Windsor. She was twenty-eight years old when she married a coachman, John Chapman, in 1869. They had three children, one of them, a boy, was possibly a cripple. The family moved to the countryside, to Clewer near Windsor, but eventually Annie's drinking habits forced John to reluctantly separate from his wife. Annie took to the roads about Clewer and Windsor like a common tramp before eventually making for London.

Chapman, by all accounts, was a clever woman. She was quiet, sociable and well educated. Occasionally she tried to earn some money by selling flowers or doing crochet work. Frequently she got drunk, usually on her favourite rum, and as she was not fussy about how she earned her living she was soon well known as a prostitute on the streets of Spitalfields and Whitechapel. In 1886 she was living with a man who made iron sieves. It was for this reason that she was nicknamed Siffey or Dark Annie Sievey.

Amelia Farmer had seen her two or three times in the week before she died. She had met her on the Monday when she had complained of feeling unwell. At the time she was sporting a black eye and had a badly bruised chest, the result of a drunken brawl with Liza Cooper, a prostitute Chapman had known for fifteen years. Dark Annie, as Chapman was also known, occasionally spent the weekend at the lodging house with a man locally known as the Pensioner. He lived only a short distance away in Osborn Street. The quarrel between the two women had started over a piece of soap that Dark Annie had borrowed for the Pensioner to wash with. She promised to return it but did not do so, and when she was asked for it the following week she contemptuously tossed a halfpenny to Liza and told her to go and buy some more. Later, they happened to meet in the Britannia public house. Liza was drunk – probably Dark Annie was also – and they started to quarrel. They were still quarrelling when they staggered back to the doss-house kitchen. Dark Annie finally slapped the other woman's face and told her, 'Think yourself lucky I did not do more.' Now Annie was about forty-one years old, stout and well-proportioned; she was described as one who had seen better days. She was a small woman, only five feet tall, with dark brown wavy hair, blue eyes, a large thick nose and two teeth missing from her bottom jaw. She was a formidable opponent. Unfortunately, she had badly underestimated Liza Cooper who mauled her and kicked her and blacked her eye and badly bruised her chest. When Amelia Farmer saw her some days later she was still creeping around like a sick cat. Next day, Tuesday, 3 September, she had met her again by the side of Spitalfields Church. Dark Annie again complained of feeling unwell and said that she thought she would go to the casual ward for a day or two. She had had nothing to eat or drink that day except for a cup of tea. Amelia Farmer had given her twopence for a cup of tea and told her not to have any rum. She didn't see her again until 5 o'clock on the Friday afternoon when she asked her if she was going to Stratford. Annie again complained of feeling too ill to do anything. She was listless and didn't want to move but said, 'It's no use my giving way. I must pull myself together and go out and get some money, or I shall have no lodgings.' That was the last time Amelia Farmer had seen her alive.

The next witness was Timothy Donovan, the deputy of the common lodging house at 35 Dorset Street. He told the court that Annie Chapman had lived in the lodging house for about the past four months except for the last week, during which time he had not seen her until the Friday evening. Around 7 o'clock she had come into the lodging house and asked him if she could go into the kitchen: Donovan had known her for about sixteen months and let her stay in the kitchen until nearly 2 a.m. when he was compelled to turn her out as it was obvious by then that she wasn't going to rent a bed. She told him that she had been ill and in the infirmary and asked him to trust her for the doss money. He told her that she knew the rules, and that she could not stay without paying. Normally, Annie would get drunk on a Saturday night, but not during the rest of the week. Tonight, however, she had been drinking, but she could walk straight. Donovan did not see which way she went out but, as she left, she told him that even though she had no money he was not to let her bed, which was still vacant, as she would soon be back.

Apart from an unconfirmed report that she had been served at a public house in Spitalfield's market less than half an hour before she was murdered, the last two people to see her alive were the nightwatchman at the lodging house, who saw her walk away in the direction of Brushfield Street, and the park keeper's wife, who saw her talking to her killer.

Not all of Dr Bagster Phillips's evidence could be published in the newspapers. Some of it could only be reproduced in *The Lancet*. In court he began by saying that the woman's face and tongue were swollen and that there was bruising on the face and chest. There were abrasions on the finger where the rings had been torn off. The incisions in the throat indicated that they had been made from the left side of the neck. There were two distinct cuts, parallel to each other, and about half an inch apart. From the way the muscles had been worried it seemed as though the killer had tried to cut through the spine and take off the head.

The abdomen had been entirely laid open and the intestines severed from their mesenteric attachments which had been lifted out and placed on the shoulder of the corpse; whilst from the pelvis, the uterus and its appendages with the upper portion of the vagina and the posterior two-thirds of the bladder had been entirely removed. Obviously the work was that of an expert – or one, at least, who had such knowledge of anatomical or pathological examinations as to be enabled to secure the pelvic organs with one sweep of the knife.

The cause of death, he concluded, was visible from the injuries he had described. From these appearances he was of the opinion that death arose from syncope, or failure of the heart's action in consequence of loss of blood caused by the severance of the throat. The report further showed that, besides being undernourished, she was already dying from chronic diseases of the lungs and brain which would have killed her within a short time.

Cross-examined by the coroner, he thought that the murder weapon must have been a very sharp knife with a thin, narrow blade, at least six inches to eight inches long, probably longer. The injuries could not have been inflicted with a sword-bayonet or bayonet. They could have been done with a post-mortem knife but ordinary surgical cases might not contain such an instrument. Knives used by slaughtermen, which were well ground down, were possible alternatives but those used in the leather trade would not be long enough in the blade. There were indications that the murderer had some anatomical knowledge. Even without a struggle he did not think that he could have committed all the injuries in under a quarter of an hour. Had he done them in a deliberate way, as a professional, it would probably have taken him the best part of an hour.

The leather apron which had been found he dismissed as of no importance. There had been no blood on it and from its appearance it had not been recently unfolded. Some staining on the wall of a nearby house looked like blood but on examination turned out to be urine. Referring again to the bruises on Annie Chapman's face he said that those about the chin and the sides of the jaw were recent but those on the chest and temple were several days older. Clearly the latter were the result of the brawl with Liza Cooper. He thought that the killer had taken hold of Chapman by the chin and made his incision from left to right. To a suggestion that she might have been gagged he could only point to the swollen face and protruding tongue, both of which were signs of suffocation.

It seemed as if society as a whole had needed some horror such as this to awaken them to the fact that within a cab-hire distance of the palaces and mansions of the West End there were 'tens of thousands of fellow creatures begotted and reared in an atmosphere of godless brutality, a species of human sewage, the very drainage of the vilest production of ordinary vice; such sewage ever on the increase, and in its increase forever developing fresh depths of degradation'.

An unknown moralist in a letter to *The Times* laid the blame for the killings squarely on society and not on the half-crazed monster terrorizing the East End in his search for blood and whose legend was even then being created. Society had sown the seed and must reap the harvest.

The Revd Samuel Barnett, vicar of St Jude's, Whitechapel, more pragmatically thought that the Whitechapel horrors would not have been in vain if 'at last' the public conscience was awakened to the life that these horrors revealed. 'The murders were, it may almost be said, bound to come; generation could not follow generation in lawless intercourse, children could not be familiarised with scenes of degradation, community in crime could not be the bond of society and the end of all be peace.' As one of those who for years had known of the conditions that the killings had brought to the general attention of the public, he offered some practical remedies to these problems. He was careful to point out that these criminal haunts were of limited extent. The greater part of Whitechapel was as orderly as any part of London and the life of most of its inhabitants was as moral, if not more so, as that lived in some of the wealthier parts of the capital. Most of its evil was concentrated in an area of about a quarter of a mile square and to deal with it, or at least to bring it under control, he offered some practical suggestions.

There could be more efficient police supervision. There had never been enough policemen to do anything more than to contain crime within certain areas. Rows, fights and thefts had been allowed to go unchecked in these rookeries of crime so long as the main thoroughfares were safe. More policemen were therefore needed to enforce the law in these areas. There should be, at least, adequate street lighting and cleaning. The back streets were gloomy and dirty and encouraged crime.

Barnett failed to point out that this was not the fault of the local authority. It was a simple question of economics. Because of the general poverty of the area the amount of money that could be raised on the rates was simply not enough to pay for these basic services. Unless some sort of financial help was forthcoming from the richer boroughs, and the East End as a whole made London's responsibility, then the squalor and vice of Whitechapel could never be mitigated.

Yet neither the Revd Barnett nor *The Times*, in which there was some quite lengthy comment on his proposals, was bold enough to suggest that this was a matter of public responsibility rather than private charity. The most sensitive of the issues that the Revd Barnett raised had concerned private property and the fat profits that could be made by landlords and tenants who let, sub-let and sub-let again, piling lease upon lease until a situation was reached, as in 29 Hanbury Street, where seventeen people could exist in grossly overcrowded squalor. He could only express the pious hope that such properties would be bought by public-spirited philanthropists who would not batten on the easy profits that could be made from prostitution and flagrant overcrowding. His final conclusion was that society had to make fresh and determined efforts to extirpate the existing evils which were an intolerable reproach to a Christian and civilized society. Either that or 'acquiesce in the desolating conclusion that our social organisation demands for its base a festering mass of unexplored and irredeemable iniquity'.

The police were criticized by press and public for their incompetence. At Chapman's inquest one witness complained that when he had told a street constable that there had been a second murder similar to that at Buck's Row, the policeman had told him that he couldn't come and that he (the witness) must find someone else. An inspector's explanation to the coroner that constables on fixed points were not supposed to leave them but to send someone else did not revive his listeners' waning confidence.

Critics were equally scathing about the casualness of the investigation. Even the coroner voiced his criticisms. He wasn't provided with plans and had nothing to show where the body was found, not even a map of the street. Clearly, however, there were severe handicaps facing the police investigation. Finger-printing as a science had yet to be proved and accepted in the English courts; seventeen more years were to pass before the first conviction was obtained from them. The difference between animal and human blood could not be told until 1901. Blood grouping was unknown until 1905. Pocket radios, telephones and wireless cars were for the future. Detection, in fact, relied very heavily on local knowledge, informers and an arrest at the time of the offence. According to Press Association reports, the police felt that they would get nowhere with their inquiries. No attempt was made to disguise the fact that such inquiries as had been made had been so fruitless as to produce in official minds a feeling almost of despair.

Tradesmen had so little confidence in the efforts being made that some of them formed a Vigilance Committee and published the following notice:

Finding that, in spite of murders being committed in our midst our police force is inadequate to discover the author or authors of the late atrocities, we the undersigned have formed ourselves into a committee and intend offering a substantial reward to any one, citizens or otherwise, who shall give such information as will be the means of bringing the murderer or murderers to justice.

Samuel Montagu, the local MP, offered £500 reward for the capture of the murderer, and the police had been bombarded as a result with literally hundreds of letters from all parts of the country offering advice.

Early on the morning of Monday, 10 September the elusive John Pizer (Leather Apron) was traced to 22 Mulberry Street. Police suspicions of him had been intensified after Timothy Donovan, Annie Chapman's lodging-house keeper, said in an interview with a Press Association reporter that not only had he ejected Pizer from the lodging house a few months earlier for attacking or threatening a woman, but that both he and another witness, when they had last seen him, had noticed that he was wearing a deerstalker hat similar to the one worn by Annie Chapman's killer.

Pizer was arrested by Sergeant Thicke, nickname 'Johnny Upright', who told him that he was wanted for questioning in connection with the death of Annie Chapman. While searching the house they found five sharp long-bladed knives, which Pizer claimed he used in his trade as a boot finisher. They also found several old hats, an unfortunate reminder that Pizer also made hats and that Polly Nichols had boasted of her new one shortly before she was murdered.

Protesting his innocence, Pizer was taken to Leman Street police station. The friends with whom he had been hiding accompanied him, and they insisted that he had not been out of the house since the previous Thursday and that he knew nothing of the affair.

The same afternoon there were crowds waiting outside Commercial Street police station when Detective Inspector Frederick Abberline arrived from Gravesend with William Piggott, a suspect who closely resembled Leather Apron. Somebody had noticed his bloodstained clothing as he was drinking in a pub in Gravesend and had sent for the police. Piggott's behaviour when he was being questioned had been so erratic that he was arrested at once. On his hands were several recent wounds. In custody he made a rambling statement that he had been in Whitechapel, walking down Brick Lane, on the Saturday morning at about half past four, when he had seen a woman fall down in a fit. Yet when he tried to pick her up she had bitten his hand. Exasperated by her behaviour he had struck her across the face and then, seeing two policemen coming towards them, run away. None of this explained the bloodstained shirts in the bundle of clothing that he was carrying, nor the blood that had recently been wiped off his boots. In London, however, none of the police witnesses could identify him. Nevertheless, rather than let him go it was thought best to keep him in custody until something more could be found out about him. But after two hours in the cells his behaviour and speech became so strange and so incoherent that a doctor was called in and on his advice Piggott was declared insane and sent immediately to an asylum in Bow.

An important point, which had to be cleared up when the inquest resumed, was the exact time of Annie Chapman's murder. According to the evidence, she must have been murdered after 5.30 a.m. which, if correct, meant that the killer must have walked through the streets in daylight with blood on his hands and clothes. There was some corroborative evidence for this. According to a police statement, a dustman had seen a man with bloodstained clothing walking down the street at about this time.

Doubts had been raised over the time of the killing. Dr Bagster Phillips had thought she might have been dead for about two hours when he saw the body at 6.30 a.m. He subsequently admitted that the heavy loss of blood and the coldness of the morning might have caused him to miscalculate the time. Another witness, who lived next door, said he was crossing the yard of 27 Hanbury Street at about 5.20 a.m. when he heard a woman's sharply uttered 'No' from the other side of the fence. A few minutes later he heard something fall against the fence. He could easily have misjudged the time as he said that he didn't get up until 5.15 and left for work at 5.30. His timing appears to be a little too rigid – a bit more flexibility might explain the discrepancy.

The first witness was John Richardson. His widowed mother rented the ground floor of 29 Hanbury Street as well as the workshop and yard at the back. It had been her habit to leave her door open, since she trusted her neighbour. But some time earlier the cellar in the yard had been broken into and a saw and a hammer stolen, and since then the cellar had been regularly padlocked at night. John Richardson used to check that the cellar flaps were secure whenever he was in the market. On the day of the murder he had gone to the house at between 4.40 and 4.45 a.m., only an hour before the body was discovered. The front door was closed and so was the yard door. He had not gone down the steps into the yard. The body hadn't been there then. Indeed, because one of his boots was hurting him he had sat down on the top step with his feet on the floor of the yard. He cut a piece of leather off his boot with a table knife that he had picked up by mistake in the morning at his house and put in his pocket. The coroner pounced on this point and questioned him closely about the knife, which the witness said was about five inches long. He was sent home to fetch it, and the coroner handed it over to the police (it was still lying on the table where he had left it).

Another point that had raised certain doubts in the coroner's mind about John Richardson's innocence had centred on the leather apron found by Dr Phillips lying half in a pan of water in the yard. Richardson's widowed mother explained that her son normally wore it when he was working in the cellar. On the Thursday she had washed it, leaving it by the fence where the police had found it on the Saturday morning. The police had wrongly assumed that it belonged to Leather Apron, John Pizer the bootmaker. Detective Sergeant Thicke said he had known Pizer for several years, and when anyone locally spoke of 'Leather Apron' they meant him.

Pizer was no longer in custody. The police had confirmed his alibi that he had been hiding with his brother and stepmother for four days and hadn't stirred out of doors until he was arrested by Sergeant Thicke on Monday morning. His brother had advised him not to leave the house as he was the prime suspect. In other words, he had an unshakeable alibi: from Thursday 6 to Monday 10 September he had not moved out of the house.

It was equally important that he should have an alibi for the night of 30–31 August, when Polly Nichols had been murdered. When questioned he told the coroner that he had spent the night at Crossman's common lodging house in the Holloway Road. It was called the Round-house. At 11 p.m. he had his supper and then walked as far as the Seven Sisters Road. He turned back and went down Holloway Road, from where he saw the glow of a large fire in the London docks. Outside the lodging house, when he got back, he spoke to the lodging-house keeper and one or two constables who were talking together. When he asked them where the fire was they could only tell him that it was a long way off. One of them had then added that he thought that it was 'down by the Albert Docks'. It was then about 1.30 a.m. as near as he could remember. He had then walked on as far as Highbury railway station before turning back to the lodging house. As it was after 11 p.m. when all the unoccupied beds were re-let, he paid the night-duty attendant 4d. for another bed. Before turning in he sat in the kitchen and smoked a clay pipe.

Next morning, he was woken up by the day attendant who told him that he must get up as he wanted to make the bed. He did so and went downstairs to the kitchen.

The coroner said that he thought it only fair to point out that this statement could be corroborated. Pizer left the court completely cleared of the allegations that had been made about him and free to begin the first of several court actions against those newspapers that had so grossly libelled him.

On 26 September Mr Wynne E. Baxter the coroner summed up the evidence. He reserved his bombshell for the end. Two things were missing from Chapman's body, he said: the rings, which had not been found, and the uterus, which had been taken from the abdomen. The body, he went on, had not been dissected but the injuries had been made by somebody with considerable anatomical skill and knowledge. There were no meaningless cuts. The amount that was missing would go into a breakfast cup, and had the post-mortem examination been less thorough it might easily have gone unnoticed. An unskilled person could not have performed such a deed nor, he added, pouring cold water on another popular theory, a mere slaughterer of animals. It must have been someone accustomed to the post-mortem room. It was impossible to escape the conclusion that a desire to possess the missing abdominal organ had been the object of the attack. If the object had been robbery, then the injuries to the viscera were meaningless, as death had resulted from the loss of blood from the cut throat. Moreover, when they found an easily accomplished theft of some paltry brass rings and an internal organ which it had taken a skilled person at least a quarter of an hour to remove, they were driven to the conclusion that the object of the attack was the abstraction of the viscera, and the stealing of the rings a thinly concealed attempt to disguise the fact.

It was not necessary to assume that the murderer was a lunatic, because there was in fact a market for such organs. After the earlier medical evidence had been published in the newspapers, the sub-curator of the pathological museum attached to one of the great medical schools had informed him of an incident that could have a bearing on the case. Some months previously an American had asked him to procure a number of specimens of the missing organ, and for these he was willing to pay £20 each; astonishingly, he planned to issue an actual specimen with each copy of a publication on which he was then engaged. Even though he was told his request was impossible, the American had persisted in his demands, explaining that he wanted them preserved in glycerine to keep them flaccid. He had afterwards made the same request to a similar institution.

Mr Baxter told the jury that he had passed this information on to Scotland Yard, and asked if it was not feasible that somebody, having heard of the American's request, had been incited to commit murder for gain.

This, as *The Times* pointed out in a leader the next day, not only threw a different light on Annie Chapman's murder but attributed to it an appalling motive. Sixty years had passed since Burke and Hare committed the series of murders that had given a new word to the English language. A few years later another resurrectionist had been convicted of the same offence. The price then for a body had been between £7 and £10, which, even allowing for the depreciation of money, was less than the sum the American was alleged to have offered. This fact, when coupled with the general conclusion that the murderer had a special method of arresting consciousness in his victim and was possessed of surgical skill, at once vastly narrowed the field of search. Obviously he was a class above the people he had killed, and considerably superior in education to the people whom the police first suspected. 'There is a perfect abundance of clues provided they are followed up . . . The police will be expected to follow up with the keenest vigilance the valuable clue elicited through the Coroner's inquest, and, since the lines of their investigation are plainly chalked out by information which they themselves failed to collect, it will be a signal disgrace if they do not succeed.'

3. Double Event

INCIDENTS RELATING TO THE EAST END MURDERS

RELATIONS OF SPIRITUALISTS. TRIAL OF BLOODHOUNDS. SIR C. WARREN VIEWING HANDWRITING ON WALL.

After a lull of some three weeks, two more equally brutal murders were committed, in the early hours of Sunday, 30 September and within a quarter of an hour's walking distance of each other.

The first body was found just after 1 a.m. in a narrow court off Berner Street, then a quiet street running down from Commercial Road to the London, Tilbury & Southend railway. At the entrance to the court were two large gates, one of them fitted with a wicket gate that was used when the gates proper were closed. On the left of the court were some terrace cottages, occupied by sweat-shop tailors and cigarette makers. Most of the residents had been in bed by midnight but some of them were kept awake by noise from the International Working Men's Educational Club on the other side of the court, where earlier in the evening there had been a heated debate followed by impromptu singing and dancing. Although it was after midnight, lights were still showing in the first-floor club windows and onto the terrace windows and roofs of the facing cottages. Otherwise the court was in darkness, and the street lights were out as well. Anyone coming into the court, therefore, had to grope his way for eighteen to twenty feet through a shroud of darkness that lay between the blind walls just inside the gates.

The steward of the club was Louis Diemschutz. He was also a traveller in cheap costume jewellery, which meant that he left the day-to-day running of the club to his wife. It was 1 a.m. when he eventually turned his pony and costermonger's barrow into the court. As he did so the pony shied to the left and wouldn't pull straight. Diemschutz thought at first that some mud or rubbish must be in the way but, when the pony shied again, he peered about and saw something bundled on the ground. He poked it with his whip before getting down and striking a match. It was a windy night and the match was instantly snuffed out, but in the spurt of light Diemschutz saw that the object was a woman, probably drunk. He hurried into the club and got a candle. Some of the club members came back with him and helped him to raise the woman's head and shoulders from the ground. It was then that they knew she was not merely drunk. Blood had coagulated on the cobbles from a gash in her throat, and a lot more – about two quarts, they thought – had flowed down the cobbles towards the club door. Her musty black clothes were wet from the rain. As they lifted her they saw that her hands were folded underneath her, one of them gripping a bag of cachous. Red and white flowers were pinned to her fur-trimmed jacket.

Several men immediately went off in search of a policeman. When they found one his whistle blasts soon brought others running to the courtyard and cottages, which were quickly sealed off. Dr Bagster Phillips examined the body and pronounced life extinct. Putting his hand inside the top of the woman's bodice and jacket, which were undone, he was heard to tell one of the policemen that she was still warm. He then examined for bloodstains the hands and clothes of everyone who had been in the club or who was living in the court, much to their indignation. They were equally enraged when their homes were thoroughly searched. Eventually the police abandoned their search about 5 a.m. By then, news was beginning to spread that there had been a second body found a mile away in Mitre Square in the City.

The Times thought that 'the assassin, if not suffering from insanity, appears to be free from any fear of interruption while on his dreadful work.' He had taken enormous risks. Mitre Square had three entrances – one from Mitre Street and passages from Duke Street and St James's Place. On two sides of the square there were warehouses belonging to Kearley and Tonge, with a watchman on night duty. On the third side, opposite where the body was found, there were two old houses, one of which was unoccupied and the other lived in by a policeman. On the fourth side were three empty houses. Every fifteen minutes during the night the square was patrolled by a police constable: at 1.30 the square had been empty when he strolled through; at 1.45 he had found a body.

In a sense this fourth killing was unique. The victim was, as it turned out, the only one to be murdered in the City of London and the investigation, unlike those of the other murders, was in the hands of the City police. They, responsible for the one square mile only, were answerable to the Corporation of the City of London, whereas Sir Charles Warren and the Metropolitan Police were answerable to the Home Office. The Commissioner was Sir James Fraser but, as he was nearing retirement and had been absent for two months, the investigation itself was in the hands of the Acting Commissioner, Major Henry Smith, described by a contemporary as a good raconteur and a good fellow. Since August he had been desperately keen to lay hands on the killer and, to guarantee success, had put nearly a third of the force into plain clothes, with instructions as he candidly admitted in his memoirs 'to do everything which, under ordinary circumstances, a constable should not do. It was subversive of discipline; but I had them well supervised by the senior officers. The weather was lovely, and I have little doubt that they thoroughly enjoyed themselves, sitting on doorsteps, smoking their pipes, hanging about public-houses, and gossiping with all and sundry.'

Smith was beginning to think that the killer had either gone abroad or had retired from business when he was woken up with the news of the Mitre Square murder. He had been spending an uncomfortable night in Cloak Lane police station, not far from Southwark Bridge. There was a railway goods depot in front of the station and a furriers behind, which meant that the sickening smell from the skins was always present. Sleep was an impossibility, and it was a relief when the bell by his head rang violently. After being told what had happened he had dressed and was in the street within a couple of minutes and boarded a hansom, which he detested:

This invention of the devil claims to be safe. It is neither safe nor pleasant. In winter you are frozen; in summer you are broiled. When the glass is let down your hat is generally smashed, your fingers caught between the doors, or half your front teeth loosened. Licensed to carry two, it did not take me long to discover that a fifteen stone Superintendent inside with me, and three detectives hanging on behind, added neither to its comfort nor to its safety. Although we rolled like a 'seventy-four' in a gale, we got to our destination – Mitre Square – without an upset, where I found a small group of my men standing round the mutilated remains of a woman.

She was lying on her back, with her left leg extended and her right leg bent. Her throat had been cut and she had been horribly mutilated. One large gash across her right cheek had severed the tip of her nose and part of her right ear, which in the mortuary fell from her clothes. She had been ripped open from the rectum to the breastbone and disembowelled. Some of the cuts had been made through the clothing which would have further reduced the risk of bloodstaining to the murderer who, the doctors deduced, had knelt on the right side of the body below its middle. Her chintz skirt with the three flounces had a jagged cut six and a half inches long from the waistband; her coarse brown bodice with the black velvet collar showed a clean cut five inches long made from right to left; a very old green alpaca skirt had a jagged downward cut ten and a half inches long in front of the waistband; a very old blue skirt with red flounces had a jagged cut ten and a half inches long through the waistband; her white calico chemise was torn at the front in the middle and was bloodstained all over. This was the only blood on the front of the clothes. The remaining clothes included a black cloth jacket with imitation fur edging; a grey stiff petticoat; a man's white vest; no drawers or stays; brown ribbed stockings which had been mended with white thread, and a pair of men's boots the right one of which had been repaired with red thread. Her black straw bonnet, trimmed with black beads and green and black velvet, was still tied to the back of her head.

In her pockets was probably everything she owned; this included two small blue bed ticking bags, two short black clay pipes, one tin box containing sugar and another with tea, one piece of flannel and six pieces of soap, a small tooth comb, a blunt white bone-handled table knife together with a metal teaspoon, a red cigarette case with white metal fitting, an empty tin match box, a piece of red flannel containing pins and needles, a ball of hemp, a piece of old white apron, a portion of a pair of spectacles, and two handkerchiefs, one with a red border. Dr Frederick Brown and Dr Sequeira carried out an initial examination in Mitre Square and a more detailed one that Sunday afternoon in the mortuary. Dr Brown said that the arms were by the side of the body, palms upwards, and that the intestines had been drawn out and placed over the right side – they were smeared over with some peculiar matter and a piece about two feet long was quite detached and had been placed between the body and the left arm apparently by design. The lobe and auricle of the right ear was cut obliquely through. There was a quantity of clotted blood on the pavement by the left side of the neck and the body was quite warm. There was a piece of red gauze silk with various cuts about the neck.

They examined the body just after 2 a.m. and death must have been within the half hour. There had been no spurting of blood on the bricks or pavement around the body. There was no trace of any recent sexual connection.

The mortuary examination showed that there was no bruising to the scalp, back of the body or elbows. The doctors believed that the wound to the throat, a cut about six inches long, was the first one inflicted and that she was lying on the ground when this was done. There would have been no noise. The throat had been severed instantly. Death would have been immediate and the mutilations inflicted after death. There would not have been much blood on the murderer who had used a pointed knife with a six-inch blade. After carefully taking out the left kidney he had still had sufficient time to nick the lower eyelids as he disfigured the corpse. A subsequent analysis of the stomach contents showed no signs of poison. At least five minutes had been needed for the disembowelment and mutilations.

One possible explanation for the severing of the tip of the nose, which never seems to have been considered, is that it was the murderer's way of branding the woman, true or not, as syphilitic. Syphilis was widespread throughout the Victorian era and, in the later stages of the disease, tertiary syphilis ate away the nose bone leaving a hole in the face. So widespread was the number of syphilitics with tertiary symptoms that artificial noses were widely available. In the Great Exhibition of 1851 one manufacturer offered sterling silver artificial noses while another from Whitechapel, where prostitution was widespread, offered a cheaper product. Removing her nose would have been the murderer's way of saying that she was both syphilitic and a prostitute.

Major Henry Smith had given orders that every man and woman seen together after midnight was to be stopped and questioned. He was convinced that if his orders were carried out, the murderer would be caught. What galled him now was the knowledge that the woman, Catharine Eddowes, had been in police custody, in a City police station, until a short while before her death.

At 8.30 p.m. on Saturday she had been found lying drunk on a pavement in Aldgate. PC 931 Robinson had picked her up and propped her against some shutters, but she had fallen down again. He had taken her to Bishopsgate police station and she had been put into a cell to sober up. At midnight she was heard singing and at about half past twelve she asked when she was going to be let out, as she was capable of looking after herself. It was normal policy, and a humane one, to let drunks out when they had sobered up rather than take them to court and punish them with a punitive fine that few of them could pay. She was let out, and with a 'Goodnight old cock' she walked out of the station towards Houndsditch and Mitre Square, which was less than a quarter of a mile away.

Somewhere on this route she met the Ripper.

When she had been discharged she had given her name as Kate Kelly (Eddowes was her maiden name), of 6 Fashion Street, Spitalfields. In her pocket were two pawn tickets, one of them in the name of Kelly. Her married name was in fact Conway but for the past seven years she had lived with a John Kelly. All three earned their livings as hawkers. Conway had left her about seven or eight years before because of her drinking (he was a teetotaller) and had taken their three children, two boys and a girl, Annie, with him. Annie, now twenty-three and married, gave evidence at the inquest. She said that she hadn't seen her mother for twenty-five months; she was expecting at the time, and her mother had asked her for money. She was purposely not told where the boys were living to stop her asking them. Her father had lived with her and her husband up until eighteen months ago but she didn't know where he and the boys – now fifteen and twenty years old – were now. The police had been unable to find them.

Eddowes must have taken up with John Kelly quite soon after her husband left her. According to Kelly they had been thrown together a good bit in the lodging house where they lived, at 55 Flower and Dean Street, which was why they had paired up. She used to get an occasional spot of charring and he picked up all the odd jobs he could get in the markets. She drank, he knew, but she was not troublesome. Most years they went hop-picking for a holiday and to make some money. They had not done too well this particular year and had walked back to town, arriving on Thursday, 27 September. Luck, as usual, was against them. They had no cash and the only thing of value that they possessed was a pair of boots, which they pawned in order to get a bite to eat. They had pledged them for one shilling and six pence, and got the same on a man's flannel shirt. Their first night back in London they spent in the casual ward in Shoe Lane. On Friday Kelly managed to earn sixpence and wanted to spend it on food, but Kate told him to take fourpence and go to the lodging house where he could at least get a decent night's lodging. She took the remaining twopence and went to the casual ward at Mile End. Kelly had seen her next morning at 8 a.m., and again on the Saturday afternoon when she had told him that she was going to Bermondsey to try to find her daughter Annie, presumably to borrow money from her. Later, he heard that she had been arrested and locked up because she'd had a drop of drink. Kelly didn't bother to go and ask about her because he was sure that she would turn up on the Sunday morning.

As the body of Eddowes was being undressed in the mortuary, the detectives noticed that part of the bloodstained apron that was around her neck had been cut away. This missing piece was found soon afterwards in Goulston Street, which was about a third of a mile away and some ten minutes' walk from Mitre Square. The scrap of material, which looked as if a knife had been wiped on it, had been discarded in a passageway to some flats. It was impossible to say if the blood was human. It was picked up by a patrolling policeman, Constable Alfred Long, who immediately searched the adjoining staircase for bloodstains. As he was shining his lamp about he saw that a message (which he was to wrongly transcribe) had been scrawled across the black dado of the wall. The message had been written in chalk – 'in a good schoolboy hand', according to one witness – and read:

> The Juwes are not
> The men that
>   Will be
> Blamed for nothing

He assumed that it must have been recently written because so many people were living in the flats that the words would certainly have been rubbed out soon after being written.

As soon as the constable had reported his discovery at Leman Street police station and handed his find to Dr Phillips, detectives converged on the building. They searched the flats and surrounding neighbourhood but, as usual, they found nothing. One of the City detectives, Daniel Halse, stayed behind, sending a message to the City head of CID, Mr McWilliam, that he would wait by the passage until it was light enough for a photograph to be taken of the words. This was because Goulston Street was on Metropolitan Police ground, and Superintendent Arnold, who was in charge of that division, wanted the words rubbed out since he thought that if they were seen they might inflame local prejudices and aggravate the danger of anti-Jewish riots. However, he was not prepared to shoulder the responsibility for the destruction of such a vital piece of evidence. His solution was to send an Inspector to wait at the spot with a dry sponge.

Sir Charles Warren, the Metropolitan Police Commissioner, had no doubts as to what must be done when he arrived at Leman Street police station shortly before 5 a.m. He hurried at once to Goulston Street and ordered the words to be rubbed out. Halse tried to persuade him to wait just one hour until it was light enough for a photograph to be taken. Afterwards, in a letter of explanation to the Home Secretary, Warren said that he thought that if they had waited so long the house might have been wrecked. Traders were just beginning to put out their stalls and the streets would soon be crowded.

Warren's explanation should be dismissed for the nonsense that it is. Safely ensconced back at Scotland Yard he must have realized that by ordering the destruction of the message he had laid himself open not only to even more press criticism but to criticism from within the police force itself. He had done something which, for any other police officer, would have justified instant dismissal: he had destroyed prima facie evidence in a major investigation. He was asked by the Home Office to submit a report justifying his behaviour and could only wriggle clear by saying that if the message had been left another hour the house might have been wrecked by anti-Semitic demonstrations. He was very economical with the truth. The doorway where the message was written is not a house. It is one of several stairways into a large, solidly built five-storey apartment block, as can still be seen today. There is no way that this building could have been wrecked in such a short time and, with all the resources available to him, it should have been ridiculous for Warren to argue that he could not secure the street and leave the message for one more hour. One possible explanation for his action is that he was a high-ranking freemason and it has been suggested that he recognized that the message had masonic connotations.

Warren had rejected a suggestion that the message be temporarily covered up, because he thought there was danger from rioting for as long as it was in place. He also rejected various compromises – from Halse, that perhaps they rub out only the top line, and, from one of his own men (probably Superintendent Arnold), that it might be enough to rub out the word 'Juwes' only. According to Major Smith, Acting Commissioner, City Police, the words, once copied down, were rubbed out by Warren personally.

What the exact wording was is still debatable. The controversy began at the inquest. Constable Long (Metropolitan) said that it was 'The Juwes are The men That Will not be Blamed for nothing'. His accuracy is questionable, as he admitted that he had not noticed the spelling of 'Juwes' until it was pointed out to him by an inspector. When Detective Halse (City) was asked for the exact wording he rendered it as 'The Juwes are not The men

That Will be Blamed for nothing'. As Halse was at the scene far longer, arranging for photographs and arguing for the preservation of the message, the balance of probabilities is that this version is the accurate one. But for either Smith or Warren to have admitted that their man was wrong would have meant an unacceptable loss of face – which is probably why there was never any common agreement on the wording. If, however, it is laid out as above, with a capital beginning each new line, then it conforms to Halse's description of it as about three lines long. (Stephen Knight's example in his Ripper book follows Long's wording and takes up six lines. He argues that the copyist tried to imitate the handwriting; but this is nonsense. It is a copy of a copy. The source was Long's pocket book, which had to be brought back from Westminster (presumably Scotland Yard) when the coroner asked the policeman to produce it as he was giving his evidence from memory.)

Smith had gone to bed by the time Warren called at City Police headquarters to tell them what he had done. It was left to his head of CID, Mr McWilliam, to tell Warren bluntly that he had made a bad mistake in destroying the writing, as a photograph might have yielded a clue.

Smith had roamed the streets for most of the night, hoping in vain for an arrest. In Dorset Street his men had been so close on the killer's trail that he had arrived there in time to see the bloodstained water where the Ripper had allegedly washed his hands. Finally, he had gone to bed about an hour before at 6 a.m., 'after a very harassing night' and feeling 'completely defeated'.

In the winter of 1887–8 relations between the Metropolitan Police Commissioner (Sir Charles Warren) and the Home Secretary (Henry Matthews) steadily worsened. Warren was also quarrelling with the head of the CID, James Monro. According to one contemporary, 'Warren was the finest man we had in Whitehall, but probably the worst appointment, because he must be independent, and the Commissioner of Police is held in very tight bonds by the Home Office. Matthews was an exceedingly able lawyer, but quite incapable of dealing with men.'

Warren's main quarrel with the Home Office was that it interfered too much in the internal administration of the force, and didn't give him the free hand to which he claimed the right under the statute appointing him Commissioner. Certainly he was justified in asking for an inquiry into the relations between the police and the Home Office. Faced with, and constantly referred to, memoranda and letters which he claimed that he had never seen, he could only take his stand and insist on the legal rights he was entitled to.

His internal quarrel with Monro, who had been the head of CID since 1884, was over the claim of his department to be an independent department – a state within a state, in fact, and free of the Commissioner's control. *The Times* related that the information which Monro gave to Sir Charles was the scantiest possible. Although he held the rank of Assistant Commissioner, Monro claimed to be independent of the Commissioner and responsible only to the Home Secretary; so much so that he refused to let Warren even see his correspondence. The Home Office played one off against the other, and Matthews annoyed Warren still more by writing to Monro direct. Such a state of affairs could not continue indefinitely and, in August 1888, Warren forced Monro to resign.

The officers of the CID, as Robert Anderson pointed out when he took over from Monro in September 1888, were already demoralized by the way their former chief had been treated. All sorts of rumours were being spread about his possible successor and for some 'occult reason' Anderson was sworn to secrecy regarding his appointment. As he had been in the habit of frequently meeting with Monro to discuss other matters on which they were engaged for the Home Office, it was immediately – and wrongly – assumed, when Warren started to make frequent calls on him, that the Commissioner was spying on him because he was Monro's friend. Indignation was so great among the senior officers that it was only with the greatest difficulty that Anderson stopped his chief subordinate from sending in his resignation.

An already serious situation was complicated still further by the fact that Anderson himself was feeling the strain of long periods of overwork and was physically unfit for his job. His doctor insisted that he should have two months' complete rest and told him that he would probably give him a certificate for a further two months' sick leave. Anderson said that was out of the question. He told the Home Secretary that 'greatly to his distress', he could not take up his new job until he had had a month's holiday in Switzerland. And so, after one week as head of CID, he crossed the Channel.

The night before he left, Annie Chapman was murdered in Hanbury Street. Soon the newspapers were beginning to comment on his absence.

Letters from Whitehall (presumably urging that he should return) forced Anderson to spend the last week of his holiday in Paris to be in closer touch with his office. He arrived in Paris on the night of the Berner Street and Mitre Square murders. Next day, an urgent appeal from the Home Secretary forced him back to London. He spent the day of his return and half the following night re-investigating the case. The next day he held a conference with Matthews, who told him that they would hold him responsible for finding the murderer, but Anderson shook his head in the negative.

'I hold myself responsible,' he said, 'to take all legitimate means to find him.'

He thought that the police methods so far had been 'wholly indefensible and scandalous, for these wretched women were plying their trade under definite police protection'. He actually suggested that all prostitutes found prowling the streets after midnight should either be arrested or warned that the police would not protect them. The first course was thought to be too drastic and, according to Anderson, the second was therefore adopted.

The Times reported that Warren sent 'every available man' into the East End in the hope of catching the killer red-handed.

In Anderson's absence, Warren decided to put the whole of the investigation into the hands of one man who would be the eyes and ears of the Commissioner. The man he put in charge was Chief Inspector Donald Swanson, not Inspector Abberline as is popularly believed. Warren thought the murders would be easily solvable and confidently, if in retrospect foolishly, wrote on 15th September, 'I am convinced that the Whitechapel Murder case is one which can be successfully grappled with if it is systematically taken in hand. *I go so far as to say that I could myself in a few days unravel the mystery if I could spare the time & give individual attention to it.*' (author's italics)

In charge locally was Inspector Frederick George Abberline. As so little is known of him it is worth putting down the few details that we do have. According to Scotland Yard records, he was born at Blandford, Dorset on 8 January 1843 and joined the Metropolitan Police on 5 January 1863. The records describe him as being 5 ft. 9½ ins. tall, with dark brown hair, hazel eyes and a fresh complexion. More mundanely, he had a varicose vein on the left leg below the knee. His wife's name was Emma, but when or where they were married is not known. He was appointed to N Division on joining, promoted to sergeant on 19 August 1865 (that's very rapid indeed), transferred to Y Division on 30 October 1865 and promoted to Inspector on 10 March 1878. He was transferred to A Division and then to CO Division on 19 November 1887. He was appointed First-class Inspector on 9 February 1888 and Chief Inspector on 22 December 1890.

Abberline had been one of the fourteen 'appointments to divisions' in 1878 to the newly formed CID which replaced the old Detective Department. He was a soft-spoken man, rather portly, with the appearance of a bank manager or a solicitor. He had unrivalled knowledge of the East End and for many years had been the detective inspector or Local Inspector for the

Whitechapel division which he had left only on promotion to the Yard. He was the best known of the squad of detectives out scouring Whitechapel. From 30 September his main aides were Inspectors Reid, Moore and Nairn, with Sergeants Thicke, McCarthy and Pearce (all of H Division). On average each of them had to follow up about thirty main enquiries per week in inner London and the suburbs.

After Emma Smith's murder back in April, people had gossiped at street corners about her death, but nothing more – brutal crime and indeed murder were not uncommon in Whitechapel. There was no hint of the panic and fear that was to come, when they began to walk about in groups, with sheer terror often reflected on their faces. But gradually, as the panic wore off, they would walk about in pairs and finally they could even joke about the murders to the local policeman, as he patrolled Flower and Dean Street, and quip, 'I'm the next for Jack' or, 'It's either the bridge or him.' Men often threatened, particularly in domestic disputes, 'I'll Whitechapel you.'

Scotland Yard's policy was to keep the newspapers at arm's length. Inevitably, the press, with so few facts to work on, turned their attention to the police and individuals such as the Commissioner, but none of them – including Abberline – was permitted to give interviews. This policy was wrong. As one policeman later wrote: 'I have always thought that the higher police authorities in ignoring the power of the Press deliberately flouted a great potential ally, and indeed might have turned that ally into an enemy.'

The first police theory was that the murders were the work of a gang levying blackmail on these women. This soon gave way to a more likely one that they were the work of one man. Once this was realized, it became much harder for the police to get information. People thought that if this theory were true, then the personal risks to themselves were much greater because he had no accomplice to betray him. Rather than jeopardize their lives, they withheld information which might possibly have led to the killer. Inevitably, there was a continuous flow of information of sorts to the police, some of it from publicity seekers who only wanted to see their name in the newspapers, and much of it was worthless.

Always there was the question of the killer's motive. The victims were too poor to be worth robbing; what they had in common was that all were prostitutes.

The Home Office refused to issue rewards for the killer's capture. (One inquest jury pointed out with some vehemence that, if the victim had come from the West End, the reverse would have been the case.) Warren was himself in favour of offering a reward, but was overruled by the Home Secretary. There were good reasons for such a decision. Experience had shown that offering rewards was often too strong a temptation for quasi-policemen and vigilantes and led to the formation of blood-money conspiracies in which the reward money led conspirators to frame innocent men, resulting in wrongful deaths and imprisonment. The last trials for such had been in 1816 and 1818. Even so, private individuals did now offer rewards.

As terror mounted, people's blood lust became sharper. Among the men concentrated in and around Hanbury Street was Constable Walter Dew, who was later to achieve fame as the man who arrested Crippen. He was standing in Hanbury Street when he saw a local villain, named Squibby, who was wanted on an assault charge (he had been throwing bricks at a policeman when one of them missed him and hit a child). As he moved in closer to arrest him Squibby dashed between the legs of a horse and ran off with Dew in hot pursuit and pulling out his truncheon as he ran. Immediately the crowd jumped to the conclusion that the man he was chasing was Jack the Ripper.

'Jack the Ripper! Jack the Ripper! Lynch him!' they shouted.

The cry was quickly taken up and, as they ran along, Dew could hear hundreds of feet running along behind him. In Flower and Dean Street, Squibby dashed into a lodging house and then into an adjoining building, where he was caught just as he tried to climb through a back window. Dew's immediate reaction was to prepare for a fight. Normally, it took six or eight policemen to bring Squibby into the station, fighting all the way. This time, however, the man was shaking with fright. Outside the crowd were shouting, 'Lynch him! Fetch him out!'

Fortunately, other policemen reached the house in time and barricaded the door against the mob while others went to Leman Street and Commercial Street police stations for reinforcements. This only confirmed the crowd's suspicions that the police had arrested the killer, and the shouts of 'Lynch him', 'Murder him' and 'Get him' became even more insistent.

As the police tried to force their way out through the crowd the screams and shouts became more furious still. The crowd surged against the lines of policemen trying to hold them back and made determined efforts to take Squibby from them. But the police managed to bundle the prisoner into a four-wheeler cab and, with an escort, get him to the station. Even so it was nearly turned over. In Spitalfields market they were forced to scramble out of the carriage and then to force their way through a double line of policemen to Commercial Street police station, through the frenzied mob. Even when they reached the station the mob didn't give up hope of lynching the prisoner. Several times they stormed the building. All efforts to convince them that the man had nothing to do with the murders were to no avail, and it was several hours before they calmed down.

All this, as Dew said, because some fool, seeing a man chased by the police, had shouted 'Jack the Ripper!'

On 1 October, the evening after her murder, the Berner Street victim was identified as Elizabeth Stride. One of the witnesses, who was taken to the mortuary to identify her, knew her also as Annie Fitzgerald. She was regularly arrested for drunkenness but whenever she was charged, she always denied that she was drunk and said that she suffered from fits. The inquest was held in the Vestry Hall, Cable Street, before Mr Wynne E. Baxter. One of the witnesses, a lodger at 32 Flower and Dean Street who had known Stride for six years, said that she had always known the woman as Long Liz. This was not a reference to her height. It was East End humour that men and women surnamed Stride should have a 'Long' put before their first name. She was also nicknamed Mother Gum because, when she laughed, a peculiarity of her mouth always displayed the upper gum. Another witness was Sven Olsson, the vestryman of the Swedish Church in Trinity Square, who had known her even longer, for about seventeen years.

Her maiden name was Elizabeth Gustafsdotter. She was born on 27 November 1843 in the parish of Torslanda, north of Gothenburg, Sweden. She was the daughter of a farmer called Gustaf Ericsson and his wife Beata Carlsdotter. Their farm was called Stora ('Big') Tumlehed. Elizabeth had one sister and two brothers. She was confirmed in Torslanda's church in 1859. On 14 October 1860, when she left school and was evidently old enough to work away from home, she took out a certificate of altered residence from the parish and moved to the parish of Carl Johan in Gothenburg, where she worked as a domestic until 1864 for a workman named Lars Fredrik Olofsson, who had four children. She moved again and on 2 February 1862 took out a new certificate to the Cathedral parish in Gothenburg but the details of her home address or place of work are not known. She still gave her profession as domestic.

In March 1865 she was registered as a prostitute by the Gothenburg police. The following month she gave birth to a stillborn girl. Possibly her pregnancy had forced her on to the streets as the only way of getting a living. According to the official ledger – she was entry No. 97 – in October the same year she was living in Philgaten in Östra Haga, a suburb of Gothenburg. She was described as being slightly built with blue eyes, brown hair, straight nose and oval face. The register entries of October and

November 1865 are for notification of communicable diseases. She had twice been in Kurhuset, the hospital for venereal diseases, the last time three weeks before. The 17 October entry specifies chancre (venereal ulcer) but the entries for 3, 7, 10 and 14 November state that she was 'Healthy'. After the last entry she was told that she no longer had to report to the police.

On 7 February 1866 she took out a new certificate of altered residence from the Cathedral parish to the Swedish parish in London. According to the certificate she could read reasonably well but had a poor understanding of the Bible and catechism. She was entered in the London register on 10 July 1866, an unmarried woman. Her first employment is thought to have been with a family in Hyde Park. In 1869 she is supposed to have married John Thomas Stride, a carpenter living at Sheerness. She subsequently claimed that he, with two of their nine children, was among the more than six hundred drowned when the pleasure steamer *Princess Alice* was rammed and sunk by a collier off Woolwich in 1878. A check of the passenger list reveals that nobody of the name of Stride was on board, however, and the only case recorded of a father and two children drowning was that of an accountant with two sons aged ten and seven.

For the three years before her death she had been living in Fashion Street with a waterside labourer named Michael Kidney. Occasionally she had earned some money by sewing and charring but, whenever the mood took her, or the restraints of their life together became too much for her, she would drift away from him for a while. During the time they were together they had separated altogether for about five months. The cause was always the same: drink. Kidney never went after her as he always knew that she would return to him in her own good time. On the previous Tuesday she had walked out on him. He didn't see her again until he identified her body in the mortuary.

She seems to have gone direct to 32 Flower and Dean Street which is where she was seen the next night by Dr Thomas Barnardo, who was himself to become a Ripper suspect, being then in his forties, a medical man and a surgeon with an intimate knowledge of the streets and East End low-life. He wrote to *The Times*:

Only four days before the recent murders I visited No. 32 Flower and Dean Street, the house in which the unhappy woman Stride occasionally lodged. I had been examining many of the common lodging houses in Bethnal Green that night, endeavouring to elicit from the inmates their opinions upon a certain aspect of the subject. In the kitchen of No. 32 there were many persons, some of them being girls and women of the same unhappy class as that to which poor Elizabeth Stride belonged. The company soon recognised me, and the conversation turned upon the previous murders. The female inmates of the kitchen seemed thoroughly frightened at the dangers to which they were presumably exposed. In an explanatory fashion I put before them the scheme which had suggested itself to my mind, by which children at all events could be saved from the contamination of the common lodging houses and the streets, and so to some extent cut off the supply which feeds the vast ocean of misery in this great city.

The pathetic part of my story is, that my remarks were manifestly followed with deep interest by all the women. Not a single scoffing voice was raised in ridicule or opposition. One poor creature, who had evidently been drinking, exclaimed somewhat bitterly to the following effect: 'We're all up to no good, and no one cares what becomes of us. Perhaps some of us will be killed next!' And then she added, 'If anybody had helped the likes of us long ago we would never have come to this!'

Impressed by the unusual manner of the people, I could not help noticing their appearance somewhat closely, and I saw how evidently some of them were moved. I have since visited the mortuary in which were lying the remains of the poor woman Stride, and I at once recognised her as one of those who stood around me in the kitchen of the common lodging house on the occasion of my visit last Wednesday week.

Doctors Blackwell and Phillips gave evidence to the Coroner's Inquest. Police had called both men to the murder scene, each arriving within a few minutes of the other. Stride's body was still warm when Blackwell examined it, apart from the hands, which were cold.

The right hand was lying on the chest, and was smeared inside and out with blood. It was quite open. The left hand was lying on the ground and was partially closed, and contained a small packet of cachous wrapped in tissue paper. There were no rings or marks of rings on the fingers. The appearance of the face was quite placid, and the mouth was slightly open. There was a check silk scarf round the neck, the bow of which was turned to the left side and pulled tightly. There was a long incision in the neck, which exactly corresponded with the lower border of the scarf. The lower edge of the scarf was slightly frayed, as if by a sharp knife. The incision on the neck commenced on the left side, 2 ½ inches blow the angle of the jaw, and almost in a direct line with it. It nearly severed the vessels on that side.

Both doctors performed the post-mortem next afternoon at St. George's mortuary in the presence of two other doctors. Phillips said that apart from the injury to the throat there were no other marks on the body except some healing sores.

The opinion of both men also agreed upon a knife which had been found at 1.20 a.m. in the Whitechapel road by another witness, Thomas Corman. A policeman saw him find it outside a laundry shop where it was lying on the bottom step of the doorway. A bloodstained handkerchief was tied around the handle with a string. The blade was dagger-shaped and about nine to ten inches long. It was a slicing knife and came from a chandler's shop. The blade was rounded at the point and both doctors thought it a highly unlikely weapon for the murderer to have used as it could only be used one way – although it would have been capable of making the incisions in the neck.

Two witnesses, who claimed to have seen the murderer, were

not called to give evidence at the inquest. The first was Matthew Packer, an elderly greengrocer and fruiterer, trading from his small shop at 44 Berner Street. When interviewed, during house-to-house inquiries, he said that he had closed up his shop at 12.30 a.m. and had seen nobody standing about, or heard any noise or anything suspicious. Two days later he gave a different story to two private detectives hired by the Whitechapel Vigilance Committee. He told them that at about 11.45 p.m. he had sold half a pound of black grapes to a man and woman who had loitered about the street for the next half hour eating them in the rain. This story underwent other modifications in its retelling to the newspapers. Bits and pieces of detail were added which Packer had either picked up from the newspapers or local gossip. As far as the doctors were concerned, when questioned on this point, they were emphatic that no grapes had been found in Stride's hands or near the body, nor had she swallowed or eaten any grapes before her death. The changes that Packer made to his story seem to be directly related to the reward that was being offered after the 'double event' of the Stride and Eddowes killings and his hopes of profiting from the murderer's capture. His differing statements were considered unreliable as evidence, which is why he never appeared before the Stride inquest as a witness.

Several people had seen Stride that evening up until a short time before her death and gave evidence to that effect. One puzzling omission was that of a local man, a Hungarian immigrant named Israel Schwarz, who saw the attack on Stride.

At 12.45 a.m. Schwarz had turned into Berner Street from Commercial Road. Ahead of him was a 30-year-old man, wearing a dark jacket and trousers, a black cap with a peak, and apparently partly drunk. He was clearly in an angry mood, which is possibly why he had been drinking, and obviously looking for a quarrel. The man was described as having a fair complexion, a small brown moustache and dark hair. At the gateway of Dutfields Yard he stopped to speak to Stride and immediately began to quarrel with her. The argument then became more physical as the man tried to pull Stride into the street, more out into the open where she could be seen, surely indicative that murder was not her attacker's original intention and, as Schwarz thought, it was some sort of domestic dispute. As they struggled, Stride screamed three times, but not very loud, obviously wanting to keep the noise of their quarrelling down to a minimum, which again suggests a possible domestic dispute, in other words, let's keep the noise down; there were people singing and talking in the club at the far end of the yard who would otherwise hear them. Schwarz crossed to the other side of the street. He was Hungarian and could not speak English and understandably was anxious not to get involved. Seeing him, Stride's attacker shouted out 'Lipski', a reference to the Lipski murder of the year before and now in common use to describe a Jew. His shout alarmed Schwarz even more. At the same time a man came out of a nearby pub holding a pipe, some theorists argue for a knife, and who, seeing what was happening, shouted something to Stride's attacker, possibly a warning to stop what he was doing. Schwarz, even more anxious, hurried away down the street followed by the pipeman who I suggest, like Schwarz, hurried away because he did not want to be involved in an unpleasant incident.

Stride was now pushed or dragged into the gateway of Dutfields Yard. She was thrown down facing the wall, her left side and face becoming plastered with mud, while some of the cachous that she had been holding in her left hand became scattered about the ground. Her attacker must have then dropped down on her, causing bruising, part kneeling on her to hold her in that position, and reaching under her chin cut her throat, the knife partially severing the left carotid artery and completely severing the windpipe causing the body to haemorrhage. He then made a smaller cut on the right side but not cutting deep enough to sever the deeper vessels on that side and which would not have proved fatal. According to Dr Phillips, the throat cutting could have been done in just a few seconds, possibly as little as two.

That night's 'double event' led to a natural assumption that both women had been Ripper victims. The newspapers certainly thought so as did the leading police investigators such as Abberline, Swanson, Smith, Macnaghten and Anderson, while others such as Walter Dew, then a young policeman, disagreed.

While it was certainly true that Eddowes was a Ripper victim, the same can't be said of Stride. All the evidence suggests that she was not Ripper victim but had been murdered by someone else.

On the day of her murder, Stride had earned 6d by cleaning rooms at her Flower and Dean Street lodgings. Later she went out and at 11 p.m. she was seen by two witnesses, J. Best and John Gardner, leaving the Bricklayers Arms in Settle Street. It was raining hard and she was with a man who was hugging and kissing her. Best and Gardner chaffed the man about his behaviour. They described him as definitely English, about 5'5" tall, with a black moustache, and wearing a morning suit and billycock (bowler) hat. At 11.45 p.m., when it had temporarily stopped raining, William Marshall, living in Berner Street, saw a few doors away a man with Stride but did not see his face; the man was decently dressed in a small black coat, dark trousers, wearing a round cap with a small peak, and with the manner and appearance of a clerk. Marshall heard him talking to Stride. It was an English voice. The man was kissing and cuddling her and had his arms about her neck. He was heard to say, 'You would say anything but your prayers'. The two of them then walked away. This lovesick swain was almost certainly the same man seen by Best and Gardner. By midnight it was raining again and Matthew Packer, who claimed to have sold Stride's companion some black grapes, commented what fools the couple were to be standing in the rain. He noted at the same time that the pubs had closed and the time was then 12.10 or 12.15 a.m. Packer described the man as about 35, about 5'7", stout and square built, wearing a wide-awake hat (a felt hat with a low crown and wide brim so called because it never had a nap), dark clothes, and the appearance of a clerk, his words uttered in a quick sharp way. As with Marshall's description, there is the same reference to a man of clerk-like appearance. A question mark, however, has to hang over Packer's description because of the discrediting of his other evidence.

PC 452H Smith saw Stride between 12.30 and 12.35 a.m. He described the man she was with as being about 5'7" tall, wearing a dark overcoat and trousers and a hard deerstalker hat. He was clean shaven and respectable. I would suggest yet again this is the same man as seen by the earlier witnesses. The slight discrepancies in description are understandable when it is remembered that it was a dark night and raining. This confusion is reflected in the fluctuating descriptions of the suspect subsequently given in the Police Gazette.

Another witness, James Brown, claimed that he had seen Stride with a man in Fairclough Street, crossing Berner Street, at 12.45 a.m. This was the same time that Israel Schwarz said that he had seen Stride attacked and thrown to the ground. The man had his arm against the wall to detain her. Brown heard the woman say, 'Not tonight, some other time'. The newspapers subsequently learned that there was a courting couple in the street and certainly the language can be seen as sexually explicit: he is asking for sex and she is putting him off. I think Brown did see Stride but it was the same man she had been with for the past hour and a half and that Brown, who self-confessedly was not very observant, simply made a mistake in the time.

What I believed happened that night was that the man with Stride for much of the late evening is someone who, from his words and behaviour, is clearly passionate about her. He has been continually with her since leaving the pub, he is extremely demonstrative both at the pub and in Berner Street; he wants sex, she is promising him that but withholding it, hence his remark 'You would say anything except your prayers'. They still stay talking, even in the rain, which prompts Packer's comment about what fools they are, and then they move away, possibly for a bit more shelter and then there is the final rejection in Fairclough Street of 'Not tonight, some other time' which is when her companion finally accepts that he is not going to get his way and leaves. Stride then moves back to Berner Street, to Dutfields Yard.

One of the puzzling factors is why Stride has been hanging around Berner Street all this time. She is with someone who she has no intention of sexually satisfying; she is not earning money; it is a dark night; it is late; the pubs have closed and it is raining, so why does not she go back to her lodgings? The only theory that fits the facts is that she was waiting for someone, almost certainly for someone with whom she is in a relationship, and this is the man who will kill her. Schwarz commented that seeing the attack on Stride he thought he was witnessing a domestic dispute, which is why he crossed the road to avoid it, and that is precisely what it was, a domestic dispute of sorts except that it would end in murder.

All the evidence points to Stride not being a Ripper victim. The murderer's first cut was sufficient to kill her. There was no attempt at mutilation such as happened in the Nichols and Chapman murders although there was a fifteen minute window between Schwarz seeing the attack and the discovery of the body. Some have argued, notably Swanson, that this fifteen minute window would have allowed time for her attacker to abscond and for her to pick up a customer. All the evidence shows, in fact, that she was not trying to pick up a customer that evening and that the fifteen minute window is not so large if Schwarz sees the attack at 12.45 a.m. By contrast, Swanson, when referring to the Mitre Square murder, thought that the ten minute window between Eddowes being seen alive and her body being found meant it was safe to say that the man she was with was her murderer. Despite the two or three minute difference in Stride's murder, the same can confidently be said that Schwarz and possibly two others did see Stride's murderer.

But almost certainly he was not Jack the Ripper.

Stride, I believe, was the victim of some sort of love triangle or domestic dispute. Looking at the Ripper's modus operandi there was no strangulation or asphyxiation before the throat cutting. There were no abdominal mutilations. Certainly the fifteen minute window allowed time for that to be done. The injuries on Polly Nichols it has been estimated could have been done in less than four minutes. Those on Eddowes could have been done in less than five. Stride's throat had been cut, not with a long straight bladed knife of about 6 to 8 inches in length and with a sharp point that could nick the vertebrae, such as was used on Eddowes less than an hour later, but with a short, broad and possibly blunt knife with a beveled end. Dr Phillips thought that Stride's injuries, the cutting of the left carotid artery and division of the windpipe, could have been inflicted in just a few seconds, possibly as little as two. He further pointed out the great dissimilarity in the throat cutting between Chapman and Stride, how in the former the neck was severed all the way down to the vertebral column and an evident attempt had been made to separate the bones. The fact that the knife used on Stride was blunt suggests that had murder been the killer's original intention he would at least have taken a sharpened knife with him.

If not the Ripper, then who was Stride's murderer? The likeliest and most obvious suspect, but there is no evidence against him, is 36-year-old Michael Kidney who had lived with Stride for most of the past three years. They had a somewhat turbulent relationship, separating on occasions totaling about four months. In July 1888 he had been sent down for three days for being drunk and disorderly and at the time of the murder had not seen Stride for about five days. On September he went to Leman Street police station asking to see a detective as he had some information about the murder but this turned out to be just drunken ramblings. In June 1889 he was treated at the

Whitechapel Workhouse Infirmary for syphilis.

What evidence we do have suggests that Kidney was never suspected of Stride's murder, although only the year before she had charged him with assault, but failed to turn up in court to give evidence against him. A possible explanation for Kidney not being considered a suspect was because the police investigators had already assumed that the 'double event' was the work of one man and that Kidney was not the man they were looking for.

What this revision of Stride's murder does suggest is that we no longer have a scenario, put forward by many, of the Ripper, psyched up by his failure to mutilate and get body parts, crossing the boundary between the two police districts, buying time as he does so, in search of a fourth victim to ease the pangs of his frustration.

Instead, what we now have is the Ripper looking for a victim on City police ground not knowing that a murder has already taken place and that he is in danger of being caught, as the two forces liaise and begin random street stops on both sides of the boundary.

Within twenty-four hours of the 'double event' the public were clamouring for the resignation of the Police Commissioner Sir Charles Warren and the Home Secretary. At a meeting of nearly a thousand people in Victoria Park, the crowd passed a resolution calling on them to make way for men who would leave no stone unturned to find the murderer. At four other meetings in Mile End there were similar resolutions passed.

A petition was presented to the Queen by George Lusk, head of the Whitechapel Vigilance Committee, on behalf of the inhabitants of Whitechapel, asking for her Government to offer a reward for the capture of the murderer. Warren had already tried to persuade the Home Secretary to agree to this but Matthews had refused him. He similarly advised the Queen that it would be bad policy to agree to this measure now. Fortunately, the City of London Corporation did not come under Home Office control and within twenty-four hours of the murders Colonel Fraser, the City Police Commissioner, offered a reward of £500 for information leading to the capture of the Whitechapel murderer.

A petition more to the Queen's liking was collected within the three days following the murders and forwarded by the St Jude's vicar's wife Mrs Barnett, who had managed to collect between four and five thousand signatures:

To our Most Gracious Sovereign Lady Queen Victoria.

Madam – We, the women of East London, feel horror at the dreadful sins that have been lately committed in our midst and grief because of the shame that has fallen on our neighbourhood.

By the facts which have come out in the inquests, we have learnt much of the lives of those of our sisters who have lost a firm hold on goodness and who are living sad and degraded lives.

While each woman of us will do all she can to make men feel with horror the sins of impurity which cause such wicked lives to be led, we would also beg that your Majesty will call on your servants in authority and bid them put the law which already exists in motion to close bad houses within whose walls such wickedness is done and men and women ruined in body and soul.

We are, Madam, your loyal and humble servants.

In vain, a harassed Warren pointed out that he had drafted as many police reinforcements into the East End as he could spare. In a long and detailed letter published in *The Times* on 4 October he refuted point by point the allegations that he had switched experienced detectives from one district to another where they had no local knowledge to help them; that he had not changed the old system of beat patrols but had kept the same one that had been in existence for the past twenty years. But the public was wanting a scapegoat and it did not matter what he said or did. The mounting opposition to him was completely summed up in one newspaper headline – WAR ON WARREN.

He was heaped with ridicule when he negotiated with a Mr

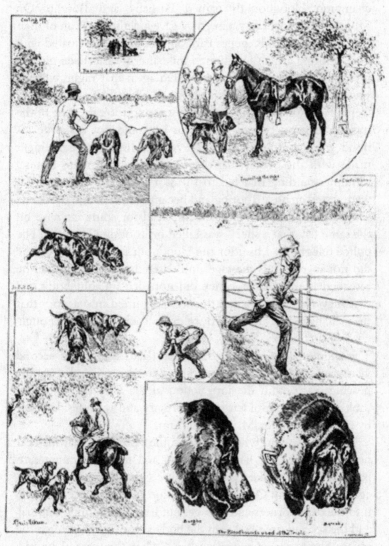

Warren and the bloodhounds

Edwin Brough of Scarborough, Yorkshire, for the use of two champion bloodhounds named Barnaby and Burgho. On Monday, 8 October at 7 a.m., they gave a demonstration of their tracking powers in Regent's Park on ground thickly coated with frost, hunting a man for about a mile after he had been given a fifteen-minute start. They were tested again that night, when it was dark, and again the next morning, when half a dozen runs were made. Warren himself was present and took the part of the hunted man on two of them. But he could not make up his mind whether to use them. There was never any agreement made with the owner that they would be. It was this general misunderstanding that led to the story that the bloodhounds were tested again at Tooting and became lost in a fog. Barnaby's keeper took him to Hemel Hempstead for some exercise on the same day that a sheep was killed on Tooting Common. The police telegraphed him for the bloodhounds to be sent but he did not receive this message until later that evening when he returned home. Because they did not turn up somebody said that they were missing and this was magnified into a story that they had been lost, although Burgho was back up in Scarborough.

The inquest on Catharine Eddowes (Kate Kelly), the second victim on 30 September, opened on Thursday 4 October. As the hearing was within the jurisdiction of the City of London, it took place at the Golden Lane mortuary and was presided over by the City coroner, Mr S. F. Langham.

PC 881 Watkins, who had found the body, said that his beat normally took him between twelve and fourteen minutes to patrol. He had walked through Mitre Square at 1.30 a.m. and again at 1.44 a.m. On the first occasion he had shone his lamp into the dark corners and passages but had seen nothing unusual, and the second time had seen the body as soon as he entered the square. She had been ripped up, like a 'pig in the market', he said, and her entrails 'flung in a heap about her neck'.

He had run across to Kearley and Tonge's warehouse, where

the door was ajar, and called to the watchman who was sweeping the stairs: 'For God's sake, mate, come to my assistance.' From his appearance the watchman thought that he was ill. As he was an ex-policeman himself, and knew what to do, he ran into the square and blew his whistle for help as this was more likely to attract attention than the policeman's old-fashioned rattle.

If his times were correct – and Watkins said that he checked his watch immediately after speaking to the watchman – then, allowing for the constable's time in entering and leaving the square and getting out of earshot, the Ripper could have had only between seven and eight minutes in which to kill the woman and do his work. This would apparently have been enough; the doctors said that he would have needed a minimum of five minutes. A search was made at the back of the empty houses but apparently not inside them. According to the medical evidence, her throat was not cut until she was lying down. Thus, if the murderer had first strangled her, there would have been no risk of her screaming or calling out, and this would have given him more chance of getting safely away.

Nobody had seen them go into the square. But a couple of witnesses who had left the Imperial Club in Duke Street, close by, just after 1.30 a.m., had seen a man and a woman standing together at the corner of Church Passage leading into Mitre Square. The woman was wearing a black jacket and bonnet, and one of the witnesses thought that clothes he later saw in the mortuary were the same. The woman was about three or four inches shorter than the man, and the witness saw her put her hand on his chest, though not apparently to push him away. She was facing him and they were talking together quietly. When the witness was asked to describe him, the prosecution asked that the description should not be given as, it was inferred, it might hinder police inquiries. Later, this description was published in the *Police Gazette*:

At 1.35 a.m., 30 September, with Catharine Eddowes, in Church Passage, leading to Mitre Square, where she was found murdered at 1.45 a.m., same date, a man, age 30, height 5 feet 7 inches, or 8 inches; complexion fair, moustache fair, medium build; dress: pepper and salt colour loose jacket, grey cloth cap with peak of same material, reddish neckerchief tied in knot; appearance of a sailor. Information respecting this man to be forwarded to Inspector McWilliam, 26 Old Jewry, London E4.

Dr Sequeira and Dr Brown, both of whom had been called to Mitre Square and been present at the post-mortem, thought that the murderer had shown no evidence of any anatomical knowledge other than that which could be expected of a professional butcher or meat cutter. Dr Saunders, who had examined the contents of the stomach for poison, and who had also been present at the post-mortem, agreed with them. Most of the relevant points of this examination were dealt with by Dr Brown, who was the surgeon of the City of London Police, in his long and detailed statement, followed by cross-examination.

The throat was cut across to the extent of about 6 inches or 7 inches. The sterno cleido mastoid muscle was divided; the cricoid cartilage below the vocal cords was severed through the middle; the large vessels on the left side of the neck were severed to the bone, the knife marking the intervertebral cartilage. The sheath of the vessels on the right side was just open; the carotid artery had a pin-hole opening; the internal jugular vein was open to the extent of an inch and a half – not divided. All the injuries were caused by some very sharp instrument, like a knife, and pointed. The cause of death was haemorrhage from the left common carotid artery. The death was immediate. The mutilations were inflicted after death. They examined the injuries to the abdomen. The walls of the abdomen were laid open, from the breast downwards. The cut commenced opposite the ensiform cartilage, in the centre of the body. The incision went upwards, not penetrating the skin that was over the sternum; it then divided the ensiform cartilage, and being gristle they could tell how the knife had made the cut. It was held so that the point was towards the left side and the handle towards the right. The cut was made obliquely. The liver was stabbed as if by the point of a sharp knife. There was another incision in the liver, and 2½ in., and, below, the left lobe of the liver was slit through by a vertical cut. Two cuts were shown by a jag of the skin on the left side. The abdominal walls were divided vertically in the middle line to within a quarter of an inch of the navel; the cut then took a horizontal course for 2½ in. to the right side; it then divided the navel on the left side round it – and made an incision parallel to the former horizontal incision, leaving the navel on a tongue of skin. Attached to the navel was 2½ in. of the lower part of the rectus musela of the left side of her abdomen. The incision then took an oblique course to the right. There was a stab of about an inch in the left groin, penetrating the skin in superficial fashion. Below that was a cut of 3in., going through all tissues, wounding the peritoneum to about the same extent. There had not been any appreciable bleeding from the vessels.

MR CRAWFORD: What conclusion do you draw from that?

DR BROWN: That the cut in the abdomen was made after death, and that there would not be much blood left to escape on the hands of the murderer. The way in which the mutilation had been effected showed that the perpetrator of the crime possessed some anatomical knowledge.

MR CRAWFORD: I think I understood you to say that in your opinion the cause of death was the cut in the throat?

DR BROWN: Loss of blood from the throat, caused by the cut. That was the first wound inflicted.

MR CRAWFORD: Have you formed any opinion that the woman was standing when that wound was inflicted?

DR BROWN: My opinion is that she was on the ground.

MR CRAWFORD: Does the nature of the wounds lead you to any conclusion as to the kind of instrument with which they were inflicted?

DR BROWN: With a sharp knife, and it must have been pointed; and from the cut in the abdomen I should say the knife was at least six inches long.

MR CRAWFORD: Would you consider that the person who inflicted the wounds possessed great anatomical skill?

DR BROWN: A good deal of knowledge as to the position of the organs and the abdominal cavity and the way of removing them.

Mr Crawford: Could the organs removed be used for any professional purpose?

Dr Brown: They would be of no use for a professional purpose.

Mr Crawford: You have spoken of the extraction of the left kidney. Would it require great skill and knowledge to remove it?

Dr Brown: It would require a great deal of knowledge as to its position to remove it. It is easily overlooked. It is covered by a membrane.

Mr Crawford: Would not such a knowledge be likely to be possessed by one accustomed to cutting up animals?

Dr Brown: Yes.

Mr Crawford: Have you been able to form any opinion as to whether the perpetrator of this act was disturbed when performing it?

Dr Brown: I think he had sufficient time. My reason is that he would not have nicked the lower eyelids if he had been in a great hurry.

Mr Crawford: About how long do you think it would take to inflict all these wounds, and perpetrate such a deed?

Dr Brown: At least five minutes would be required.

Mr Crawford: Can you as a professional man assign any reason for the removal of certain organs from the body?

Dr Brown: I cannot.

Mr Crawford: Have you any doubt in your mind that there was no struggle?

Dr Brown: I feel sure that there was no struggle.

Mr Crawford: Are you equally of opinion that the act would be that of one man, one person, only?

Dr Brown: I think so; I see no reason for any other opinion.

Mr Crawford: Can you as a professional man account for the fact of no noise being heard by those in the immediate neighbourhood?

Dr Brown: The throat would be so instantaneously severed that I do not suppose there would be any time for the least sound being emitted.

Mr Crawford: Would you expect to find much blood on the person who inflicted the wounds?

Dr Brown: No, I should not.

At the conclusion of the hearing on 12 October the jury brought in a verdict of 'Wilful murder by some person unknown'.

4. Miller's Court

THE SEVENTH HORRIBLE MURDER BY THE MONSTER OF THE EAST-END.

THE SEVENTH VICTIM! PICKED OUT FOR SLAUGHTER BY THE EAST-END FIEND.

Number 26 Dorset Street was less than a quarter of a mile away from Hanbury Street where Annie Chapman had been murdered. The rooms were let to anyone who wanted them by the lodging-house keeper, John McCarthy, who also kept a small chandler's shop close by. The original back parlour had been cut off from the rest of the house by a false partition and this was now known as Room 13. Although it was only a single room, and as such was part of the house, it had its own entrance (the second door on the right) into Miller's Court; this was a narrow court about a yard and a half wide at the side of the house. Further up this court, which was approached through a narrow arch, there were six more houses with whitewashed fronts, three on each side, two of which were certainly occupied by prostitutes (and so, one suspects, were the rest). Most of the slum housing in the area had been converted into common lodging houses. One of them, directly opposite Miller's Court, had three hundred beds which were taken every night.

Earlier in the year, in February or March, Room 13 had been let for four shillings a week to an attractive 24-year-old, Mary Jane (or Mary Ann) Kelly. She shared the room with her common-law husband Joseph Barnett until 30 October when they had a violent quarrel, breaking a window in the process. According to Barnett, who left her and went to live in a lodging house in Bishopsgate, they broke up because Kelly brought home another prostitute and insisted on their sharing the room with her. After two or three nights he had refused to do so any longer and this had led to the violent quarrel and break up. He apparently made no attempt to move back, not even when this prostitute, Mrs Harvey, moved out to lodgings in nearby New Court.

Kelly was desperately short of money and went back to soliciting in the Aldgate and Leman Street area. She owed over three months' rent and was drinking more heavily than usual. She spent part of the last night she was seen alive, 9 November, in the public houses in Commercial Street. It was probably in one of these that she picked up a client and took him back home. Mrs Cox, one of the Miller's Court prostitutes, followed them into the court at about 11.45 p.m. Kelly was very drunk. She was with a short stout man, shabbily dressed, with a billycock hat on his head and a quart can of beer in his hand; he had a blotchy face and a heavy carrotty moustache. Mrs Cox said, 'Goodnight Mary,' and as the man banged the door behind them Kelly called out, 'Goodnight, I'm going to have a song.' She began to sing 'Only a violet I plucked from my Mother's Grave when a Boy.' She was still singing when Mrs Cox went out again about quarter of an hour later and when she returned home at 1 a.m. At about 3.10 a.m., when Mrs Cox returned for the last time, wet through from the rain, the light was out in Room 13 and the court was quiet.

Directly above Mary Kelly's room was No. 20, occupied by Elizabeth Prater. She was separated from her husband and almost certainly a prostitute like the others in the court. She went wearily to bed about 1.30 a.m. and fell asleep still wearing her clothes. About 3.30 or 4 a.m., she wasn't sure which, she was woken up by her cat. At the same time she heard a low cry of 'Oh! Murder!' coming from somewhere close by. The voice was a woman's but she wasn't sure whether it came from the court or one of the houses. She said later that Kelly had only to move about in her room and she could hear her. As she didn't hear it again she dropped off to sleep once more. This wasn't callousness. She didn't pay any attention because such shouts were a normal occurrence in the neighbourhood. She slept on until 5 a.m. when she got up and went to the Ten Bells pub for her morning tot of rum and to solicit for custom among the market porters.

At 10.45 a.m. the lodging-house keeper sent his shop assistant, Thomas Bowyer, to ask Kelly if she could pay the rent as she was twenty-nine shillings in arrears. Bowyer knocked on the door and, as he couldn't get an answer, he went to the side and poked his hand through the broken pane of glass (it had been stuffed with rags ever since the final quarrel with Barnett) and pulled back the muslin curtain inside. He was horrified by what he saw. The first thing he observed was what appeared to be two pieces of flesh on the table in front of the bed. When he could steel himself to look again he saw the body, which was lying on the bed, and a pool of blood on the floor. He went back to the shop and told McCarthy what he had seen.

'Good God, do you mean that, Harry?' McCarthy said. They ran back together to Miller's Court, and the sight was even more ghastly than McCarthy had expected. He sent Bowyer to the police station. Inspector Beck soon arrived and after he had confirmed the accuracy of Bowyer's report he sent a telegram to Divisional Superintendent Arnold telling him what had happened. Shortly afterwards Inspector Abberline arrived and gave orders to seal off the court. Nobody was to enter or leave without his permission. At Dr Phillips's suggestion he refused to let anyone enter the house until the bloodhounds had been given a chance to show what they could do. He cabled a telegram to Commissioner Warren requesting that they be brought immediately.

Unfortunately, none of them there knew that Warren had resigned the day before.

Monro's resignation in the summer as head of the CID had only added to the Commissioner's troubles. Monro had transferred to the Home Office but, even though no longer at Scotland Yard, he still retained his hold over the CID. He was only able to maintain his grip on the plain-clothes department with the support of the Home Secretary, Henry Matthews, who was just as much a misfit as was Warren himself. Warren had vigorously campaigned against this twin-pronged attack and against the constant undermining of his authority, but his complaints had been ignored and for the past few weeks he had been given only the scantiest details of the daily conferences held at the Home Office between Monro, Anderson and the heads of the CID. In November Warren forced a crisis by writing an article for *Murray's Magazine* on 'The Police of the Metropolis'. In it he stressed that the head of CID should be subordinate to the Commissioner of Police, and that it was impracticable for police work to be done efficiently when one was independent of the other.

Matthews angrily drew his attention to a Home Office circular forbidding police to discuss internal matters in the press and Warren replied by tendering his resignation for the second time on 8 November, the day before Kelly's murder. This time it was accepted. The pill was made even more unpalatable for him by Matthews then appointing Monro as Commissioner in his place.

His resignation momentarily paralysed the police machine and was the reason for the hesitation and indecision next morning after Kelly's body had been found. Nobody in Miller's Court knew, as they waited, that Warren, even then, was still undecided about the merits of buying the dogs Burgho and Barnaby. Burgho was sent back, at the owner's request, to compete in some dog shows, while Barnaby stayed in London at a house in Doughty Street. After the Mitre Square murder, his temporary keeper was asked to take him to a nearby shop that had been burgled that same night, just in case the two incidents were linked and the dog might be able to pick a scent. This was an impossibility as any scent that might have existed had been scoured from the ground by the large number of curious policemen blundering in and out of the shop. Barnaby's owner was furious when he heard that his dog had been used for such a purpose and demanded its return at once. His greatest fear was that, if it became known that his dogs were being used to track burglars, certain 'ruffians of the night' might try to kill them by putting down poisoned meat. As the police hadn't bought his dogs it was unlikely that in this event they would compensate him for their loss.

Throughout the morning the crowds steadily gathered in Dorset Street. It was Lord Mayor's Day, but Jack the Ripper had stolen the show. When the procession had turned into Ludgate Hill in front of St Paul's Cathedral, the newsboys burst through the crowds with their newspapers and placards screaming '*Murder – Horrible Murder*'. At the same time scores of medical students dashed along the wet and greasy pavements of the street, knocking off hats in their exuberance. One policeman was pushed to the ground by a student who jumped on his back and bit his thumb. All the 'circus element was let loose' and, for the Lord Mayor, Sir James Whitehead, the day was ruined. If, as *The Star* thought, the Ripper was craving notoriety and wanted to 'be the sensation of the hour', then he had chosen his time well. 'He got his sensation. While the well-stuffed calves of the City footmen were being paraded for the laughter of London his victim was lying cold in a foul, dimly-lit court in Whitechapel.'

At 1.30 p.m. Superintendent Arnold decided that they could wait for Warren no longer and ordered one of the windows to be taken out. The investigators were appalled by what they saw. The *Illustrated Police News* reported:

Miller's Court. Mary Kelly's lodgings

The throat had been cut right across with a knife, nearly severing the head from the body. The abdomen had been partially ripped open, and both of the breasts had been cut from the body, the left arm, like the head, hung to body by the skin only. The nose had been cut off, the forehead skinned, and the thighs, down to the feet, stripped of flesh. The abdomen had been slashed with a knife across downwards, and the liver and entrails wrenched away. The entrails and other portions of the frame were missing, but the liver etc., it is said, were found placed between the feet of this poor victim. The flesh from the thighs and legs, together with the breasts and nose, had been placed by the murderer on the table, and one of the hands of the dead woman had been pushed into her stomach.

A photographer arrived and took pictures of this butcher's shambles. There was a popular theory that in cases of violent death the last images were permanently fixed on the retina of the eye and that by photographing them the killer could be identified. This was the basis of Jules Verne's story 'Les Frères Knap'. Surprisingly, the killer had not mangled the eyes at all. Possibly he had left them alone as some sort of unspoken challenge to the police to do their best – or worst. According to a German correspondent there were three ways of photographing the retina. The eye had to be drawn a little way out of its socket and a small incandescent lamp placed behind the eye. Three photographs had to be taken: of the illuminated pupils, of the illuminated pupils with the nerves of the eye excited by electricity, and the eye not illuminated but again with the nerves electrically excited. Other than the official statement that the eyes were photographed now, nothing more is known.

To enter the crime scene, McCarthy had broken open the door with a pickaxe. This again is an unexplained mystery. According to Inspector Abberline, giving evidence at the subsequent inquest, the murderer had not locked the door and walked off with the key as some newspapers supposed. The key, he said, had been missing for some time. Joseph Barnett confirmed this. He said that he and Kelly used to open the door by reaching through the broken window at the side and pulling back the bolt. Yet this window was not broken until their quarrel on 30 October. After that, Barnett had visited Kelly several times, on friendly terms – indeed, he brought her money – and it is only on these subsequent visits that he could have used this means of entrance. It also means that the key was lost only within the last ten days. Yet *someone* had a key, and used it, which is why the door had to be forced.

As Dr Phillips pushed the door back it knocked against a table by the bed. The first thing he noticed was how sparsely the room was furnished. It was about twelve feet square, and apart from the bed the only furniture was a chair and two tables. The body was wearing a chemise or some linen undergarment and was lying on the edge of the bed nearest to the door. The other side of the bed was touching the wooden partition. From the amount of blood on the floor and on the sheets nearest to the partition Phillips was sure that the body had been moved after the carotid artery had been cut (this having been the immediate cause of death). The bedclothes had been rolled back, presumably by the murderer, but the dead woman's clothes were still neatly folded on one of the chairs. There were no signs of a struggle, and no knife.

A large fire had been burning in the grate. The ashes were still warm, even seven hours after the estimated time that the Ripper had left the house. When they were sifted it was evident that he had burnt some women's clothing, and it was presumed that he had done this to enable him to see what he was about. There were parts of a skirt and the rim of a woman's hat in the grate.

Phillips ordered the body to be taken to Shoreditch mortuary for a detailed post-mortem and inquest. A one-horse carrier's cart trundled into Dorset Street at 3.45 p.m. and the crowds of horrified but interested bystanders watched as a scratched and dirty coffin which had seen a lot of use was carried into the court. When it was realized that the body was to be brought out there was an immediate rush of spectators into Dorset Street from the surrounding area, and a determined effort was made to break through the police lines. 'Ragged caps were doffed and slatternly-looking women shed tears as the shell, covered with a ragged-looking cloth, was placed in the van' and taken away.

After it had gone, the windows of Room 13 were boarded up, a padlock was put on the door and a policeman had to be stationed temporarily by the court to keep sightseers away.

Dr Roderick MacDonald MP, who was the coroner for the district, fixed the following Monday morning for the inquest.

From the police inquiries, it transpired that only Mrs Prater and Sara Lewis, a laundress who was visiting a friend in Miller's Court, had heard a cry for help. Barnett, the main suspect until he had satisfied the police about his quarrel with Kelly, was soon eliminated from the inquiry. His story of the quarrel was confirmed by Mrs Maria Harvey, the prostitute who was its cause. She told the police that Kelly was a better educated woman than most of her class, and that she had last seen her alive on the Thursday night. In spite of a few drinks Kelly had been quite sober when they split up, and she had gone on to her beat in the Leman Street area. That was the last time that Mrs Harvey had seen her alive.

Already there was a flood of new rumours and scare stories in the newspapers. The latest was that the murderer might be a butcher or drover on one of the cattle boats that usually docked in the Thames on a Thursday or Friday night and left again for the Continent on Saturday or Sunday. This schedule explained why the murders had been committed at weekends, and also how the murderer had made his escape. This theory had a lot of support, including that of the Queen, who mentioned it in one of her letters and asked if the cattle boats had been searched. Another argument in its favour was that it fitted in with the assertion made at some of the inquests that a butcher might have sufficient knowledge of anatomy as well as the skill to perform the mutilations.

Filed away amongst the police correspondence was a long and extremely detailed memorandum from an official at the Customs House Statistical Department identifying two particular cattle boats, *City of Cork* and *City of Oporto*, regularly sailing between London and Portugal, with Portuguese crews and cattlemen, with sailing times that neatly dovetailed with the murders. An English sailor in New York, where the case had aroused considerable interest, identified another suspect as a Malay ship's cook called Alaska who had been robbed of two years' savings and had been heard threatening to murder and mutilate every woman in Whitechapel unless he recovered his money; he was thought to be on a ship making short trips in and out of London.

The Whitechapel Vigilance Committee called a special meeting for the following Tuesday at the Paul's Head tavern to discuss further ways in which they could help the police. Certainly people were not slow in coming forward to say that they had been accosted by or had seen the Ripper. Mrs Paumier, who sold roasted chestnuts at the corner of Widegate Street, only two minutes' walk away from Miller's Court, said that on the day the body was found a man, dressed like a gentleman but clearly not one, asked her if she had heard that there had been another murder. When she replied that she had he had grinned and said that he knew more about it than she did. From her description – black moustache, black silk hat, black coat, and speckled trousers, carrying a black shiny bag – he was the same man who had accosted three of her friends on the night that Kelly was murdered. When one of them had asked him what was in his bag he told her, 'Something the ladies don't like,' and walked away. A man carrying a similar bag was arrested and taken to Leman Street police station. Another, arrested near Dorset Street, was followed by a howling mob to the police station in Commercial Street.

There were more sensations when the inquest opened on the following Monday morning at Shoreditch Town Hall. The hearing, to everyone's astonishment, lasted less than half a day. Several newspapers commented unfavourably on the unnatural brevity of the proceedings and on the behaviour of the coroner, who told the jury that he was going to take only the preliminary part of Dr Phillips's evidence, which would be heard in full at an adjourned date. His abrupt termination of the hearing thus allowed for only a minimum of evidence to be given, and he went out of this way to stifle the criticisms from the inquest jury.

The jurors' main objection to the hearing was that it should not have been held in Shoreditch at all. The murders had happened in Whitechapel and came within Mr Wynne E. Baxter's district. Some of them resented having to hear cases which didn't properly belong to their district, and others to the hearing being presided over by Dr McDonald instead of Mr Baxter. Dr McDonald was a former police surgeon for K Division and was clearly determined to have his own way from the beginning:

JUROR: I do not see why we should have the inquest thrown on our shoulders when the murder did not happen in our district, but in Whitechapel.

CORONER'S OFFICER (*severely*): It did not happen in Whitechapel.

CORONER'S (*severely*): Do you think that we do not know what we are doing here? The jury are summoned in the ordinary way, and they have no business to object. If they persist in their objection I shall know how to deal with them. Does any juror persist in objecting?

JUROR: We are summoned for the Shoreditch district. This happened in Spitalfields.

CORONER'S: It happened within my district.

ANOTHER JURYMAN: This is not my district. I come from Whitechapel, and Mr Baxter is my coroner.

CORONER'S: I am not going to discuss the subject with the jurymen at all. If any juryman says he distinctly objects, let him say so. (*After a pause*). I may tell the jurymen that jurisdiction lies where the body lies, not where it was found.

He stressed this point a little later by saying that he hadn't been in touch with Mr Baxter, as some newspapers had suggested. 'The body is in my jurisdiction, it was taken to my mortuary, and that is the end of the matter,' he said stiffly.

Before the evidence was given, the jury were taken to the mortuary to see the body. A dirty grey sheet covered it to the neck, so that the mutilations mercifully couldn't be seen. The face itself was slashed and disfigured beyond recognition. Only the eyes showed any signs of humanity. It resembled, according to the *Pall Mall Gazette*, 'one of those horrible wax anatomical specimens'.

After viewing the body, the jurors went on to Miller's Court and then back to the town hall to hear the first witness, Joseph Barnett. He told the court that he had last seen Kelly alive between 7.30 and 7.45 p.m. on the Thursday evening when she was talking to Maria Harvey. He was questioned in some detail about her background. He said she had told him several times that she had been born in Limerick but had been taken when she was quite young to Wales, where her father had been employed at an ironworks in Carmarthenshire. She had also mentioned that she had six brothers and sisters; one of the brothers was in the army. When she was sixteen she had married a collier named Davis but a year or two later he had been killed in an explosion. Apparently it was the delay in paying her compensation which first drove her onto the streets. This is unconvincing, as she had no children of her own to look after, wasn't quite eighteen and was capable of earning a living other than as a prostitute. She was twenty-one when she moved to London in 1884. It is difficult to separate fact from fancy at this point, but she allegedly lived in a 'gay house' (a high-class brothel) in the West End and then for a short time with a gentleman in France, but she didn't like the life and returned to England. Hard facts creep into her story once again with Barnett's disclosures that she had subsequently lived with a man named Morganstone in the infamous Ratcliffe Highway running east from the Tower of London, and in Bethnal Green with a mason named Joseph Fleming.

From the medical and other evidence, the time of death had

been established as being between 3.30 and 4 a.m. The laundress Sara Lewis was one of the witnesses who confirmed this timing. She lived at 24 Great Pearl Street but had gone to Miller's Court at 2.30 a.m. on Friday morning to visit Mrs Keyler, who lived in the house opposite Room 13. One strongly suspects that she was a prostitute and that possibly she had gone there to shelter from the rain or, like Mrs Harvey, who had shared Kelly's room for a while, had nowhere else to sleep. She said that she had seen a man standing outside the lodging-house door. He was stout, not very tall and had on a black wide-awake hat. She didn't hear any noise as she went down the court, but she heard a woman's scream later on. At the time she was sitting in a chair in Mrs Keyler's house, having been unable to sleep, and it was just before 4 a.m. when she heard a woman's voice shout 'Murder!' quite loudly. Her impression was that it was a young woman's voice and that it came from just outside the door.

She was asked if she was frightened or if she woke anyone up. Mrs Lewis shrugged her shoulders. 'No,' she said. She had taken no notice as the woman screamed only once. Mrs Prater confirmed that she had heard the scream at about that time.

Yet the evidence of another witness, Mrs Maxwell, contradicted them both. According to her, she had spoken to Kelly at 8 a.m. *the next morning*. This was in such direct conflict with all the evidence that had already been given – including the medical – that the coroner warned her to be careful about what she said. She told him that she was the wife of the lodging-house keeper at 14 Dorset Street and had known Kelly for about four months although she had spoken to her only about twice. She was positive that she had seen Kelly between 8 and 8.30 a.m. at the corner of Miller's Court, less than three hours before her body was found, as this was the time that her husband normally left off work. It was so unusual to see her at such an hour that Mrs Maxwell had asked her to have a drink. Kelly explained that the reason why she was up so early was because she felt so bad. She had drunk a glass of beer and brought it up again. Mrs Maxwell sympathized and said that she could pity her feelings. Half an hour later she saw her outside the Britannia public house talking to a man. She could see that Kelly was wearing a dark skirt, velvet bodice, maroon shawl and no hat. The man she was with was wearing dark clothes and seemed to have a plaid coat on. He was little taller than Mrs Maxwell herself, and stout.

Almost the last witness was Dr Bagster Phillips. The coroner said that he would not go into all the medical details at this stage and that his more detailed evidence could be given at a later date. Dr Phillips complied with this directive and said that the immediate cause of death was the severing of the carotid artery.

Shortly after Phillips finished giving his evidence, the coroner, to the astonishment of his listeners, said that he did not propose to take any more evidence that day and, turning to the jury, asked if they had heard enough to reach their verdict. He said that if they were satisfied that Mary Kelly had died as the doctor said, by having the carotid artery cut, then they could bring in a verdict to this effect and leave the rest of the investigation in the hands of the police. Of course, if they disagreed with this he would adjourn the inquest for a week or fortnight, when they could hear the evidence they wanted.

The foreman stood up and said that the jury considered that they had heard enough to return a verdict of wilful murder by some person or persons unknown.

This abrupt termination of the inquest was instantly criticized by several newspapers including the *Daily Telegraph*, which gave a plain hint that the Home Secretary should order a new inquiry. By hurriedly closing the hearing, it pointed out, the opportunity had been lost to take statements while the evidence of witnesses was still fresh in their minds. Such mishandling of the most sensational murder of all might, if the killer was ever caught, materially affect the outcome of any further trial and might possibly be the flaw in the case which could lead to his acquittal.

Incredibly there was one witness who didn't come forward until after the inquest. His name was George Hutchinson and he had been out of work for several weeks. He had known Mary Kelly for about three years, and was occasionally able to give her a few shillings. Whether this was meant to imply that he was a casual client is not clear. His statement to the police was the most important one to date as he said that he had met Kelly at 2 a.m. in Thrawl Street, about an hour and a half to two hours before she was murdered. If true, he was the last man to see her alive, apart from the killer.

He said that at 2 a.m. he was walking down Thrawl Street, without the money for a bed, and just before he reached Flower and Dean Street he met Kelly who asked him to lend her sixpence. He told her, 'I can't. I have spent all my money going down to Romford.' She shrugged and said, 'Good morning. I must go and find some money.'

As she walked away, a man coming in the opposite direction tapped her on the shoulder and said something, and they both burst out laughing. Hutchinson was surprised to see her with such a well-dressed man and he stared curiously at them. The man was about thirty-five years old, 5 ft. 6 ins. tall, with a pale complexion, dark hair and a slight moustache which was curled up at each end. He wore a long dark coat, with collar and cuffs of trimmed astrakhan and a dark-coloured jacket underneath, and a light-coloured waistcoat holding a very thick gold chain.

He also wore dark trousers and button boots and gaiters with white buttons. His white shirt and black tie were fastened with a horseshoe pin. In appearance he was Jewish and quite respectable.

In his left hand he had a kind of parcel with a strap around it.

Hutchinson heard her say, 'All right,' and the man reply, 'You will be all right for what I have told you.' He then placed his right hand around her shoulders and Hutchinson, who was standing against the lamp outside the Queen's Head public house, watched them as they walked back towards him. The man kept his head down and his dark felt hat over his eyes. Hutchinson was so curious to know what he looked like that he bent down and looked him in the face. This would explain the 'surly face' in his description. He followed them into Dorset Street and watched as they stood talking at the corner of Miller's Court for about three minutes. He said something in a low voice and Hutchinson heard Kelly say, quite clearly, 'All right, my dear. Come along, you will be comfortable.' He then placed his hand on her shoulder and gave her a kiss. She said that she had lost her handkerchief, whereupon the man pulled out his, a red one, and gave it to her before they went up the court together. Hutchinson was curious enough to follow them, but he couldn't see them. He waited for about three-quarters of an hour to see if they came out again, but they didn't. And so he went away.

It is probable that Hutchinson was the man whom the laundress saw waiting outside the court when she went in to Mrs Keyler at 2.30 a.m. The probable sequence of events that night was that Kelly took home a man from the pub and got rid of him pretty quickly. This would be sometime between midnight and 2 a.m. when she met Hutchinson. She told Hutchinson that she hadn't got any money and so we can assume that either the first client didn't pay her, which is unlikely, or that she was pretending poverty and had some reason for doing so. At this point it is worth referring back to the lodging-house keeper McCarthy and his behaviour the next day. Both he and Joe Barnett tried to pretend ignorance of the fact that Kelly was a prostitute or, in McCarthy's case, that he had only just learned that she walked the streets in Aldgate. As almost every woman in Miller's Court was a known prostitute this is hard to believe, especially as he rented them their rooms and houses; these were known locally as McCarthy's Rents, which was probably a local phrase referring to the prostitutes in Miller's Court controlled by McCarthy and not the houses that he owned, as has been often assumed.

This interpretation might explain certain other puzzling facts about the Kelly case. All the sources agree that she was owing three months' rent to McCarthy, amounting to twenty-nine shillings. However, according to the *Illustrated Police News*, Mrs McCarthy adhered very 'strictly to the principle of "ready" cash in dealing with lodgers. It is usually her practice to wait on them in the course of the morning, and receive each day's rent in advance.' This was normal practice throughout the area. Why then was Kelly privileged? According to neighbours, Barnett had done his best to keep her off the streets. In spite of his efforts she might have continued with a certain amount of casual prostitution, but her earnings would have been minimal.

The room was in Kelly's name and possibly she was drinking the money that Barnett gave her for the rent. McCarthy probably allowed her to run up the debt so that he could make even more out of her when he chose. From the facts it seems likely that at the end of October, to get her back to work, he told her that she had to share her room with Mrs Harvey, knowing that this must force Barnett to leave until the debt was paid. This was possibly what the real quarrel with Kelly was about, that they were twenty-nine shillings in debt to McCarthy and that Kelly had to pay it off the only way that she could. This would also explain why, even after Mrs Harvey had moved out, Barnett did not move back into Room 13 and why he continued to visit Kelly almost daily to give her money and even, the last time that he saw her alive, to tell her that he had not got any.

Possibly Kelly had been given an ultimatum that she had to earn more money or get out of her room. This would explain why she was so desperate for money on the night she was murdered and why she was ready to pound the streets on a rainy night long after everyone else had gone to bed. It might also offer an explanation for the behaviour of McCarthy's other 'rents' who felt equally impelled to stagger about the streets until after 3 a.m. and then get up to go to work only two hours later.

In fact, Kelly needed quite a lot of customers to raise the twenty-nine shillings owing in rent. Barnett had given her all the money that he could, and she might have been paid something by the man she took home from the pub, but Hutchinson could give her nothing. And then she meets the stranger. There is some haggling, which Hutchinson witnesses. Probably it was about how much he was willing to pay for spending what was left of the night with her. This might explain the remark that Hutchinson overheard him make: 'You will be all right for what I had told you.'

Between 3.30 and 4 a.m., according to an independent medical report, Mary Kelly's killer partly smothered her with a sheet as he killed her, probably by stabbing. Because of the extensive mutilations it was not possible to say how the first blow was struck.

At 6.15 a.m. Mrs Cox heard someone walking down the court. As she didn't hear a door bang it might have been the local policeman but she couldn't be sure. It might just as easily have been Jack the Ripper. This, like so much else, is only conjecture.

One of the mysteries the police found when they broke down the door was the remains of the fire in the grate. According to Inspector Abberline the heat had been so intense that it had burnt off the handle and spout of a tin kettle. The ashes were still warm when they entered the house at 1.30 p.m. Assuming 6 a.m. to be roughly the time that the killer left Miller's Court, this means that the ashes had been cooling for over seven hours. When the ashes were sifted they found some pieces of skirt and the brim of a woman's hat, the latter presumably one of the items of clothing left by Maria Harvey. At the inquest she said that it consisted of two men's dirty shirts, a boy's shirt, a black overcoat (which was all the police could find), a black crepe bonnet with black satin strings and a girl's white petticoat. Yet this would not have created a great blaze. Mary Kelly's own clothes were lying folded up on the bedside chair, and so the unanswered question is: what had been burnt in that grate?

There have been various suggestions. It might have been clothing that the killer himself wore. But the only reason he could have for burning it would have been if it was bloodstained; and as such it is only likely that it would smoulder, and not flare – certainly it would not throw out enough heat to burn the handle and spout off a tin kettle that was designed to withstand intense heat. Even ordinary combustibles such as coal and coke would have to have the help of a bellows to throw out that sort of heat. Another suggestion is that these things were burnt to give him light. If light was what he needed, why had he not used the candle which stood there? Surely the risks were much smaller with one small flickering flame than with a roaring fire?

Hutchinson's description is the most detailed we have of a Ripper suspect and yet Hutchinson is someone who is quickly dropped from the subsequent investigation. Abberline initially thought Hutchinson's evidence genuine and sent him with two detectives to scour the area to see if he could identify the man. Hutchinson said the suspect lived in the area and thought that he had seen him in Petticoat Lane market on a Sunday morning. Possibly he did and I suspect that the man was probably a street trader, somebody Hutchinson knew by sight, if not by name, and giving his description was an act of spiteful resentment or jealousy on his part at the man's sexual friendship with Kelly. This suspect seems to have been identified, and both he and Hutchinson are quickly dropped from the investigation.

In effect, this means after the Kelly murder and dismissing Stride's as a non-Ripper killing, we have only three eyewitness descriptions left for a possible identification. All that remains are: Mrs Long who saw the man with Chapman but only in part profile; Joseph Lawende who saw a man talking to Eddowes but doubted that he would recognize him again; and Mrs Cox who saw Kelly's drinking partner, the man with a carroty moustache, and who may just have been that and nothing more.

In 2006 ten leading historians were asked to name the ten worst Britons, one for each century, of the past thousand years. Professor Clive Emsley named Jack the Ripper as the worst Briton of the 19th century. The harsh fact is that we don't know that Jack the Ripper was a Briton. We know so little about him that we don't even know his nationality.

While Inspector Abberline was busily following up these

clues, the newspapers and public at large were rejoicing over the downfall of Sir Charles Warren. *Punch* jeeringly published a parody of the nursery rhyme which they called 'Who Killed Cock Warren?':

> Who chased COCK WARREN?
> 'I', said the Home Sparrow
> 'With my views cramped and narrow,
> I chased COCK WARREN.'
>
> And who'll fill his place?
> 'I', said Monro, 'I'm the right man, I know,
> And I'll fill his place.'
>
> And who'll tie your hands?
> 'I', said Routine, 'That my business has been,
> So I'll tie his hands.'
>
> Who'll see fair play?
> 'I', said John Bull, 'For I'm quite a fool;
> I'll see fair play!'

Warren had tendered his resignation on 8 November but he didn't remove his papers from his office until 12 November when it was officially announced in the House of Commons to the cheers of the Opposition.

One of his last acts had been to put his name to a document that was nothing more or less than a confession of a failure. It was an official pardon and read:

MURDER – PARDON. Whereas, on November 8 or 9 in Miller's Court, Dorset Street, Spitalfields, Mary Jane Kelly was murdered by some person or persons unknown, the Secretary of State will advise the grant of Her Majesty's pardon to any accomplice not being a person who contrived or actually committed the murder who shall give such information and evidence as shall lead to the discovery and conviction of the person or persons who committed the murder.

Ironically, within a few months it was evident that the murders had come to an end, and it was widely assumed that the Ripper was dead.

5. From Hell

THE "FIFTH" VICTIM OF THE "WHITECHAPEL" FIEND.

FINDING THE MUTILATED BOD.   MITRE SQARE.

At the peak of the murders, the police were being bombarded with an estimated one thousand letters per week. The Lord Mayor, bishops, spiritualists and the newspapers were similarly deluged. Few of them were of any genuine help. Many were from cranks. All of them had to be bundled up and passed on to the hard-pressed police, who had to sift through them and decide which were worth following up. Occasionally one gets more than a hint of the exasperation they felt at this correspondence. Scribbled across many of them in red ink now are such remarks as 'Take no notice of this', 'The man must be a lunatic!' and 'Not acknowledged'. Letters were still coming in at such a rate the following July that the Yard was forced to go to the unusual length of having acknowledgement slips, headed 'Whitechapel Murders', printed. The newspapers suffered from the collective madness only slightly less. After *The Star* published a leader on the murders, it was inundated with letters and for several days it overflowed with correspondence on the question 'Is Christianity a Failure?' Two of the many letters not accepted for publication were signed respectively 'J.C.' and 'Shendar Brwa' – the latter being an anagram of Bernard Shaw. The Shavian wit is evident throughout the first letter, too, blasphemously signed 'J.C.' (Jesus Christ):

> Sir,
> Why do you try to put the Whitechapel murders on me? Sir Charles Warren is quite right not to catch the unfortunate murderer, whose conviction and punishment would be conducted on my father's old lines of an eye for an eye, which I have always consistently repudiated. As to the eighteen centuries of what you call Christianity, I have nothing to do with it. It was invented by an aristocrat of the Roman set [St Paul], a university man whose epistles are the silliest middle class stuff on record. When I see my name mixed up with it in your excellent paper, I feel as if nails were going into me – and I know what the sensation is like better than you do. Trusting that you will excuse this intrusion on your valuable space.
>
> > I am, Sir &c., J.C.

Most readers could not grasp that the murders were being committed by an individual such as themselves. There had to be something extraordinary about such a man. One woman, writing 'In confidence' from the Isle of Wight, thought that he might be a large ape belonging to some wild beast show. Clearly she had been reading Poe's *The Murders in the Rue Morgue*, for she continues, 'This animal would be swift, cunning, noiseless and strong, standing over its work until a footstep was heard and then vaulting over a fence or wall, disappearing in a moment, hiding its weapon high up in a tree [in Whitechapel?] or other safe place, and returning home to lock itself up in its cage.'

A 46-year-old widow, however, believed that respectable women such as she had nothing to fear from the Whitechapel murderer as she thought it was true that he 'respects and protects respectable females'. His manners were none too gentlemanly, it seems, for she continued, 'I feel certain it was him whom I saw one night in the Devonshire Street end of Cavendish Court on or about the 30th of August. Although conducting himself in a disgusting manner he allowed one to pass without a murmur.' Piously she hopes that, 'when in the agony of his own death he takes the last look for mercy, may the sigh of his soul be Jesus, sweet Jesus'.

One popular theory was that the criminal had been 'badly disfigured by disease – *possibly had his privy member destroyed* – and he is now revenging himself on the sex by these atrocities'. Somebody else, who had reached the same conclusion, thought that he might be 'suffering from syphilis and is using the part cut off from the woman as a kind of poultice to suck off the virus from his ulcers. This is a vile superstition of the Chinese and Malays who commit this kind of crime for this very purpose.' If true, it pointed to a man who had travelled in the China Seas.

The alternative, which another correspondent suggested, was that he was a hill tribesman. 'In the sanscrit mythology, particular reverence is paid to the male and female generative organs. I have been informed by old soldiers who had been admitted to the home life of the *Hill Tribes*, the very organs themselves, preserved are hung up as *Amulets* &c.' Warming to his theme he asks, 'Has a gang of these Hill tribes started to work? They would be scarcely distinguished from Europeans in a dimly lighted street. Murder for obtaining the female organ among them is a sacred action.' The other possibility – too dreadful to contemplate – was that it might be a white man who had adopted their customs while on civil or military duties: 'Sunstroke would then loose all civilized restraints on such matters.' The same correspondent, in further conversations with this old soldier, had been told by him that it was quite common for the East Indian tribes to carry a concealed weapon with a fine point like a needle, dipped in poison, of which one prick in the vein would mean instantaneous death. A man armed with such a weapon could, while caressing a woman, deliver 'the fatal prick on the spine or veins of the neck', and she would fall to the pavement with very little noise. 'The cutting of the throat diverts suspicion and complies with the savage ritual.' He forwarded with his second letter thirty copies of his pamphlet

'The Apocalypse Unveiled and a Fight with Death and Slander', which was his own translation of the Book of Revelation into plain everyday speech; he didn't guarantee the correctness of his explanations of the symbols but had simply thrown the pamphlet out as a challenge in order that a fuller understanding could be attempted.

An English teacher who had been in Turin for the past twenty-two years thought that a follower of Buddha might be the killer – perhaps one of the Thugs, who were practised killers and 'bound to offer human victims to their deity . . . The murders taking place at given periods in the month may be some indication as to the time such human sacrifices are offered – perhaps at different phases of the moon.'

Dreams often suggested ways of tracking down the killer. A clergyman in Newmarket dreamed that the culprits were two men named Pat Murphy and Jim Slaney, and that they would walk past 22 Gresham Street in the City at 4.10 p.m. on Wednesday, 18 November. As he couldn't leave Newmarket on that day, would the police kindly send a couple of detectives to watch for two young men? As proof that this wasn't a hoax he had asked his churchwarden to countersign his letter, which was politely acknowledged, as was another from B. Barraclough of York who said that he had sent a telegram two days before that read: 'Watch the house 20 Wurt Street, W.C.' He explained why in the letter that followed. His children had been experimenting with the table to see if it would rap out a message, as it was supposed to do in a seance. It did, in fact, rap out, 'More murders tonight in London'. In reply to further questioning it said that another woman would be killed by the same man, whose name and address were 'Tom Totson, 20 Wurt Street, W.C.' Furthermore, the spirit had told the sender to warn the police by telegram, which he had done, partly to relieve himself of the heavy responsibility lying on him and partly from a belief that there may be 'more things on heaven and earth than are dreamt of in our philosophy'.

Equally receptive to these unseen influences was Josiah E.

Boys, late Private, King's Own Scottish Borderers, who wrote a warning to Sir James Fraser, the City Police Commissioner, that he had seen a message scrawled on one of the walls of a water closet in Guildhall and reading: 'I am Jack the Ripper and Intend to do another murder at Adelphi Arches, at 2 a.m.' Mr Boys thought that this warning might be a hoax but as the writer had added: 'I will send the ears to Colonel Frazer', he thought that he had better communicate these facts at once, as he thought there was striking similarity in the handwriting to the letters which had been published in the newspapers. The message, he concluded lamely, had been scrawled on the wall in lead pencil.

The commonest suggestion of all was that the killer could be trapped by disguising policemen as women. These letters nearly all stress that the men must be clean shaven and armed with snaps (handcuffs) and revolvers. Richard Taylor, who gave his address as the Public Baths, Endell Street, Long Acre, asked for the following suggestion to be forwarded to the Vigilance Committee as he couldn't find out their address:

... in addition to the ordinary costume, I would suggest that a kind of corset of metal (ring mail would be most efficient) should enclose the trunk and that, as broad a band as possible of thin flexible steel be worn round the throat, this being light could be made with a suitable covering to represent an ordinary collar, and if a broad tapering piece were attached to that and bent up under the jaw, it would shield the throat from anything like serious injury. This collar would be further utilized as the terminal of a powerful storage battery, to be varied a`la dress improver, the terminals could be on either side of the collar, or, assuming the victim is (as is most probably) grasped from the rear, a pair might be led up the headgear and discharged if grasped from that position. The shock would possibly so seriously disconcert the assassin, that it would be a comparatively easy matter to secure him.

A gentleman in Cheshire, not quite so vicious, suggested that women should carry a piece of paper liberally pasted with bird lime which they could slap upon the Ripper's rear shoulder or back and which he would not observe but which would identify him to the police. Precisely at what stage of the attack they were to get this out of their handbag he does not make plain. An extra precaution, wrote an ex-patriate Yorkshireman from Cleveland, Ohio, would be an alarm wire fixed to the pavement kerbs with electric warning buttons about thirty feet apart; these would lead to a shop or store, 'where the police have got to warm themselves on winter nights', where there would be a panel of alarm bells, each of which would indicate the street that they were connected to. Prostitutes would be additionally armed with revolvers so that, when attacked, they could keep the Ripper at bay and ring one of these bells for help. A policeman on horseback, so the same writer calculated, should be capable of galloping to any one of these points within half a minute. He stressed that on no account must the recipient (the Lord Mayor) let an Irish detective peep at his plan. It must be an Englishman. Should the police wish to make him an offer . . .

A more practical suggestion was that there should be better street lighting and that the police, by means of their whistles, should develop a rapid warning system to alert colleagues on other beats.

Of course, some of the letters were decidedly odd. The instructions in the following letter are so explicit that it is a reasonable assumption that the writer was himself some kind of fetishist. He asks for locks of hair from the last two victims to give to a friend of his who, so he says, by similar means had brought to justice persons who were guilty of cruelty to animals when there was no other evidence to convict them. (Did he use hair from these animals?) He instructs: 'cut the hair with any human hand and send it to me . . . If the hair cannot be procured send on something belonging [to] the victims [that] they were wearing at the time and worn close to the skin.'

A number of letters had quite hilarious origins. A telegram from Dublin warned 'Arrest Palermo Nagro, Alias Wilmo, ht.

5 feet to 5 feet 9, as Whitechapel Murderer.' It was signed 'I. Fogarty, 47 North Strand Road'. The report which followed from the Dublin CID, who interviewed the sender, was that 'Fogarty is and for some days past suffering from Delirium Tremens. He is aware that he sent a telegram to London, but respecting what he cannot say.' Apparently his friends had telegraphed his wife in Cork to come and fetch him, which she did, but she had managed to get him only as far as Dublin when he gave her the slip. He got away for only a few minutes but this was long enough for him to send the telegram. He was horribly frightened when he was questioned about it and thought that he was going to be prosecuted for causing a public mischief. The officer charitably concluded: 'There is no doubt that the fellow was mad when sending the telegram,' and presumably recommended no further action.

Some writers thought that the Ripper was a foreigner and that he should be kicked out of the country with other political refugees and into the sea. 'If the government don't act plucky ... the City is doomed to destruction,' said one. He added that the murders were committed from anti-police motives and that they were calculated to overthrow the Empire. He explained:

A week or two ago I noticed a poster of *The Star* saying 'War on Warren'. I have been daily looking for the outbreak in any form and I admit it is apparent [that] in the Horrors they thought [that] by demoralising the Police force [that] they would make government impossible [and] that Lord Salisbury would resign and Gladstone come in and the ruin of the Empire certain – and their distinguished object gained – A Republic – *God Forbid*.

The safety of the public has depended very much upon the Salvation Army who have been going about the country, amongst the labouring classes especially, making good citizens and antagonistic to the Socialists who hates them and would like to destroy them.

Another writer took the opposite view. He thought that, because the victims were working class, the Ripper must be of the 'upper or wealthy sort' who think that the world and its inhabitants exist 'for their pleasures – that of revenge being included – as a life business; without regard to any law but their own will'.

Yet another thought that the Ripper might be one of the socialist pedagogues who nearly every day hoisted the red flag in Hyde Park. He had overheard one of them say, 'Wait till we get a few murders done up here in the West End and then you'll see what a howl there'll be.'

A number of the many suspects were named. They included the lunatic living in Fulham who used to recite and sing tragical stories, accompanying his gestures with an ivory-handled knife which he used to keep in a black shiny leather Gladstone bag; Herbert Freund, who used to create disturbances in St Paul's Cathedral; the Germans who worked in the Sugar House in Hanbury Street (and seldom leaving it), who had come to England to avoid army conscription in their own country; Richard Mansfield, the star of a successful stage production of *Dr Jekyll and Mr Hyde* (the writer accusing Mansfield had not been able to rest for a day and a night after seeing the performance, claiming that no man could disguise himself so well and that, since Mansfield worked himself up into such a frenzy on stage, he probably did the real life murders too); William Onion, who had been released from Colney Hatch lunatic asylum and who had 'ginger whiskers' and 'a Crucked flatish nose' with a faint scar, the result of being hit by a pepper box. One correspondent was positive that the Ripper could be identified by procuring *Davidson's Illustrated Comprehensive Bible*. This, if it were to be opened at the Lord's Supper, would show 'a knife clearly visible, but who is the holder of that knife, I seem to think he will be found out. I may be saucy when I am irritated but I would shrink from those deeds. Yours respectfully John Legg Bagg Junior. P.S. I do not think it is my Father because I know he would not do it neither do I think he had been to London.' Another anonymous correspondent signed himself 'Richard Whittington the Second'. Another forwarded his suggestions on Home Office notepaper. A popular suspect was the watchman in Mitre Square; one writer said she had dreamt she had seen him peeping out of the warehouse door and laughing at the policemen as they turned the corner. A writer from Australia thought the murders were the work of Germans who skinned people and wore these second skins as disguises which they pasted on with American glue; their motives were that they were working in league with their men in the Colonial Office, and in time hoped to get the Crown of England, the Colonies and India and the New World. (The Commissioner, not surprisingly, scribbled across the letter: 'This appears to be the work of a lunatic'.)

There was no lack of volunteer detectives ready to help the police. Ladies offered to take the place of the prostitutes and were quite willing to be martyred for the sake of their country. A father of five daughters, four of them living with him, asked that, should his help be needed, advertisements be placed as follows in the *Evening Standard*:

Nemo Come – I should then present myself in Old Jewry
Nemo Go – I should then present myself at Scotland Yard
Nemo Remain – In this latter case I should present myself at Leman Street Station at 7 o'clock in the evening of the day on which the advertisement appears.

One of the Ripper's hiding places, it was suggested, might have been an old vault in the Jews' Cemetery. Alternatively, he could have escaped through the underground sewers which would account for his sudden disappearances; at the same time he could tear into shreds the dark woollen serge coat which he would have been wearing and scatter its bloodstained pieces underground. Other letter writers were obviously having a good laugh at the expense of the police, including Andy Handy who 'saw A man go into Mr Barclay & Son he had A bag in his hand and it snap open and I saw two feet and A head of A human Person he had A large knife in his pocket'. Another prayed that God would show him the murderer. Apparently He did better than usual;

He showed him the Ripper in his three disguises, one of them involving a black turban cap of Scotch pattern, which led the writer to conclude that the Ripper might be a Frenchman, a German, or an Italian, a soldier or a lord. A final bonus, granted to this same visionary, was the vision of an unknown woman who could be identified by her missing nose – and who was the missing link in the case (she was apparently the woman whom the Ripper had been searching for and now that he had killed her there would be no further killings). Of course, if the police have no faith and didn't believe him . . .

There were many suggested ways of trapping Jack. One nineteenth-century Emmett suggested that female dummies should be placed in the darkest and loneliest spots; their arms and legs would be powerful springs 'capable of being released by moderate force, such as raising the chin or pressing the throat. Once released these springs would act like the arm of an "Octopus" and hold the person entrapped, while a sound resembling a police whistle might proceed from the machine.'

Another was that women should wear velvet-covered steel collars and, something far nastier, a soft-covered collar with

fine, sharp pointed stings (thorns), that the infernal assassin will be thus hardly wounded . . . At the same moment the officer will turn round and take hold of the murderer *above the hand, turning it with all the power of his two hands against the breast* of the scoundrel; thus, that this monster must *bore his own knife into his own breast* or *must let fall it* . . . and don't give this *Idea* to any one except the *Chief of Police* (as your Lordship would warn unconscious that way the blood-hound). For – *who can say, that this criminal don't belong to a rich family.* The officer or officers should look at every suspicious woman or all women in general . . . The *D—* may know what is often in such a *petticoat*!!!!

This was as about as sensible as the suggestion that suspicious-looking couples should have corrosive matter discharged onto their clothes by means of glass syringes, so that there would be a distinctive mark by which to identify them. When the next victim was found her killer could be then traced both through the description of him that the police would already have, and by matching up the stains on his clothes.

The three hundred to five hundred detectives that would be needed for this manhunt could be recruited, one writer felt sure, from the young Emperor of Germany who was known to be very fond of his royal grandmother Queen Victoria and who would willingly loan her a thousand detectives from Berlin. The Emperor of Russia and the French President would, he felt sure, be equally agreeable to loaning her a similar number of men.

Another writer warned that the policemen must be constantly on their guard as he felt sure the Ripper was stupefying his victims with a chloroform-soaked handkerchief before killing them; therefore, as an urgent precaution, they were to arrest anyone who came near them and tried to blow his nose. As a final precaution, all detectives were to act drunk, and wear iron collars and body armour.

Of course, there was always the possibility that the killer's vanity might lead to his downfall. Why could he not be traced through the newsagents and newsboys when he bought the newspaper accounts on the mornings after his murders? This was assuming that it was only at such times that he bought newspapers. No doubt the newsagents could identify such a monster. Every one of them should keep a list of clients and against the ones that they most suspected they should scribble the word 'horrible'.

With so much activity in Whitechapel it was clear that the police were going to be stumbling over each other every few yards. This led to a suggestion that Whitechapel should be cleared of policemen, except for one hundred pairs of detectives and the prostitutes they could hire for two shillings a night as decoys. Otherwise, too much activity was only going to frighten the Ripper away. Alternatively, since he took such an interest in the efforts that were being made to catch him, why not call a public meeting in a hotel to discuss these ways, and as he was bound to attend, lock him in once the meeting had started.

One anonymous correspondent, far ahead of his time, did appreciate something about the correspondence that police and public didn't. He wrote to the City police that having read that a postcard sent to the Central News Agency had the impression of a thumb he suggested that as 'no two person's thumbs are alike, the impression of one suspected person's thumb should be taken and microscopically examined tested'. His letter was read and dutifully filed away with the rest. It would be another seventeen years before the first fingerprint conviction.

The final suggestion was perhaps the best of all. The following advertisement was to be inserted in the newspapers to trap the medical man that the Ripper was thought to be:

Medical Man or Assistant Wanted in London, aged between 25 and 40. Must not object to assist in occasional post mortem. Liberal terms. Address stating antecedents. PTR [Please to reply]

NAME   STREET

If only he had!

Few of the letters signed 'Jack the Ripper', or purporting to come from him, are of any real value – in fact, a ruthless weeding out process leaves just one. Of interest, however, is the first letter to use the name. It was posted on 28 September 1888, and had a London East Central postmark. It read:

25 Sept. 1888

Dear Boss, I keep on hearing the police have caught me but they won't fix me just yet. I have laughed when they look so clever and talk about being on the right track. That joke about Leather Apron gave me real fits. I am down on whores and I shan't quit ripping them till I do get buckled. Grand work the last job was. I gave the lady no time to squeal. How can they catch me now. I love my work and want to start again. You will soon hear of me with my funny little games. I saved some of the proper red stuff in a ginger beer bottle over the last job to write with but it went thick like glue and I can't use it. Red ink is fit enough I hope *ha ha*. The next job I do I shall clip the lady's ears off and send to the police officers just for jolly wouldn't you. Keep this letter till I do a bit more work, then give it out straight. My knife is nice and sharp I want to get to work right away if I get a chance. Good luck.

> Yours truly

> JACK THE RIPPER

Don't mind me giving the trade name.
Wasn't good enough to post this before I got all the red ink
off my hands curse it.
No luck yet they say I am a doctor now *ha ha*.

As it was posted two days before the 'double event' of the Stride and Eddowes murders on 30 September, he was clearly referring to the Hanbury Street murder (Annie Chapman on 8 September) when he says 'Grand work the last job was. I gave the lady no time to squeal.' Did he mean that he took her by surprise or – recalling the witness who remembered hearing a woman call out 'No!' and then heard something fall against the fence – did he mean that he killed her before she could call out again? Unfortunately the wording is too ambiguous to decide one way or another. However, the threat to 'clip the lady's ears off ' meant that the letter had to be taken seriously, as the killer tried to do precisely that with both Eddowes and Stride. The ugly slash that can still be seen on the post-mortem photographs of Eddowes is where he drew his knife across her face with the apparent intention of cutting off her right ear as well as her nose. Yet, if this letter was genuine, and he really wanted to send the ears to the police as he had threatened, why didn't he? It could hardly have been for lack of time, since he had enough to disembowel the unfortunate woman – it would have required but a second's further work to cut off an ear.

A second communication was posted on 1 October, the day after the 'double event'. This time it was a postcard and, like the first, was sent to the Central News Agency. It read:

> I was not codding dear old Boss when I gave you the tip. You'll hear about Saucy Jack's work tomorrow. Double event this time. Number one squealed a bit. Couldn't finish straight off. Had not time to get ears for police. Thanks for keeping last letter back till I got to work again.
>
> JACK THE RIPPER

Some details of the 'double event' had been published in the Sunday newspapers of 30 September. The text of the 'Dear Boss' letter was published in a Monday newspaper next day and so the 'Saucy Jack' postcard might have been an imitative hoax. The actual postmark – 'OC 1' – suggests that it was posted when the details were public. The police tried to trace the writer, by publishing a facsimile poster of both items. This was circulated within three days of the 'double event' and asked for anyone who recognized the handwriting to communicate with the nearest police station.

The most apparently genuine letter of all was not received until 16 October. It was sent to George Lusk, who was head of the Whitechapel Vigilance Committee, and was enclosed within a small parcel containing part of a kidney. Lusk was a builder who specialized in the redecoration and reguilding of music hall interiors. He was a freemason, the local churchwarden, and lived at 1 Alderney Road, Mile End. The letter was addressed 'From Hell' and read:

> Mr. Lusk
> Sir I send you half the Kidne I took from one woman prasarved it for you tother piece I fried and ate it was very nise I may send you the bloody knif that took it out if you only wate a whil longer
>   signed Catch me when you can Mishter Lusk

HANDWRITING SAMPLES

Jack the Ripper

25 September, the first 'Ripper' signature.

Jack the Ripper

30 September, details of the double event.

Catch me when you can Mishter Lusk

6 October, 'From hell' to Mr Lusk.

Jack the ripper

29 October, 'Old boss' to Dr Openshaw.

Interestingly, it was not signed 'Jack the Ripper' almost as if the murderer, if he was the letter writer, was repudiating his public christening. The phrase 'Catch me when you can', which concludes the Lusk letter, was discovered by art historian Anna Gruetzner Robins to be the slight reworking of the title of a popular piece of music written by Imanuel Liebich in 1866 called 'Catch me if you can!'

When Eddowes's body had been examined by the police surgeon, one of the kidneys was indeed found to be missing. This letter and the kidney were sent on to Major Smith of the City Police who asked the police surgeon to consult with the most eminent specialists in the medical profession about it and get a report to him without delay. Unfortunately, as he later wrote, some clerk or assistant in the office was got at, and the whole affair was public property next morning. 'Right royally did the Solons of the metropolis enjoy themselves at the expense of my humble self and the City Police Force.' 'The kidney was the kidney of a dog, anyone could see that,' wrote one. 'Evidently from the dissecting room,' wrote another. 'Taken out of a corpse after a post-mortem,' wrote a third. 'A transparent hoax,' wrote a fourth.

The kidney was examined by Dr Openshaw, the Pathological Curator of the London Hospital Museum. Initial press reports had him saying that the kidney was a 'ginny' kidney of the sort found in an alcoholic, that it belonged to a woman of about forty-five, and that it had been removed within the last three weeks. The kidney was in an advanced state of Bright's disease, and the one that had been left in Eddowes's body was in an exactly similar state. This was denied by Dr Openshaw who said that he had made no such comments and that he had only been able to say that it was half of a left human kidney. Alcohol does not damage the kidneys and there was no such thing as a 'ginny' kidney.

As proof that it did indeed come from the same body, Smith added that of the renal artery (which is about three inches long) two inches remained in the body and one inch was still attached to the kidney. Dr Henry Sutton, a leading authority on the kidney and its diseases, who was consulted by Smith, said that he would pledge his reputation that the kidney had been put in spirits within a few hours of removal. This meant that it could not have come from a dissecting room where the body would have been kept for one or two days prior to the inquest.

Dr Frederick Gordon Brown, the City police surgeon, also examined the kidney. His most important assertion was that no portion of the renal artery adhered to the Lusk kidney because the organ had been 'trimmed up'. This contradicts Smith and would seem to put his case out of court for the kidney coming from Eddowes. Dr Sedgwick Saunders, the City's Public Analyst, thought the Lusk kidney a student hoax. Opinion is divided now, as it was then, over the Lusk kidney. If genuine, as many believe it is, then the unsigned letter 'From Hell' that accompanied it came from the murderer. It would be the only letter that we could say, with any certainty, came from Jack the Ripper.

After the Eddowes inquest a jeering letter, postmarked 29 October, was sent to Dr Openshaw of the London Hospital. This he handed to Major Smith. It said:

> Old boss you was rite it was the left kidney i was goin to hoperate agin close to your ospitle just as i was going to dror mi nife along of er bloomin throte them cusses of coppers spoilt the game but i guess i wil be on the job soon and wil send you another bit of innerds
>
> Jack the ripper

> O have you seen the devle with his mikerscope and scalpul a-looking at a kidney with a slide cocked up.

How authentic were these letters? Of which of them could it be said that the writer was definitely 'Jack the Ripper'? Sir Robert Anderson, in his book *The Lighter Side of My Official Life*, threw considerable doubts on the first two by saying: 'So I will only add here that the "Jack the Ripper" letter which is preserved in the Police Museum at New Scotland Yard is the creation of an enterprising journalist.' And Sir Melville Macnaghten, who was to become head of the CID in 1903, confirmed that this was so by commenting in his own memoirs: 'In this ghastly production I have always thought I could discern the stained forefinger of the journalist – indeed, a year later I had shrewd suspicions as to the actual author! But whoever did pen the gruesome stuff, it is certain to my mind that it was not the mad miscreant who had committed the murders.'

The mystery appears to have been solved by Stewart Evans's discovery in 1993 of a letter from Chief Inspector John George Littlechild, head of the Secret Department (Special Branch) at Scotland Yard, asserting that Tom Bulling, who forwarded the Jack the Ripper letters from the Central News Agency to the police, was the originator and Charles Moore, his boss, was the inventor of the original letter. Another journalist called Best subsequently claimed that he and a provincial colleague were responsible for all the 'Ripper' letters. Allowing for the exaggeration, he and his colleague may have written some but certainly not all of them. Their understandable motive was to keep the story in print, 'to keep the business alive'.

Assuming this identification of Bulling and Moore as the originators to be correct, why was the name of 'Jack the Ripper' chosen? There is a possible explanation in the events of some fifty years before when in 1837–8 London was being terrorized by a strange bat-like creature called Spring Heeled Jack. He had fiery eyes, according to witnesses from his mouth would shoot blue and white flames, and with claw-like hands he would tear at his victim's clothes before escaping with huge spring-like bounds and screams of maniacal laughter. After a two-year reign of terror he disappeared, just as mysteriously as he had come, but 'Spring Heeled Jack, the Terror of London' quickly gained popular notoriety in the penny dreadfuls and stage melodramas of the day. The fictions about him continued to be published well into the next century. Possibly it was capitalizing on this well-known notoriety that the name of Jack was chosen. It was a name already familiar to the public and had connotations of terror. 'Ripper' is more obviously explainable but possibly, and I only throw this out as a suggestion, someone was recalling the notorious Hannibal Chollop in Dickens's *Martin Chuzzlewit* who, besides carrying a brace of seven-barrel revolving pistols in his pockets, also carried a swordstick which he called his 'Tickler' and 'a great knife, which (for he was a man of pleasant turn of humour) he called "Ripper", in allusion to its usefulness as a means of ventilating the stomach of any adversary in a close contest.'

This being so, it does suggest that both the letter and the postcard were hoaxes. Until now, it has generally been assumed that the early reference to the 'double event' before the newspapers carried the story was proof positive that it must have come from the Ripper. If, as both Anderson and Macnaghten say, they had strong suspicions as to the identity of the author and that he was a journalist (and one probably working on the case for Anderson, at least, to have known him), then the case for their being genuine falls down. Certainly it would explain how the writer knew in advance of the 'double event'.

Donald McCormick disputes this and offers the evidence of Dr Thomas Dutton who, prior to the murders, had specialized in micro-photography and who was a prominent figure in the Chichester and West Sussex Microscopic Society. Apparently he had made a hundred and twenty-eight micro-photographs of the Jack the Ripper correspondence and of these at least thirty-four were in the same handwriting.

The writing was disguised to appear to be that of an uneducated man on some occasions; on others it was that of a painstaking clerk. The same with the phraseology. But even that was marked by 'lapses' into literacy, especially in Jack's effective essays into verse. To quote one example:

Eight little whores, with no hope of heaven,

Gladstone may save one, then there'll be seven.
Seven little whores begging for a shilling,
One stays in Henage Court, then there's a killing.
Six little whores, glad to be alive,
One sidles up to Jack, then there are five.
Four and whore rhyme aright, So do three and me,
I'll set the town alight
Ere there are two
Two little whores, shivering with fright,
Seek a cosy doorway in the middle of the night.
Jack's knife flashes, then there's but one,
And the last one's the ripest for Jack's idea of fun.

It may not be verse in the accepted sense, but this is certainly not the composition of an illiterate. Jack would sometimes mis-spell words deliberately, then forget later on and write a word correctly. It was the same with his punctuation. He wrote 'Jewes' with an extra 'e' when he scrawled his message in chalk on the wall, and which the police so stupidly washed off. But he also spelt the word correctly in some letters.

I was asked by the police to photograph the message on the wall before it was washed off, but Sir Charles Warren was so insistent that the message must not be preserved in any form that he ordered the police to destroy the prints I sent them.

This I find frankly incredible. Even if true, why did Dr Dutton never keep copies and what, in fact, did he do with the originals? Did they ever exist? As he had apparently full police co-operation with the other hundred and twenty-eight micro-photographs, why should they jib at this particular message when, according to Dutton, he 'definitely established that the writing was the same as that in some of the letters'? His micro-photograph would have settled once and for all the doubts that still exist about precisely what was written on that wall. Even the police constable who found it in Goulston Street reported it wrongly when he was giving evidence at the inquest. He said the message was 'The

Jews are The men That Will not be Blamed for nothing', and it was only after persistent cross-examination that he revealed that 'Jews' should have read 'Juwes'. The correct wording was 'The Juwes are not The men that Will be Blamed for nothing'. According to a BBC television presentation of the case in 1973, this spelling of Jews has a masonic connotation. The biblical Solomon ordered the three Jews who had murdered the Grand Mason Hiram Abiff to be killed with 'due ceremony and *formal ritual*'. The wording is, '. . . for the murder of J-U-W-E-S . . . Let the breast be torn open and the heart and vitals be taken from thence and thrown over the shoulder.' This recalls the following cross-examination at the Eddowes inquest:

DR BROWN: . . . The abdomen was all exposed; the intestines were drawn out to a large extent and placed over the right shoulder; a piece of intestine was quite detached from the body and placed between the left arm and the body.

MR CRAWFORD: By 'placed' do you mean put there by design?

DR BROWN: Yes.

MR CRAWFORD: Would that also apply to the intestines that were over the right shoulder?

DR BROWN: Yes.

A similar sort of thing had happened to Annie Chapman. Dr Phillips had said of the body in the back yard at Hanbury Street: 'The intestines, severed from the mesenteric attachments had been lifted out of the body and placed on the shoulder of the corpse.'

At the time several newspapers had said that the Yiddish spelling of Jewes was 'Juwes', but in *The Times* of 15 October Warren asked the newspaper to report that he had made inquiries about this very point, his attention having been drawn to the newspaper reports, and that the Yiddish equivalent was 'Yidden'. The report concluded: 'It has not been ascertained that there is any dialect or language in which the word "Jews" is spelt "Juwes".' However, there is a spelling which approximates to it so closely that one can't help speculating that, had Police Constable Long taken a little more care in copying down the message, the investigation might have taken a slightly different turn. The spelling is the French word for Jews, the feminine form of which is 'Juives' (masculine 'Juifs'). On the black fascia on which the message was written, it is possible that he didn't see or else ignored the dot over the 'i'; and in an italic hand the 'i' and 'v' when they are joined together could quite easily be mistaken for a 'w'.

When all is said and done there is only one letter which has real credibility and that is the letter addressed 'From Hell'. The others may or may not have been written by the Ripper. It is unlikely that we shall ever know. Most writers have made the mistake, when they have been comparing specimens, of looking for similarities between such normal signatures as the suspects Druitt's and J. K. Stephen's and the Ripper letters. This is a mistaken approach, as was thoroughly proved at the trial of Peter Kürten, who in Düsseldorf fifty years later deliberately modelled himself on the Ripper even to the extent of writing to the newspapers. Under stress his handwriting became unrecognizable – so much so that he showed the 'murderer's' letters to his wife, when they were published in facsimile in the newspapers, and although she looked at them carefully she saw no resemblance between them and her husband's handwriting.

In August 1968 a Canadian graphologist, C. M. Macleod, published in *The Criminologist* an article called 'A "Ripper" Handwriting Analysis'. This was prompted by Professor Camps's article 'More About "Jack the Ripper" ' which had appeared in the February issue and which had reproduced in facsimile some of the letters. The specimens he chose for analysis were the letter addressed 'From Hell' and the one beginning 'Old Boss you was rite . . .'

In Macleod's opinion, 'they are the efforts of two persons having similar perversions but important personality differences. Both specimens reveal a propensity to cruelly perverted sexuality to a degree that even the most casual amateur graphologist could hardly mistake.' The most obvious thing about both letters is their untidiness. The blotting and smearing suggest that the writers were addicted to drink or possibly drugs. Both were certainly sadists, as indicated by the 'sharp angles and dagger strokes' which 'can only be produced by a violently jerky thrust of the hand, suggesting extreme tension finding a vent in anger'. Their ages would have been somewhere between twenty and forty-five, and both were probably 'working class'. If he had had to pick one of them as being the real Jack the Ripper then he would go for the writer of the letter 'From Hell', who 'shows tremendous drive in the vicious forward thrust of his overall writing, and great cunning in his covering-up of strokes; that is, the retracing of one stroke of a letter over another, rendering it illegible while appearing to clarify. While Sample 1 appears to be written better than Sample 2, it is in fact extremely difficult to decipher; whereas Sample 2, except for the atrocious spelling is fairly readable.' Macleod continues:

I would say that this writer was capable of conceiving any atrocity, and of carrying it out in an organised way. I would say he had enough brains and control to hold down some steady job which would give him a cover for his crimes. He has imagination, as revealed in the upper-zone flourishes. Those hooks on the t-bars, among other signs, indicate tenacity to achieve a goal.

I could have looked for this killer among men such as cab-drivers, who had a legitimate excuse to be anywhere at any time. I should have sought a hail-fellow-well-met who liked to eat and drink; who might attract women of the class he preyed on by an overwhelming animal charm. I would say he was in fact a latent homosexual (suggested by lower-zone strokes returning on the wrong side of the letter) and passed as a 'man's man'; the roistering blade who made himself the life and soul of the pub and sneered at women as objects to be used and discarded. He would, of course, have had wits enough to stop short of explaining how he used them.

6. Aftermath

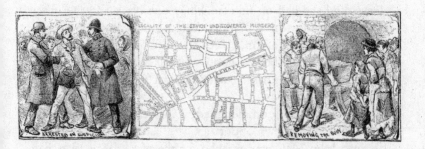

The following year, 1889, new fears began to spread that Jack the Ripper was not dead and that another wave of killings was about to start.

On 17 July 1889 a woman was murdered in Whitechapel. In almost every respect the killing, in Castle Alley, was a Ripper event. Shortly before 1 a.m. Police Constable Walter Andrews met the duty sergeant on his nightly rounds and, after a few words of desultory greeting, continued his patrol. The sergeant had only gone about 150 yards when he heard Andrews blow his whistle for help. He ran back to see what was the matter and followed the constable as he ran up Castle Alley. Lying on the pavement, close to two vans, was the body of a woman. She was on her right side with her clothes half up to her waist. The constable pointed to the pool of blood under her head and said, 'Another murder.' He had already knelt down and felt the body which, in spite of a slight drizzle, was still warm.

Close by was a man whom the constable had seen walking along the street with a plate in his hand innocently going for his supper. As he had been the only person in the street the constable had made him wait with him until he could prove his innocence, which he soon did. As soon as police reinforcements arrived they were sent immediately to the lodging and coffee houses to make searches.

The top of the woman's left thumb was missing, as was a tooth from the upper jaw. The dress was patched under the arms and sleeves and she had on odd stockings, one black and the other maroon. Her brown stuff skirt, kilted brown linsey petticoat, white chemise and apron, paisley shawl (which was still around her shoulders) and button boots were all old clothes. Her only possessions were a farthing and an old clay pipe, which were found under her body.

The woman was soon identified as 'Clay pipe' Alice McKenzie. Not much was known about her. She had been living with a labourer, John McCormack, who for the past sixteen years had done casual work for Jewish tailors in Hanbury Street (where Annie Chapman had been murdered) and for other people in the neighbourhood. He had met McKenzie in Bishopsgate and they had been living together in lodging houses in the Whitechapel area for the past six or seven years and at 52 Gun Street for the past twelve months. According to the other lodgers they had lived comfortably together. Previously McKenzie had lived with a blind man. In spite of their intimacy McCormack could tell the police little else about her background except that she had said that she came from Peterborough and had sons who were living abroad.

McCormack told the police that he had come home from work at about 4 p.m. on 16 July and had given McKenzie some money (one shilling and eight pence) before he went to sleep. When he woke up between 10 and 11 p.m. he found she had gone out. He did not see her again until he was taken to the mortuary to identify her body.

McKenzie often went out at night but whether she was a prostitute or not is doubtful, although the police certainly regarded her as such. Like the other women, she drank heavily.

Dr Bagster Phillips carried out the initial post-mortem but Robert Anderson, the head of CID, for some unknown reason wanted a second opinion and asked Dr Bond of the Great Western Railway to confirm the findings. On 18 July Bond went to the mortuary with Dr Phillips, who explained to him that the wounds on the throat had been so disturbed that any examination he might make would convey no definite information as to the injuries. He pointed out the original wounds, their character and direction, and Bond formed an opinion, as far as he was able to, that the cuts were made from left to right. He also thought, as far as he could make out, that the knife had been plunged deeply into the left side of the neck, behind the sternomastoid muscle, and brought out by an incision above the larynx on the same side. There appeared to have been two stabs in the throat. The knife had been carried forward into the wound, leaving just a small tongue of skin between the two stabs. (If this was a Ripper killing, then the murderer had changed his methods from the customary practice of severing the throat with two deep cuts.) There were several small superficial cuts on the throat but the two main thrusts were about two inches long and had been made by a knife which had been driven in from above, in a downward and forward motion.

The weapon, Bond thought, was a sharp-pointed knife and he believed that the cuts had been made while the woman's head was thrown back upon the ground. Phillips thought that the knife must have been a smaller one than any that had been used before. There were no bruises on her face and lips, nor on the back of her head, but there were two bruises high up on the chest which indicated that the killer had stabbed her with his right hand while he held her down with his left.

On the right side of the abdomen and extending from the chest to below the level of the umbilicus there was a jagged incision made up of several cuts; these extended through the skin and subcutaneous fat. At the bottom of this cut there were seven or eight superficial scratches each about two inches long and lying parallel to each other. There was a small stab wound, one eighth of an inch deep, on the mons veneris.

Death had been instantaneous from the stab wounds in the throat; the abdominal wounds had been inflicted afterwards. There was some disagreement as to whether the killer had been left- or right-handed. Dr Phillips thought that the bruises on the left side of the stomach had been caused by the murderer pressing down with his right hand while he used the knife with his left; Dr Bond thought that they indicated the exact opposite. Bond concluded:

I see in this murder evidence of similar design to the former Whitechapel murders, viz. sudden onslaught on the prostrate woman, the throat skilfully and resolutely cut with subsequent mutilation, each mutilation indicating sexual thoughts and a desire to mutilate the abdomen and sexual organs.

I am of the opinion that the murder was performed by the same person who committed the former series of Whitechapel murders.

However, Dr Phillips disagreed with this conclusion. He did not believe that all the Whitechapel killings had been the work of one man. After long and careful deliberation he had arrived at this conclusion 'on purely anatomical and professional grounds'. He stressed this point by emphasizing that he was not taking into consideration all the circumstantial evidence and the facts in favour of the one-man theory. He had ignored all evidence which he hadn't had at first hand.

As he had himself carried out or assisted in five out of the seven post-mortems under discussion (Chapman, Eddowes, Kelly, McKenzie and Coles) his evidence on this point must carry a lot of weight.

Yet another murder, two months later, was thought to be the Ripper's handiwork. Fortunately, it can be proved to be otherwise. At 5.20 a.m. on 10 September 1889, a patrolling policeman found the naked trunk of a female body in some railway arches in Pinchin Street, not far from Berner Street where Long Liz Stride had been murdered. The street was a lonely spot but was patrolled every half hour by the night duty constable.

From the post-mortem report, the time of death fixed the murder as probably happening thirty-six hours before on the Sunday night, 8 September, which was the anniversary of Annie Chapman's murder just one year before. If this was a Ripper killing, then the murderer had once more changed a now well-established technique.

It would also mean that for the first time the murder had been committed in the murderer's house.

However, there was no evidence to show that death had been caused by cutting the throat; there was no mutilation of the body although there was dismemberment, no removal of organs or intestines; further, the murder had not been committed in the streets or in the victim's house. There was none of the frenzied mutilation of the body, as there had been with Mary Kelly, and which might have been expected as the murder had happened indoors.

There was a gash on the trunk but according to the doctor this had been done after death, probably to confuse the police and make them think that this was another Ripper killing. In fact, it looked as if the knife had slipped. The whole of the wound looked as though the murderer had intended to make a cut preparatory to the removal of the intestines but had then changed his mind.

On medical grounds and the evidence of the modus operandi, any suggestion that this unidentified woman was a Ripper victim can be dismissed.

7. Suspects

The best known of all the Ripper documents are the legendary
Macnaghten papers. These are not a large manuscript collection,
as is often supposed, but a single document written by Sir
Melville Macnaghten several years after he joined Scotland
Yard as an assistant chief constable in 1889 and before he was
appointed head of the CID in 1903. There are two versions of
these notes. One forms part of the Ripper case papers which
are deposited in the MEPOL (Metropolitan Police) papers in
the National Archives (Kew). The other set of papers was in
the possession of Lady Aberconway, Sir Melville Macnaghten's
daughter, who made them available to the writers Dan Farson
in 1959 and to Tom Cullen in 1965. The former quoted from

them in a television documentary which he made at the time, although only the initials of leading suspects were given. Tom Cullen was more fortunate, and could print the names in full; Farson was able to do the same thing eight years later when he published his own account of the same story.

Yet although both sets of papers are supposed to emanate from the same source, there are very important differences between them.

For example, Farson and Cullen quote Macnaghten as saying that the main suspect was:

Mr M. J. DRUITT, a doctor of about 41 years of age and of fairly good family, who disappeared at the time of the Miller's Court murder, and whose body was found floating in the Thames on 3rd December, i.e. seven weeks after the said murder. The body was said to have been in the water for a month, or more – on it was found a season ticket between Blackheath and London. From private information I have little doubt but that his own family suspected this man of being the Whitechapel murderer; and it was alleged that he was sexually insane.

Whereas the Scotland Yard version is:

A Mr M. J. Druitt, said to be a doctor and of good family – who disappeared at the time of the Miller's Court murder, and whose body (which was said to have been upwards of a month in the water) was found in the Thames on 31st December – or about seven weeks after that murder. He was sexually insane and from private information I have little doubt but that his own family believed him to have been the murderer.

Which, we have to ask ourselves, is the original?

Some light was shed on this problem by Philip Loftus when he reviewed Farson's book in the *Guardian* on 7 October 1972. His own interest in Druitt had started several years earlier, in fact in 1950 when he was staying with a friend, Gerald Melville

Donner, who happened to be the grandson of Sir Melville Macnaghten. Donner owned a Jack the Ripper letter, which Loftus thought was a copy, written in red ink, framed and hanging on the wall.

'Copy be damned,' Donner said, 'that's the original.' As proof that he owned some original documents he pulled out Sir Melville Macnaghten's private notes which Loftus described as being 'in Sir Melville's handwriting on official paper, rather untidy and in the nature of rough jottings'. Loftus thought that they mentioned three suspects: a Polish tanner or cobbler; a man who went around stabbing young girls in the bottom; and a 41-year-old doctor, Mr M. J. Druitt.

Donner died in 1968 and the notes then seemed to have disappeared. Loftus wrote to his family inquiring of their whereabouts, but the family told him that they did not know. He also wrote to Lady Aberconway, who was Donner's aunt – Sir Melville had two daughters – asking her the same questions. She explained: 'My elder sister, ten years older than myself, took all my father's papers when my mother died – which is why Gerald has them: I have never seen them. But in my father's book "Days of My Years" he talks of "Jack the Ripper" . . . that is all the information I can give.'

The notes that were in the elder sister's possession and which Farson and Cullen both quoted from, are *typewritten copies*. Farson says 'she was kind enough to give me her father's private notes which she had copied out soon after his death.' Tom Cullen also told me, in conversation, that the notes he had seen were typewritten.

So, in addition to the two existing sets of notes, whose whereabouts are known, there must be added those untidy 'rough jottings' which disappeared after Donner's death. This immediately prompts one to ask how many other papers have disappeared. As most of them have been in the possession of the police for over a hundred years one might imagine the answer to be 'very few, if any'. Unfortunately this is not the case. But before anyone begins attributing sinister motives to the police for the destruction or disappearance of relevant papers, certain explanations must be made to put the problem in its proper perspective.

It sounds unbelievable, but it is only in the last thirty years that the police generally have taken an interest in their own fascinating past. It was then realized, however, that in many forces much of the early history had already been lost. My own experiences in this field might help to clarify this point.

Some years ago I wrote a social history of police and crime in the City of London from Elizabethan to Victorian times. Although the City police force is the oldest in the country, far older than the Metropolitan (which serves Greater London), it has nothing in the way of early documentation. Had it not been for papers in the possession of the Corporation of the City of London it would have been nearly impossible to write a history of this force. The police themselves were not entirely to blame for this situation. A number of their stations had been badly blitzed in the 1939–45 war (one was completely wiped out). Inevitably, quite a lot of documents were destroyed but tragically, of the papers that remained, nearly all were scrapped. Only a few letters, such as those from the Governor of Newgate Prison written when hangings were still public, were snatched from the shredding machines and retained as curiosities. Much later, I was fortunate enough to salvage case papers relating to the Siege of Sidney Street in 1911 following the murder of three City of London policemen by Latvian anarchists and to use them in a book. The maps were so brittle that the binder who restored them thought that they had been baked!

The point that I am making is that these papers were destroyed, as others have been, through indifference or ignorance – not through a desire to conceal or to protect some great name.

This record of neglect is just as true of other police forces, including Scotland Yard. The late Mr Heron, its first archivist, told me that until 1959, when the Yard's files came under the

control of the National Archives office at Kew (being Home
Office papers), it was quite customary when more space was
needed for the porters to yank out handfuls of papers from old
files to make way for new ones. Some, I imagine, were a bit
selective about what they took, and hopefully one day some of
these papers will be returned. A Superintendent I once heard
lecturing to the Metropolitan Police History Society touched on
this same point. He told us that most of the early papers of the
Special Branch were thought to have been destroyed in 1884 by
a Fenian bomb which was planted against the wall of their office.
Yet some papers had recently come to light. The widow of a
Special Branch pensioner asked them to buy the contents of a
large suitcase which she brought into their office. It was full of
Special Branch papers which her husband had kept under the
bed.

Therefore, anyone who is hoping for startling revelations from
the Jack the Ripper files will be very disappointed with what
they find. They are incomplete. When I first examined them in
the early 1970s there were three bundles of loose-leaf papers in
brown wrap-round files tied up with tapes. They are now even
more incomplete because of thefts by so-called researchers. This
has led to the documents being individually sealed and bound.
Some of the documents are only known now from the
photocopies made by genuine researchers.

Two of the original Ripper files contained letters from the
general public offering advice on the best way to catch the
Whitechapel murderer. They contained nothing of any apparent
importance. The third originally consisted of a number of thin
brown folders – some of them very thin – which related not
only to the five accepted Ripper murders but to others such as
Alice McKenzie and Frances Coles which some contemporaries
attributed to him. Each of the folders had the victim's, or alleged
victim's, name across the top. There were very few documents in
each file. The Eddowes murder, investigated by the City of
London Police, contained only a single newspaper cutting. Some

of the other files contained little more. Through the permission of the Commissioner of the City police, I was able to place in the Eddowes and Kelly file copies of the original photographs which were in their possession and to deposit similar sets with the Black Museum and the now defunct Bow Street Historical Museum. One can only assume that the Kelly photograph was removed at a much earlier date, since Sir Melville Macnaghten refers to it in his notes. Stranger still was the fact that this photograph was apparently the work of the City police, in spite of the dressing down they had received from Sir Charles Warren for being in Whitechapel. A story which explains this, although it is at variance with the newspaper accounts and comes from police pensioners I once worked with, is that although the Metropolitan Police did not dare to disobey Warren's order and break down Kelly's doorway before the bloodhounds arrived, the City police did so as they ran no such risks. Apparently, as the morning dragged on, and nothing happened in Miller's Court, somebody quietly asked the City police for their help, which they gave by breaking into Kelly's room and taking the photograph of her body as their justification for doing so. Whatever the truth of the story, the City police photographs of Eddowes must have been taken by a professional photographer as there was no official City police photographic department until the early 1950s. Curiously enough, they may have had others taken. The photograph of Miller's Court is now a well known one, but it was only by chance that I found it and published it in the *Police Journal* in 1969. Its discovery can be seen as backing up the claim that the City police were involved in the taking of the Kelly photographs. In 1967 their photographic department were clearing out a lot of old negatives, including some glass ones, and I happened to spot them. Two were of immediate interest. One was of some Metropolitan policemen, taken about 1870, and the other – which I instantly recognized – was of Miller's Court, of which no photograph was known to exist. When I tried to trace their source, I was told that they had come from a large album of photographs which disappeared when the force museum was broken up in 1959 and lost at the same time as the 'From Hell' letter, which vanished with it.

In general, the documents are a haphazard collection and their very haphazardness suggests that they have been well picked over in the past hundred years. The only recorded destruction of any part of them is attributed to Sir Melville Macnaghten who is alleged to have burned the most incriminating of the papers to protect the murderer's family. His daughter denies this story and says that her father probably said that he had done this to stop himself from being pestered by people at his club.

His notes are reproduced below in full for the first time anywhere. There are seven foolscap pages, in his handwriting, with hardly a blot or deletion throughout. Presumably this copy was written from those rough jottings that were in the possession of his grandson. As such, and as it is dated, it must be regarded as the prima facie document.

Confidential

The case referred to in the sensational story told in 'The Sun' in its issue of 13th inst. & following dates, is that of Thomas Cutbush who was arraigned at the London County Sessions in April 1891 on a charge of maliciously wounding Florence Grace Johnson, and attempting to wound Isabella Fraser Anderson in Kennington. He was found to be insane, and sentenced to be detained during Her Majesty's Pleasure.

This Cutbush, who lived with his mother and aunt at 14 Albert Street, Kennington, escaped from the Lambeth Infirmary, (after he had been detained only a few hours, as a lunatic) at noon on 5th March 1891. He was rearrested on 9th idem. A few weeks before this, several cases of stabbing, or jobbing, from behind had occurred in the vicinity and a man named Colicott was arrested, but subsequently discharged owing to faulty identification. The cuts in the girl's dresses made by Colicott were quite different to the cut(s) made by Cutbush (when he wounded Miss Johnson) who was no doubt influenced by a wild desire of morbid imitation. Cutbush's antecedents were enquired into by C.Insp. (now Supt.) Chis(holm) by Inspector Hale, and by P. S. McCarthy CID – (the last named officer had been specially employed in Whitechapel at the time of the murders there,) – and it was ascertained that he was born, and had lived, in Kennington all his life. His father died when he was quite young and he was always a 'spoilt' child. He had been employed as a clerk and traveller in the Tea trade at the Minories, and subsequently canvassed for a Directory in the East End, during which time he bore a good character. He apparently contracted syphilis about 1888, and – since that time – led an idle and useless life. His brain seems to have become affected, and he believed that people were trying to poison him. He wrote to Lord Grimthorpe and others, – and also to the Treasury, – complaining of Dr Brooks, of Westminster Bridge Road, whom he had threatened to shoot for having supplied him with bad medicines. He is said to have studied medical books by day, and to have rambled about at night, returning frequently with his clothes covered with mud; but little reliance could be placed on the statements made by his mother or his aunt, who both appear to have been of a very excitable disposition. It was found impossible to ascertain his movements on the nights of the Whitechapel murders. The knife found on him was bought in Houndsditch about a week before he was detained in the Infirmary. Cutbush was the nephew of the late Supt. Executive.

Now the Whitechapel murderer had 5 victims – & 5 victims only, – his murders were

(1) 31st August '88. Mary Ann Nichols – at Buck's Row – who was found with her throat cut – & with (slight) stomach mutilation.

(2) 8th Sept. '88. Annie Chapman – Hanbury St – throat cut – stomach & private parts badly mutilated & some of the entrails placed round the neck.

(3) 30th Sept. '88. Elizabeth Stride – Berner's [*sic*] Street – throat cut, but nothing in shape of mutilation attempted, & *on same date*

Catharine Eddowes – Mitre Square, throat cut & very bad mutilation, both of face & stomach.

9th November, Mary Jane Kelly – Miller's Court, throat cut, and the whole of the body mutilated in the most ghastly manner.

The last murder is the only one that took place in a *room*, and the murderer must have been at least 2 hours engaged. A photo was taken of the woman, as she was found lying on the bed, without seeing which it is impossible to imagine the awful mutilation.

With regard to the *double* murder which took place on 30th September, there is no doubt but that the man was disturbed by some Jews who drove up to a Club, (close to which the body of Elizabeth Stride was found) and that he then, 'nondum satiatus', went in search of a further victim who he found at Mitre Square.

It will be noticed that the fury of the mutilations *increased* in each case, and, seemingly, the appetite only became sharpened by indulgence. It seems, then, highly improbable that the murderer would have suddenly stopped in November '88, and been content to recommence operations by merely prodding a girl's behind some 2 years and 4 months afterwards. A much more rational theory is that the murderer's brain gave way altogether after his awful glut in Miller's Court, and that he immediately committed suicide, or, as a possible alternative, was found to be so hopelessly mad by his relations, that he was by them confined in some asylum.

No one ever saw the Whitechapel murderer; many homicidal maniacs were suspected, but no shadow of proof could be thrown on any one. I may mention the cases of 3 men, any one of whom would have been more likely than Cutbush to have committed this series of murders:

(1) A Mr M. J. Druitt, said to be a doctor & of good family – who disappeared at the time of the Miller's Court murder, & whose body (which was said to have been upwards of a month in the water) was found in the Thames on 31st December – or about 7 weeks after that murder. He was sexually insane and from private information I have little doubt but that his own family believed him to have been the murderer.

(2) Kosminski – a Polish Jew – & resident in Whitechapel. This man became insane owing to many years indulgence in solitary vices. He had a great hatred of women, specially of the prostitute class, & had strong homicidal tendencies: he was removed to a lunatic asylum about March

1889. There were many circumstances connected with this man which made him a strong 'suspect'.

(3) Michael Ostrog, a Russian doctor, and a convict, who was subsequently detained in a lunatic asylum as a homicidal maniac. This man's antecedents were of the worst possible type, and his whereabouts at the time of the murders could never be ascertained.

And now with regard to a few of the other inaccuracies and misleading statements made by 'The Sun'. In its issue of 14th February, it is stated that the writer has in his possession a facsimile of the knife with which the murders were committed. This knife (which for some unexplained reason has, for the last 3 years, been kept by Inspector Race, instead of being sent to Prisoner's Property Store) was traced, and it was found to have been purchased in Houndsditch in February '91 or 2 years and 3 months *after* the Whitechapel murders ceased!

The statement, too, that Cutbush 'spent a portion of the day in making rough drawings of the bodies of women, and of their mutilations' is based solely on the fact that 2 *scribble* drawings of women in indecent postures were found torn up in Cutbush's room. The head and body of one of these had been cut from some fashion plate, and legs were added to shew a woman's naked thighs and pink stockings.

In the issue of 15th inst. it is said that a *light overcoat* was among the things found in Cutbush's house, and that a man in a *light* overcoat was seen talking to a woman at Backchurch Lane whose body with arms attached was found in Pinchin Street. This is hopelessly incorrect! On 10th Sept. '89 the naked body, with arms, of a woman was found wrapped in some sacking under a Railway arch in Pinchin Street: the head and legs were never found nor was the woman ever identified. She had been killed at least 24 hours before the remains which had seemingly been brought from a distance, were discovered. The stomach was split up by a cut, and the head and legs had been severed in a manner identical with that of the woman whose remains were discovered in the Thames, in Battersea Park, and on the Chelsea Embankment on 4th June of the same year; and these murders had no connection whatever with the Whitechapel horrors. The Rainham mystery in 1887 and the Whitehall mystery [when portions of a woman's body were found under what is now New Scotland Yard] in 1888 were of a similar type to the Thames and Pinchin Street crimes.

It is perfectly untrue to say that Cutbush stabbed 6 girls' behinds. This is confounding his case with that of Colicott. The theory that the Whitechapel murderer was left-handed, or, at any rate, 'ambi-dexter', had its origin in the remark made by a doctor who examined the corpse of one of the earliest victims; *other doctors did not agree with him.*

With regard to the 4 additional murders ascribed by the writer in 'The Sun' to the Whitechapel fiend:

(1) The body of Martha Tabram, a prostitute was found on a common staircase in George Yard buildings on 7th August 1888; the body had been repeatedly *pierced*, probably with a *bayonet*. This woman had, with a fellow prostitute, been in company of 2 soldiers in the early part of the evening: these men were arrested, but the second prostitute failed, or refused, to identify, and the soldiers were eventually discharged.

(2) Alice McKenzie was found with her throat cut (or rather *stabbed*) in Castle Alley on 17th July 1889; no evidence was forthcoming and no arrests were made in connection with this case. The *stab* in the throat was of the same nature as in the case of the murder of

(3) Frances Coles in Swallow Gardens, on 13th February 1891 – for which Thomas Sadler, a [ship's] fireman, was arrested, and, after several remands, discharged. It was ascertained at the time that Sadler had sailed for the Baltic on 19th July '89 and was in Whitechapel on the nights of 17th idem. He was a man of ungovernable temper and entirely addicted to drink, and the company of the lowest prostitutes.

(4) The case of the unidentified woman whose trunk was found in Pinchin Street: on 10th September 1889 – which has already been dealt with.

M. L. Macnaghten
23rd February 1894

As Macnaghten did not join the Yard until 1889 he had no firsthand experience of the case and must, one assumes, have been drawing on Abberline's reports to compile this particular document some six years after the events. Unlike some of the other policemen involved, Abberline never published any account of the murders – or of his subsequent investigations into the Cleveland Street scandal centering on a homosexual brothel in the West End to which the Duke of Clarence was supposed to have gone, and which implicated some of the highest in the land.

Soon after completion of this case Abberline resigned, having completed twenty-nine years service, on 8 February 1892. He was then living in south London at 41 Mayflower Road, Clapham. He took with him the walking stick (now at Bramshill Police College) presented to him by the seven detectives who had worked with him on the Whitechapel murders. The handle is of a face covered by a cowl. Perhaps it has some special significance, we don't know. There are rumours that several of these sticks abound and, if so, my own guess would be that someone was capitalizing on a contemporary pamphlet 'The Curse Upon Mitre Square' and that the features are those of the mad monk Brother Martin; possibly the detectives were sporting these sticks, much as their successors do today with ties flaunting the logo of a major criminal case.

Abberline then worked as a private enquiry agent and in 1898 took on the European Agency of the Pinkerton Detective Company of America. In 1904 he retired to Bournemouth where he died, aged eighty-six, on 10 December 1929, some forty years after the murders.

Appropriately local newspapers were carrying stories of the Düsseldorf Ripper, whose reign of terror was nearing its peak.

The following document, which is also reproduced for the first time, was written by Dr Thomas Bond, who carried out the post-mortems on both Alice McKenzie and Mary Kelly. Besides being a lecturer in Forensic Medicine and consulting surgeon to A division and to the Great Western Railway, he was also the author of several publications, including one on the 'Diagnosis and Treatment of Primary Syphilis'.

7 THE SANCTUARY
WESTMINSTER ABBEY
November 10th '88

Dear Sir, *Whitechapel Murders*

I beg to report that I have read the notes of the four Whitechapel Murders viz-:

1. Buck's Row
2. Hanbury Street
3. Berners [*sic*] Street
4. Mitre Square

I have also made a Post Mortem Examination of the mutilated remains of a woman found yesterday in a small room in Dorset Street-:

1. All five murders were no doubt committed by the same hand. In the first four the throats appear to have been cut from left to right, in the last case owing to the extensive mutilation it is impossible to say in what direction the fatal cut was made, but arterial blood was found on the wall in splashes close to where the woman's head must have been lying.

2. All the circumstances surrounding the murders lead me to form the opinion that the women must have been lying down when murdered and in every case the throat was first cut.

3. In the four murders of which I have seen the notes only, I cannot form a very definite opinion as to the time that had elapsed between the murder and the discovery of the body. In one case, that of Berners [*sic*] Street the discovery appears to have been immediately after the deed. In Buck's Row, Hanbury St, and Mitre Square three or four hours only could have elapsed. In the Dorset Street case the body was lying on the bed at the time of my visit two o'clock quite naked and mutilated as in the annexed report. Rigor Mortis had set in but increased during the progress of the examination. From this it is difficult to say with any degree of certainty the exact time that

had elapsed since death as the period varies from six to twelve hours before rigidity sets in. The body was comparatively cold at two o'clock and the remains of a recently taken meal were found in the stomach and scattered about over the intestines. It is therefore, pretty certain that the woman must have been dead about twelve hours and the partly digested food would indicate that death took place about three or four hours after food was taken, so one or two o'clock in the morning would be the probable time of the murder.

4. In all the cases there appears to be no evidence of struggling and the attacks were probably so sudden and made in such a position that the women could neither resist nor cry out. In the Dorset St case the corner of the sheet to the right of the woman's head was much cut and saturated with blood, indicating that the face may have been covered with the sheet at the time of the attack.

5. In the first four cases the murderer must have attacked from the right side of the victim. In the Dorset Street case, he must have attacked from in front or from the left, as there would be no room for him between the wall and the part of the bed on which the woman was lying. Again the blood had flowed down on the right side of the woman and spurted on to the wall.

6. The murderer would not necessarily be splashed or deluged with blood, but his hands and arms must have been covered and parts of his clothing must certainly have been smeared with blood.

7. The mutilations in each case excepting the Berners [sic] Street one were all of the same character and showed clearly that in all the murders the object was mutilation.

8. In each case the mutilation was inflicted by a person who had no scientific nor anatomical knowledge. In my opinion he does not even possess the technical knowledge of a butcher or horse slaughterer or any person accustomed to cut up dead animals.

9. The instrument must have been a strong knife at least six inches long, very sharp, pointed at the top and about an inch in width. It may have been a clasp knife, a butcher's knife or a surgeon's

knife, I think it was no doubt a straight knife.

10. The murderer must have been a man of physical strength and of great coolness and daring. There is no evidence that he had an accomplice. He must in my opinion be a man subject to periodical attacks of Homicidal and erotic mania. The character of the mutilations indicate that the man may be in a condition sexually, that may be called Satyriasis. It is of course possible that the Homicidal impulse may have developed from a revengeful or brooding condition of the mind, or that religious mania may have been the original disease but I do not think either hypothesis is likely. The murderer in external appearance is quite likely to be a quiet inoffensive looking man probably middle-aged and neatly and respectably dressed. I think he must be in the habit of wearing a cloak or overcoat or he could hardly have escaped notice in the streets if the blood on his hands or clothes were visible.

11. Assuming the murderer to be such a person as I have just described, he would be solitary and eccentric in his habits, also he is most likely to be a man without regular occupation, but with some small income or pension. He is possibly living among respectable persons who have some knowledge of his character and habits and who may have grounds for suspicion that he isn't quite right in his mind at times. Such persons would probably be unwilling to communicate suspicions to the Police for fear of trouble or notoriety, whereas if there were prospect of reward it might overcome their scruples.

(This letter went to Robert Anderson, head of CID)

These are the two major documents, and most of the arguments for or against the respective theories hinge on them to some extent. The suspects who are now to be discussed are the main contenders for the shroud of Jack the Ripper. They will not be the only ones. In such a popular game as Hunt the Ripper there will always be new contenders.

Past contenders have included Oscar Wilde's boyfriend George

Francis 'Frank' Miles; Charlie the Ripper, a pasty-faced fish gutter who could never make love (*Reveille*, 12 March 1976); Lewis Carroll, the author of 'Alice in Wonderland'; Lord Randolph Churchill, Winston Churchill's father, a suspect according to my unladylike informant because he lived in London and died of syphilis, which could have been said of many other men at the time. More suspects are continually being put forward such as Robert Mann, a pauper inmate and mortuary attendant; Carl Feigenbaum, a German merchant seaman; John Silver described as a 'brothel owner, pimp and trafficker in women on four continents'; and Sir John Williams, a Welsh gynaecologist who murdered the prostitutes to transfer their 'fertile organs into his sterile wife'.

The suspects' list has now grown to over two hundred and more are almost certainly in the pipeline.

The trouble with these and many other theories is that the so-called evidence is nothing of the sort. The standard of evidence that is offered is frequently such that if any of the 'names' were alive today they would win a fortune in libel actions. If one is asked: 'Is the murderer among the following suspects?', one can only try to be objective and say that, without a lot more new evidence, the answer must always be 'Perhaps'. It can only remain conjecture. I have always had the feeling that on the Day of Judgement, when all things shall be known, when I and the other generations of 'Ripperologists' ask for Jack the Ripper to step forward and call out his true name, we shall turn and look with blank astonishment at one another as he does so and say 'Who?'

The Lodger

The Bible-spouting lodger with a 'down on whores' is probably the most popular image of the Ripper. The factual basis for Mrs Belloc Lowndes' fictional character 'The Lodger' began with the newspaper claims of Dr L. Forbes Winslow, who describes himself in his memoirs, *Recollections of Forty Years*, as a medical theorist and practical detective. His earliest theory, published in *The Times* after Annie Chapman's death, was that the killer was a lunatic who had recently been released from an asylum or had escaped from one. He became so interested in the case that he soon found himself actively engaged in the hunt for the Ripper, pursuing clues and searching for facts to prove his deductions. 'Day after day,' he wrote, 'and night after night I spent in the Whitechapel slums. The detectives knew me, the lodging-house keepers knew me, and at last the poor creatures of the street came to know me. In terror they rushed to me with every scrap of information which might to my mind be of value. To me the frightened women looked for hope. In my presence they felt reassured, and welcomed me to their dens and obeyed my commands eagerly, and found the bits of information I wanted.'

It is not surprising that he subsequently went on to claim that it was he and not the detectives of Scotland Yard who had reasoned out an 'accurate scientific mental picture of the Whitechapel murderer'. He actually claimed that not only had he been able to prove beyond any doubt the identity of the murderer but also, by his revelations to the newspapers, he had also been able to stop the Ripper killings.

Forbes Winslow soon abandoned his original theory of the escaped lunatic. He changed it to a more firmly held belief that the murders were committed by a homicidal lunatic who was goaded by a religious monomania and a warped sense of duty, and that it was his mission in life to exterminate this class of woman from the face of the earth. One of Winslow's many suggestions was that the police should be replaced by warders from lunatic asylums, who would be stationed in Whitechapel to look for possible lunatics, since they were experienced in dealing with such persons while the police were not. Much to his annoyance, the only reply was the usual printed acknowledgement from the Commissioner.

Pointing out that lunatics could be caught in their own traps if their ideas were humoured, he suggested that he might insert in the newspapers an advertisement reading: 'A gentleman who is strongly opposed to the presence of fallen women in the streets of London would like to co-operate with someone with a view to their suppression.' He then proposed to have half a dozen detectives waiting at the prearranged meeting place to seize and question everyone who replied to the advertisement.

Forbes Winslow never doubted that if the police had acted on his suggestions they would have caught the Whitechapel killer. He was astonished that they did not appreciate their own incompetence and he was dismayed by their reluctance to allow others – himself – who were far more competent to handle the case, to take over the investigation.

He was not the only one obsessed with his own theories. Among the amateur detectives prowling Whitechapel was a director of the Bank of England who disguised himself as a labourer and roamed the lodging houses clad in heavy boots, a fustian jacket and with a red handkerchief around his head and a pickaxe in his hand.

Unfortunately, it wasn't until the following year, 1889, that Winslow was given the slender clues on which he built his shaky case. His theory rested on the initial acceptance that the Ripper had killed eight women, the earliest of his victims being an unknown woman who was allegedly murdered in Christmas week of 1887, and the last, Alice McKenzie, on 17 July 1889.

He says that he was given the first clue on 30 August 1889 when a woman, with whom he was in communication, told him that she had been spoken to by a man in Worship Street. He had asked her to come down a court with him and had offered her £1 to do so. She had refused, but with some of her neighbours had followed him instead to a house in Finsbury out of which she had seen him coming some days before. Subsequently, after Alice McKenzie's murder on 17 July, she had seen him washing his hands in the yard of the house. He was in his shirtsleeves at the time and had a peculiar look on his face. This was about

4 a.m. in the morning. The inference was that he was washing off bloodstains.

The lodging-house keeper where the man had lived told Forbes Winslow that in April 1888 the man had rented a large bed-sitting room in his house. The man had said that he was in England on business and that he might stay there for a few months or perhaps even a year. The keeper and his wife noticed that each time he went out he wore a different suit of clothes, and would often change three or four times a day. He had eight or nine suits and the same number of hats. He used to stay out late and when he came home creep silently into the house. He had three pairs of rubber-soled shoes, one pair of which he always used to wear when he was going out. (Winslow subsequently showed a pair to a *New York Herald* reporter who tried them on: 'Here are Jack the Ripper's boots,' said the doctor, taking a large pair of boots from under his table. 'The tops of these boots are composed of ordinary cloth material, while the soles are made of india-rubber. The tops have great bloodstains on them.')

On 7 August, the night that Martha Tabram was stabbed thirty-nine times, the landlord was sitting up late with his sister waiting for his wife to return home from the country. About 4 a.m. their lodger crept into the house and told them that he had had his watch stolen in Bishopsgate. This turned out to be false. Next morning, when the maid went to make his bed she found a large bloodstain on the bedding. His shirt was found hanging up, with the cuffs recently washed. A few days later the lodger left, allegedly for Canada, but apparently in September he was seen getting into a tram car in London.

He was thought by everyone who met him to be mad. He frequently expressed his disgust at the number of prostitutes in the streets and vented some of his spleen by scribbling fifty or sixty pages of foolscap with his own blend of religion, morality and 'bitter hatred of dissolute women'. Sometimes he would read these diatribes to his landlord.

As soon as Winslow was in possession of this information he

knew instantly:'That's the man!' Had he constructed an imaginary man, he wrote, out of his experience 'of insane people suffering from homicidal religious mania, his habits would have corresponded almost exactly with those told me by the lodging-house keeper'.

At this point in the story, Winslow's published account begins to diverge from his statement of 23 September 1889 to Chief Inspector Swanson and which is now filed away in the case papers in the National Archives at Kew.

In his book Winslow says that once he was in full possession of these facts he told the police and suggested to them a plan to capture this lunatic on the steps of St Paul's Cathedral where he went every morning at 8 a.m. To his dismay the police would not co-operate. He finally warned them that, 'unless they assisted me in the capture of Jack the Ripper on a certain Sunday morning, and if they allowed the mysterious red tape-ism and jealousy surrounding Scotland Yard to interfere', he would publish his clue to the world. This is precisely what he was forced to do, he says, since, according to his memoirs, the police ignored his threats, and so he published his story in the *New York Herald*.

When the story was picked up by the British newspapers Chief Inspector Swanson was sent from Scotland Yard to take a statement from him. It is from this document, which is now quoted for the first time, that the truth of Winslow's story emerges.

Winslow denied that the story was an accurate account of his interview with the reporter. In fact, it was a misrepresentation of the whole conversation. The original purpose of the reporter's visit had not been to discuss Jack the Ripper but an autograph book that Winslow possessed. Gradually the reporter had got him into a discussion of the Whitechapel murders and Winslow had not objected to this line of questioning as he had understood that the conversation would not be published. In fact, he says that he was much surprised and annoyed to see it in print, especially as it so misrepresented what he had said. Frankly, it is hard to believe that Forbes Winslow was as naive as this.

Chief Inspector Swanson forcibly pointed out that Winslow had not given any information to the police about any suspect bar one (the escaped lunatic), yet there was a statement in the newspapers saying that he had. Winslow denied any responsibility for this story. He had then produced a pair of Canadian felt galoshes and an old boot. The felt boots were moth-eaten and the slough of the moth worm remained on one of them. So much for the bloodstains.

He then related the previous story together with a few additional particulars which he did not publish in his book. The entire story, he said, had been told to him on 8 August 1889 by Mr E. Callaghan of 20 Gainsborough Square, Victoria Park. In April 1888 Mr Callaghan and his wife had been living at 27 Sun Street, Finsbury Square, and they had let a room to a Mr G. Wentworth Bell Smith, whose business it was to raise money for the Toronto Trust Society. The details about the writing, the suits, hats, late hours and the stolen watch are much the same as before. The household regarded him as a lunatic because of his delusions about 'Women of the Streets', who he frequently declared should be drowned.

His frequent complaint was that the prostitutes walked up and down the aisles of St Paul's during morning service. His other delusions were about his wealth and great brain power. Frequently he would talk and moan to himself. He kept three loaded revolvers in a chest of drawers in his room. If anyone knocked at his door he would stand with his back against this chest so that they were within easy reach. Because his lodger's behaviour was so erratic, the landlord had given this information to the police only after he had left.

He was described as about 5 ft. 10 ins. tall; he walked with his feet wide apart, and he was somewhat knock-kneed. His hair and complexion were dark, his moustache and beard so closely cut that he appeared to be merely in need of a shave; his teeth were probably false. He could speak several languages, was well dressed and told the household that he had done some wonderful surgical operations.

This was the only information that Winslow had except for that relating to the woman who had been accosted by (apparently) the same man who carried the proverbial small black bag. All the withering scorn which he fires at the police in his book for their lack of action on his suggestions is only the mirror of his own incompetence. Certainly he was not the great detective he claimed to be. The only clues he possessed, and these are totally worthless, were given to him a year after the murders started. He did not even know the name of the woman who had seen the lodger washing in the yard (though in fairness he said that he could get the information from Mr Callaghan).

Chief Inspector Swanson reported to his superiors that he was unable to find a record of any information having been given to the police by Callaghan. Any such would have been given after the Tabram murder on 7 August and before 31 August when the investigation was still in the hands of H division. Inspector Abberline had no record of any such information.

Happily for Forbes Winslow, the police made none of this public when he published his book.

M. J. Druitt

Montague John Druitt's parents had been married for three years when he was born on 15 August 1857, at Wimborne in Dorset. He was to be the second of their seven children. His mother, Anne Druitt, was twenty-seven years old, ten years younger than her husband, William, who was the town's leading surgeon just as his father had been before him. Medicine seems to have been a Druitt family tradition – William's brother Robert and his nephew Lionel were both doctors.

When Montague was thirteen years old he won a scholarship

to Winchester College, where he spent the next six years. From his school record it is clear that he enjoyed both sport and polemics. His only recorded failure was as Sir Toby Belch in a school production of *Twelfth Night*, which earned the college magazine comment: 'But of the inadequacy of Druitt as Sir Toby, what are we to say? It can be better imagined than described.' In November 1873 he defended the French Republic in debate, and it was presumably his post-Sedan sympathies which led him on another occasion to denounce the influence of Bismarck as 'morally and socially a curse to the world'. He championed Wordsworth as a bulwark of Protestantism. In a more lighthearted mood he defended the fashions of the 1870s as a graceful combination of beauty and utility, not the social evil that his opponents represented them to be. In his final debate he defended his contemporaries against the older generation which had subjugated women and tolerated slavery, by proclaiming, 'The old theory of government was, man is made for States. Is it not a vast improvement that States should be made for man, as they are now?'

He was a good sportsman. He was the school Fives champion in 1875 and he played cricket for the school First Eleven at Lord's in 1876. The same year he was awarded a scholarship to New College, Oxford, where he seems to have been popular with the other undergraduates and was elected Steward of the Junior Common Room. A classics scholar, he graduated Bachelor of Arts in 1880. Three years later he could purchase, as was then the privilege with Oxford and Cambridge graduates, his master's degree on payment of a small fee.

He applied for admittance to the Inner Temple in May 1882 and was called to the bar in April 1885. He rented chambers at 9 King's Bench Walk, Temple and joined the Western Circuit and Winchester Sessions as a barrister. Without private income or an exceptional talent, the failure rate of such fledglings was very high: a contemporary wrote that, of eight thousand barristers, only one in eight could make a living. He was made Special

Pleader, Western Circuit, in 1887, which did not involve courtroom appearances. In 1882 he had begun to earn extra money by teaching at a small crammer's school in Blackheath, south-east London. This, however, came to an abrupt end at the end of Michaelmas term 1888 when he was dismissed. For what reason is not known. It has been suggested that there was a homosexual explanation for his dismissal, but it is equally plausible that it was because of his erratic behaviour, since he believed he was going insane. His mother was already confined in a private mental home at Chiswick, where she died on 15 December 1890 of 'melancholia' and 'brain disease'.

Montague was last seen alive on 3 December 1888. Soon afterwards, and probably in a state of acute depression after visiting his mother, he weighted his pockets with stones and threw himself into the Thames. His body was found floating in the water at Thorneycrofts, near Chiswick, on 31 December. It was fully clothed and in a state of decomposition. At the inquest, held at the Lamb and Tap in Chiswick, his brother William, a solicitor living at Bournemouth, told the coroner that the last time he had seen his brother was when he stayed overnight at Bournemouth towards the end of October. It wasn't until 11 December that he heard from a friend that Montague had been missing from his chambers for more than a week. He went to London to make inquiries and at the Blackheath school learned for the first time that his brother had got into some serious trouble and had been dismissed. Among his things he found a paper addressed to himself which read: 'Since Friday I felt I was going to be like mother and the best thing for me is to die.'

There were no other clues in his pockets. When he was searched he was in possession of £2 10s. in gold, seven shillings in silver, twopence in bronze and two cheques drawn on the London Provincial Bank, one for £50 and the other for £16; they could have been his school wages but an alternative put forward is that they were drawn to pay off a blackmailer. There was also a first-class season ticket from Blackheath to London, a second half return from Hammersmith to Charing Cross (dated 1 December), a silver watch, a gold chain with a spade guinea attached, a pair of gloves and a white handkerchief. In his top coat were the four large stones with which he had weighted himself down.

The one obvious thing that is missing is any shred of evidence that Montague John Druitt was Jack the Ripper.

Among the Scotland Yard papers there is a letter that refers to some inquiries made about three medical students who were allegedly insane. The police had evidently managed to trace two, but the third had eluded them. The Home Secretary wanted to know what inquiries had been made about this third, and when. According to Inspector Abberline's reply, which is dated 1 November 1888, searching inquiries had been made by an officer at Aberdeen Place, St John's Wood, the last known address of the medical student known as John Sanders. The only information he had managed to glean was that a lady named Sanders had lived at No. 20 but had left and gone abroad about two years before. In fact, Abberline had mistranscribed the address which should have read Abercorn not Aberdeen Place, which is where Mrs Sanders lived and where Abberline would have learned that her son was in an asylum in England which is where he died in 1901. This failure to locate him may have been the reason why the murderer was sometimes suspected of being a medical student.

Sir Melville Macnaghten has been put in the unusual position of having given the vital clue that makes a slightly more than satisfactory solution possible. Whether he would have appreciated this position is a matter of doubt. One of his great disappointments in life was that he became 'a detective officer six months after Jack the Ripper committed suicide', which deprived him of 'having a go at that fascinating individual'. (His other disappointment was not playing cricket for Eton against Harrow.) No doubt he would be surprised that every one of his facts – precisely because they are so few – have been wrung dry of every possible shade of meaning. Even these can be wrong. He made obvious mistakes, such as saying that Druitt's age was forty-one. Even this can be explained away if we remember that he was copying from the police file and notes about a case of which he knew nothing at first hand – as we may presume, from the rough jottings in the possession of his grandson, that he was – and that he might have been copying precisely this error as it was given in the *County of Middlesex Independent* of 2 January 1889, which reported the finding of Druitt's body and which would have been filed, as we have shown, along with the rest of the case papers:

FOUND IN THE RIVER

The body of a well-dressed man was discovered on Monday in the river off Thorneycroft's torpedo works, by a waterman named Winslow. The police were communicated with and the deceased was conveyed to the mortuary. The body, which is that of a man about 40 years of age, has been in the water about a month. From certain papers found on the body friends at Bournemouth have been telegraphed to. An inquest will be held today (Wednesday).

From this it seems perfectly reasonable to assume that Macnaghten was referring to Druitt, although he doesn't mention him by name, for he says, referring to his principal suspect, 'I have always held strong opinions regarding him, and the more I think the matter over, the stronger do these opinions become. The truth, however, will never be known, and did indeed, at one time lie at the bottom of the Thames, if my conjections be correct!'

This statement was made some years after his original notes, in which he was not quite so sure. In fact he hedged his bets: 'A much more rational theory is that the murderer's brain gave way altogether after his awful glut in Miller's Court, and that he immediately committed suicide, or, *as a possible alternative, was found to be so hopelessly mad by his relations, that he was by them confined in some asylum.*' (My italics.)

Major Arthur Griffiths, the author of *Mysteries of Police and Crime*, draws much the same conclusions. In fact, his wording is so similar that it is positively certain that he was quoting from Macnaghten's notes which, as an Inspector of Prisons, he would almost certainly have had access to. Other people have made much the same statements, but as they seem to be quoting from a common source – generally Macnaghten – it is fair to ask whether there is any independent evidence pointing to Druitt.

Strangely enough, there is, although once again the original notes have disappeared. It is in a statement made by Albert Bachert who, according to Donald McCormick in his book on the Ripper, was a prominent member of the Whitechapel Vigilance Committee. After the Miller's Court murder on 9 November he became alarmed at the way that the police reduced the number of their patrols in the area and eventually, in March 1889, he complained to the senior officers 'that there seemed to be too much complacency in the force simply because there had been no more murders for some months'.

He was asked if he would be sworn to secrecy on the understanding that he was given certain information.

Foolishly, I agreed. It was then suggested to me that the Vigilance Committee and its patrols might be disbanded as the police were quite certain that the Ripper was dead. I protested that, as I had been sworn to secrecy, I really ought to be given more information than this. 'It isn't necessary for you to know any more,' I was told. 'The man in question is dead. He was fished out of the Thames two months ago and it would only cause pain to relatives if we said any more than that.'

I again protested that I had been sworn to secrecy all for nothing, that I was really no wiser than before: 'if there are no more murders, I shall respect this confidence, but if there are any more I shall consider I am absolved from my pledge of secrecy'.

The police then got very tough. They told me a pledge was a solemn matter, that anyone who put out stories that the Ripper was still alive might be proceeded against for causing a public mischief. However, they agreed that if there were any other murders which the police were satisfied could be Ripper murders, that was another matter.

If true, this means that the police had positively identified Druitt as the Ripper in January 1889 soon after his body was found.

But on what evidence? Why should they pick on this cricket-playing barrister?

One theory, which has been developed, links him with the painter Walter Sickert who thought that he knew the identity of the murderer. According to Sickert, some years after the murders he was living in a London suburb in lodgings which were looked after by an old couple. One day his landlady, as she was dusting, asked him if he knew the identity of the person previously occupying his room. When told that he didn't, she replied that it was 'Jack the Ripper'.

The writer Osbert Sitwell, a friend of Sickert's, gave the details in his autobiography *Noble Essences*:

Her story was that his predecessor had been a veterinary student. After he had been a month or two in London, this delicate-looking young man – he was consumptive – took to occasionally staying out all night. His landlord and landlady would hear him come in about six in the morning and then walk about in his room for an hour or two, until the first edition of the morning paper was on sale, when he would creep lightly downstairs and run to the corner to buy one. Quietly he would return and go to bed. But an hour later, when the old man called him, he would notice, by the traces in the fireplace, that his lodger had burnt the suit he had been wearing the previous evening.

Gradually the old couple came to the reluctant conclusion that their lodger was none other than the Ripper. But before they could make up their minds whether to warn the police about him, his health suddenly deteriorated and his mother, who was a widow, came and took him back to Bournemouth where she lived and where, says Donald McCormick, he died three months later.

According to McCormick's source, Walter Sickert told this story to Sir Melville Macnaghten, who became convinced that the young man in question must have been Druitt because 'he had a widowed mother living in Bournemouth, the same as Druitt.' This is clearly nonsense. Druitt's brother William certainly lived in Bournemouth, but their widowed mother had been confined in a mental asylum since July 1888 and was incapable of fetching home her son – who, by the bye, was not a veterinary surgeon. And Osbert adds that not only did the landlady confide in Sickert and name Jack the Ripper but that he had scribbled it down in a French edition of Casanova's memoirs which he happened to be reading at the time, and which he had subsequently given to artist Sir William Rothenstein's brother – and where it could be found now, Sickert had added, if Sitwell wanted to know the name. When, years later, Sitwell tried to trace the book it was only to learn that it had been lost in the bombing of London 'and that there had been several pencil notes entered in the margin, in Sickert's handwriting, always so difficult to decipher'. Two things are clear. Had Macnaghten been given the name he would not have been forced to speculate on the identity. The other point is that since Sickert's talk 'contained in its web certain invariable strands, certain immutable monuments that could be invoked for purposes of reference, allusion, comparison and simile', one of which was the mystery of Jack the Ripper, it is equally clear that Sickert couldn't have taken the landlady's story very seriously – which is why he only thought it worth a note in the margin of the book that he happened to be reading, although he painted a picture of the lodger's room titled 'Jack the Ripper's Bedroom'.

McCormick's same anonymous source says that Druitt was being blackmailed and that he confided this to his mother, whom he told 'about the whole affair and she presumably told the police when he was reported missing some time during December 1888. Anyhow, my father was emphatic that Druitt was living at Bournemouth when the first two Ripper crimes were committed.'

And, says McCormick, 'this seems finally to dispose of the case that Druitt had any connection with the crimes.'

Unfortunately it does not.

Even if we assume that Druitt was living in Bournemouth – which I do not for one moment believe – there is fortunately independent evidence to show that he was in London for one of these murders, at least.

According to an article by Irving Rosenwater in *The Cricketer* of January 1973, he was playing cricket at Blackheath at 11.30 a.m. on the very morning that Annie Chapman was murdered at 5.30 a.m. (8 September) only half a dozen miles away. This fact alone is enough to destroy the uncorroborated gossip of McCormick's witness that he could not have killed Chapman because he was living in Bournemouth when the first two murders were committed. Even if we concede to McCormick's theory that Chapman was the third victim and not the second (he makes Martha Tabram – 7 August – the first) there is again the confirmatory evidence from the cricketing records that he was playing in a match at Canford on the same day that Nichols's body was found, 31 August.

As Donald McCormick rightly says, 'What other evidence is there to support Sir Melville's claim to name him as chief suspect? He was never seen in the vicinity of the crimes.'

This point was challenged by Dan Farson who says in his book *Jack the Ripper* that Montague's cousin, Dr Lionel Druitt, had a surgery at 140 Minories, on the City's eastern boundary. It was an important discovery, as the Minories is only a few minutes' walk from Mitre Square, where Eddowes was murdered, and might have been Druitt's hide-out.

Farson's new evidence was that Lionel Druitt was assisting Dr Thomas Thyne at his surgery in the Minories in 1879. Farson believed that Montague Druitt visited his cousin there and that later, when Lionel became a junior partner in Dr Gillard's practice at 122 Clapham Road, he stayed on and may even have rented a room there. This, if true, would explain the ease and speed of the

Ripper's disappearance as he would be living on the City/ East End boundary.

There are several factors which throw doubts on these conclusions. Only the *Medical Register* (1879) lists Lionel Druitt as being at 140 Minories. The *Medical Director*, for the same year, lists him in the Scotland section as being assistant house surgeon to a hospital in Edinburgh. The same 1879 Directory lists the practitioners at the Minories address as Dr J. O. Taylor and Dr Thyne. The two points together prove fairly conclusively that Druitt's stay at the Minories could only have been a short one. For the following year (1880) only Dr Thyne is listed at the Minories address. Both the *Medical Register* and the *Medical Directory* for 1880 give Lionel's address as 8 Strathmore Gardens which is the same as in the 1878 editions.

A cursory stay then, if it took place at all, would explain his omission from the Register of Voters for the City of London, which includes the names of lodgers as well as of tenants and owners. I have searched these registers from 1878 to 1889 and have not found the name of Druitt mentioned anywhere. Clearly, then, neither Lionel and certainly not Montague were ever lodgers for any length of time – although there is always the possibility that they might have stayed there occasionally, as infrequent guests. Had Montague's stay, however, coincided with each of the murders then surely he would have come under suspicion. Unfortunately, without more facts this line of speculation is useless. The only conclusion that can be reached with any certainty is that Lionel Druitt was probably Dr Taylor's locum when he resigned in 1879 (he is not mentioned in the obituaries) and that when he left after a brief stay the only practitioner in residence at 140 Minories was Dr Thyne, who is the only doctor registered at that address in 1880.

This still leaves us with Cullen's other alternative that he might have changed his bloodstained clothes in his chambers in King's Bench Walk. Yet this does not explain why, if he was going to the Temple, or even to the Minories, after leaving Mitre Square he should have walked in completely the opposite direction to both. The one fact which both men ignore is that he dropped part of Eddowes's apron in Goulston Street. This means that the Ripper, like a fox, was doubling back towards the police who were running in his direction. At some point, with so many police in the area, they must have met.

How, then, did he get away?

The only way he could have done so was by bolting into one of the hundreds of lodging houses in the area. There has been a general refusal to accept that this was possible because they were so public and he would have been too bloodstained to have escaped notice. But would he? On 11 September *The Times* published the following piece in a long article about Annie Chapman's murder and the inquiries that were then being made:

The woman Chapman was known in appearance to the policemen on the night beats in the neighbourhood, but none of those who were on duty between 12 and 6 on Saturday morning recollect having seen her. It is ascertained that several men left their lodgings after midnight with the expressed intention of returning who have not returned. Some men went to their lodgings after 3 o'clock, and left again before 6 in the morning, which is not an unfrequent occurrence in those houses. None of the deputies or watchmen at the houses have any memory of any person stained with blood entering their premises but at that hour of the morning little or no notice is taken of persons inquiring for beds. They are simply asked for the money, and shown up dark stairways with a bad light to their rooms. When they leave early, they are seldom noticed in their egress. It is then considered quite probable that the murderer may have found a refuge for a few hours in one of those places, and even washed away the signs of his guilt. The men in these houses use a common washing place, and water once used is thrown down the sink by the lodger using it. All this might happen in a common lodging house in the early morning without the bloodstained murderer being noticed particularly. The conviction is growing even, that taking for granted that one man committed all the recent murders of women in the Whitechapel district, he might in this fashion, by changing his common lodging house, evade detection for a considerable time.

It is also worth remembering that after the double event of 30 September he washed some of the blood away in a street sink, as Henry Smith alleges. Just how many other times did he do this? And depending on just how these murders were committed hangs the whole question of how bloodstained he would have been.

Trying to work out the practicalities that he must have faced when he killed these women gives some of the answers. Assuming that these women went with him expecting to have normal sexual intercourse, it is hardly likely that they – and certainly not their clients – would have been lying down on one of those filthy courts or alleys in autumn and early winter weather. On the night of the 'double event' it had been raining quite heavily. If not oral sex, penetration would have been done standing up, with the woman facing the man or with her back against a wall. This would seem the logical position in view of the clothing they would be wearing. Eddowes that night was wearing two ankle length petticoats and two ankle length skirts. The probability is that with this amount of clothing on she would face the wall and, bending forward, flip petticoats and skirts on to her back to make penetration easier, if that was what was wanted. Many prostitutes used anal sex as a form of birth control. In this position she was completely vulnerable to any attack.

For a long time I assumed that she must have been standing so because of the bruising on nearly all the victims' faces and to explain away the absence of any stab wounds in the chest or throat. The bruising is generally one of the things which is ignored, although a contemporary newspaper said at the time of Eddowes's murder that one eye had been knocked out; this was wrong, but certainly it was very badly bruised and swollen, as the mortuary photographs show. Polly Nichols and Annie Chapman were similarly badly bruised about the face. From this, I thought that probably the Ripper had punched them several times in the face, which would have stunned them and given him enough time to get his hands round their throats to strangle them. This would explain why Annie Chapman was able to call out, which she could not have done if she had been seized from behind and her throat cut. Once they had been strangled, into unconsciousness at least, it would have been a simple matter for the Ripper to have knelt by their heads and swiftly cut their throats. This would explain why in the case of the four women he murdered in the street there was no bloodstaining except under the bodies. If they had been alive when their throats were cut the blood would have spurted out in a three-foot jet.

There would be very little bloodstaining on the killer. Blood would have seeped on to the ground and been soaked up by the clothing, as did happen, and after the mutilation the Ripper would have had bloodstains on his hands, cuffs, the bottoms of his trousers and his boots. Much has been made of the question of whether he was ambidextrous or left-handed, but this is hard to judge, particularly if he was kneeling by their heads when he cut their throats, as I believe he was. According to Sir Melville Macnaghten, 'The theory that the Whitechapel murderer was left-handed, or, at any rate, "ambidexter", had its origin in the remark made by a doctor who examined the corpse of one of the earliest victims; *other doctors did not agree with him.*' According to the Westminster notes, the throats in the first four murders were cut from left to right, which makes the Ripper right-handed, and the women were lying down when murdered. Professor Cameron of the Department of Forensic Medicine at the London Hospital thought, from the Mitre Square drawings and photographs, that he was right-handed as the incision drags to the right, as would happen, and is deeper as more viscera are exposed.

Both Professor Cameron and his predecessor, Professor Camps, thought that the Ripper had probably always strangled his victims first. Professor Camps, however, pointed out a difficulty in *The Investigation of Murder*:

The approach of the doctors in all the Ripper cases appears to have been on the basis of accepting the obvious. Viewed in the light of other sadistic sexual murders, strangulation would usually be a very significant feature. It seems very possible that the Ripper silenced all his victims by strangling them for, in at least two cases, obstruction to the mouth is mentioned and the absence of bleeding is also a matter for comment. In all cases there was no sign or sound of a struggle, which tends to confirm this. Yet no effort was made to trace the typical injuries associated with this, with the result that the knife became at once the murder weapon and the means of mutilation. If this hypothesis were correct and had been realised, it is possible that the later victims might have escaped their fate, for throat-cutting is neither silent nor neat, whilst all prostitutes fear strangulation. To look for such marks is not a matter of inspired guesswork but a simple extension of the maxim that it is safer to proceed by excluding all possibilities than by taking the short cut of accepting what is obvious. It is a major and very dangerous temptation to find what is expected and look no further.

The kind of injuries that Professor Camps was referring to are the showers of pin-prick haemorrhages (petechiae) which in cases of strangulation occur in the face and in and around the eyes, and the damage to the laryngeal structures, particularly the hyoid bone which is usually fractured. In fairness, however, to doctors such as Dr Phillips, the conditions they worked in were impossible. Most of their work had to be carried out in badly equipped workhouse mortuaries or in sheds like those which Dr Phillips and the coroner had protested about quite strongly at the early inquests, and which helps make the doctors' acceptance of the obvious at least understandable.

In discussing these points, Professor Cameron offered me an alternative theory of his own. It was based on a case that he had investigated in 1968. The insight that it gives into this particular killer's mind also suggests a motive for the Ripper killings that is at least as satisfactory as any other so far presented.

Briefly the facts of the case are that on 7 February 1968 a young bride was found brutally murdered in the bedroom by her husband when he returned home to the flat in Bromley, Kent. It was a seemingly 'motiveless' murder. She had fourteen incised wounds in the throat and four stab wounds to the neck, one of which had penetrated through to the front of the spine on the right side. There was bruising round the neck which indicated that there might have been partial asphyxiation at or shortly before death. There were marks on the right side of her mouth which might have been done by the left hand, if she was gripped from behind, leaving the right hand free. A knife with a serrated edge was the probable weapon but this was never found. Nor was there any evidence of sexual assault. A 26-year-old bank clerk was later convicted of the murder and sentenced to life imprisonment.

The case was discussed at a meeting of the Medico-Legal Society on 10 June 1971. During it, the following exchange took place, the relevance of which is immediately apparent:

Mr Taylor asked whether Dr Cameron was satisfied that the actual blows and wounds could have been inflicted in the way suggested. It seemed a rather peculiar attack from behind, with one hand over the mouth of a girl who obviously struggled, to use a long knife, which had to be low down quite far in front and pushed in, causing four wounds which were so very close together through the neck and all accurately placed. This was done to a girl who was, no doubt, screaming and struggling. There was also a slit across, which apparently would have been taken with a knife held in probably a different manner. It all seemed to be 'a bit too good to be true'.

Dr Cameron recalled his remarks that the deceased had exhibited evidence of asphyxia in the form of petechiae (pin-point haemorrhages) and that there was bruising around the voicebox. On examination he assumed that she could well have been partially asphyxiated and rendered unconscious before the actual knife assault occurred.

He was under the impression that, if the knife assault was from in front, it would have to be from the left hand in view of the distribution of the fourteen undercut-from-below-up wounds that were partly superficial and partly deep across the neck. His opinion was that it was more likely to have been inflicted from behind or certainly, if the body was on the floor, from the head end, with the hand gripping the face to give the abrasions to the right side of the mouth. In that position, to cause the fourteen wounds in the neck would be a sort of violin-playing effect with the serrated edge of a knife and undercut from below up. It would not then require much force to bring an eight-inch blade into contact four times through the already gaping hole.

Professor Simpson said that he could support those views from a similar kind of case which occurred on a railway train from Basingstoke. He thought that Dr Cameron had given a soundly based reconstruction of the infliction of the wounds.

The president asked whether there was a great deal of bloodstaining. The photographs did not appear to show very much bloodstaining in the room.

Dr Cameron replied that there was quite extensive bloodstaining, but it was only beneath the body. His impression was that the body had been assaulted actually in the bedroom, where it was found.

The president remarked that that suggested that 'the deceased was possibly at least semi-conscious before the knife attack took place'.

Dr Cameron said he would have thought that she was probably partially assaulted near the kitchen and ran, losing her slipper outside the door, towards the bedroom to get away. The bedroom was the furthest part of the flat, and probably that was where she was actually attacked.

The president asked whether the strangling component might have occurred first.

Dr Cameron replied that in his opinion, it did occur first.

The main points which have to be borne in mind are that there was a partial strangulation of the victim, bruising on the face and very little blood in the flat, most of it being under the body and soaked up by the victim's clothes, as happened with the Ripper's victims.

Now with this case in mind, Professor Cameron thought that the most likely position that the Ripper and each of his victims would have taken up would have been with her bending forward and the Ripper standing behind; again, remembering her heavy garments – four in all – she would have found it easier in this position to have flicked them forward over her back. Possibly, she might have had anal intercourse – which used to be a common way of birth control with these women – rather than normal vaginal penetration. In this position, anyway, it would have been a very simple matter for the Ripper to have strangled her. As he was doing so, he could have battered their faces against the wall, which could explain the facial bruising. If the Ripper had then cut their throats while still holding them from behind, the risk of staining his clothes with blood would have been minimal.

Such an explanation also gives us a possible motive for the murders other than the normal one of sadistic cruelty. The murderer, in the 1968 case referred to by Professor Cameron, had assaulted two previous victims in precisely the same manner from behind and each time with a knife. When he was seventeen he had been put on probation for three years for breaking into a girl's house armed with a knife and attempting to have sexual intercourse with her. Six years later he was sentenced to three months' imprisonment for assault occasioning actual bodily harm against a middle-aged woman whose bedroom he had broken into. Apparently he was impotent but he could overcome this by a sudden attack on a woman.

According to the Canadian graphologist's analysis of the 'From Hell' letter that was sent to Mr Lusk, the writer was probably a latent homosexual. Might this suppressed homosexuality have created a similar impotency in Jack the Ripper and caused him to act in identical manner? Such a possibility makes a much more acceptable theory than the one which sees him as a social reformer dedicated to the cause of slum clearance in Whitechapel and the erection of model dwellings. Tom Cullen puts forward this latter, very persuasive theory; but it ignores the reforms which had been going steadily forward for more than a decade and wrongly credits the Whitechapel murderer with reforms which rightly belonged to the newly created London County Council.

This has taken us slightly away from Montague Druitt but it does help us towards a more convincing picture of the Ripper.

The question has already been asked as to whether the Ripper was homosexual. Alternatively, was Montague Druitt homosexual, and was it perhaps homosexual activity that brought about his sudden dismissal from the Blackheath school? Whatever it was, it was this dismissal and a letter he wrote to the headmaster threatening suicide that probably brought him to the attention of the police. Attempted suicide was a criminal offence and was then punished with the gaol sentence, but this would have been preferable to the tragic and unnecessary waste of this young man's life. Possibly the headmaster, when he received Druitt's letter, tried to trace him through his friends who probably went to the police to help them only as a last resort, before they contacted Druitt's brother one week later. Naturally the police would have gone to the Temple and searched his rooms and it is there that they might have found either Druitt's bloodstained clothing or some other evidence which suggested that they had found the Whitechapel murderer.

And this is where my contribution to the Ripper story comes in.

When I was researching my first book *I Spy Blue* I shared the Guildhall Records Office every Monday afternoon with the Inspectress of the Sir John Soane museum, Miss Dorothy Stroud, who was also researching a book. Gradually she discovered my interest in crime and one day she gave me Jack the Ripper's knife. I must admit that I groaned inwardly, as I thought it most unlikely that it was the actual weapon until she told me the following story. In 1937 she was an assistant editor on *Sporting Life*. The editor was Hugh Pollard, whose pro-Fascist sympathies led him to fly Franco into Spain for the civil war. One day he was getting rid of many of his personal things. He came into the office and plumped on the desk in front of her a box which he said contained Jack the Ripper's knives. The box had two knives, of which I now have one, and was lined with blue silk, heavily bloodstained. Miss Stroud took one knife and her friend took the other. (They then burned the box because of the bloodstains.) During the war Miss Stroud used hers as a carving knife and later as a gardening knife. The blade became very nicked and eventually she broke it when cutting a privet bush. Fortunately she kept the pieces, which she gave to me. The Guildhall Museum, without knowing what it was, told me that it had been made in the last quarter of the nineteenth century. The knife is a nineteenth century surgical amputation knife made by Weiss, the name is stamped on the handle, a firm of surgical instrument makers of Bond Street, London.

Major Hugh Pollard was a partner of Robert Churchill the gunsmith, who was closely involved with Scotland Yard for many years as their 'gun expert'. Pollard, apparently played a similar role. He had been employed as an Intelligence Officer by the Irish Office after the 1914–18 war. The amputation knife in my possession is almost certainly a murder weapon but I no longer believe it to be Jack the Ripper's. In his book *The Secret Societies of Ireland* (1922), Pollard talks about the Phoenix Park murders. These were the murders in the spring of 1882 of Thomas Burke, Permanent Secretary in the Dublin Civil Service, and Lord Frederick Cavendish, the newly appointed Chief Secretary for Ireland. It was Burke's opposition to Irish nationalism that made him a target for the Invincibles, a splinter group that had broken away from the Fenian Society of Irish Americans. A dozen of these boxed Weiss amputation knives, with twelve inch blades, were bought from Weiss and smuggled across to Ireland to the conspirators. On Saturday 6th May 1882, a small group of

Invincibles attacked Burke as he walked through Phoenix Park in the early evening. Burke was knifed in the back, this first blow proving almost instantly fatal, and a flurry of blows by the other Invincibles brought down Cavendish as well who had gone to Burke's assistance. The two surgical knives were abandoned and these were possibly the murder weapons that came into Pollard's possession. Two more knives, not actually used, were later recovered by the police. In an attempt to intimidate the jury system, knives were again used, but not abandoned, when a juror was stabbed seven times by two Invincibles but survived the attack. Although orders were given by the Invincible leadership for the remaining knives to be broken up into little bits and burned, which would have been difficult, possibly this was not completely done as had been hoped as at least one of the conspirators, James Carey who turned informer and was subsequently murdered, had 'thought bad of it' (the idea) and jokingly had wanted them kept for display at the Dublin exhibition later that year.

N.P. Warren suggested in *The Mammoth Book of Jack the Ripper* that Pollard's knives were part of the evidence that the British government agreed to suppress that Irish Nationalists had been involved in the Phoenix Park murders, if the Fenians in return would agree to cancel their plot to dynamite Queen Victoria's Jubilee in 1887. It was for this reason that the knives might have been passed off as belonging to Jack the Ripper.

Druitt is still a favourite with many Ripperologists as the man most likely to have been Jack the Ripper. By chance, I happened to be looking through some old cuttings pasted in a battered three-volume edition of Griffiths's *Mysteries of Police and Crime*. Among them was one from the *People's Journal* issue of 26 September 1919, on the retirement of a detective named 'Steve' White who had spent many nights as a young policeman loitering about the evil-smelling alleys of Whitechapel in search of Jack the Ripper. His story is quoted below in full. Clearly it refers to the Mitre Square murder, as it is the only murder which fits the facts; it also confirms a long-held suspicion of mine that Constable Watkins was probably on the other side of Kearley & Tonge's warehouse door, either talking or drinking tea with the watchman who happened to be an ex-policeman.

Certainly White's description of the Ripper, when it is compared with the photograph of Druitt, is one of the most uncanny things about the whole story. One of his reports included the following passage:

For five nights we had been watching a certain alley just behind the Whitechapel Road. It could only be entered from where we had two men posted in hiding, and persons entering the alley were under observation by the two men. It was a bitter cold night when I arrived at the scene to take the report of the two men in hiding. I was turning away when I saw a man coming out of the alley. He was walking quickly but noiselessly, apparently wearing rubber shoes, which were rather rare in those days. I stood aside to let the man pass, and as he came under the wall lamp I got a good look at him.

He was about five feet ten inches in height, and was dressed rather shabbily, though it was obvious that the material of his clothes was good. Evidently a man who had seen better days, I thought, but men who have seen better days are common enough down East, and that of itself was not sufficient to justify me in stopping him. His face was long and thin, nostrils rather delicate, and his hair was jet black. His complexion was inclined to be sallow, and altogether the man was foreign in appearance. The most striking thing about him, however, was the extraordinary brilliance of his eyes. They looked like two very luminous glow worms coming through the darkness. The man was slightly bent at the shoulders, though he was obviously quite young – about thirty-three, at the most – and gave one the idea of having been a student or professional man. His hands were snow white, and the fingers long and tapering.

As the man passed me at the lamp I had an uneasy feeling that there was something more than usually sinister about him, and I was strongly moved to find some pretext for detaining him; but the more I thought it over, the more was I forced to the conclusion that it was not in keeping with British police methods that I should do so. My only excuse for interfering with the passage of this man would have been his association with the man we were looking for, and I had no real grounds for connecting him with the murder. It is true I had a sort of intuition that the man was not quite right. Still, if one acted on intuition in the police force, there would be more frequent outcries about interference with the liberty of subject, and at that time the police were criticized enough to make it undesirable to take risks.

The man stumbled a few feet away from me, and I made that an excuse for engaging him in conversation. He turned sharply at the sound of my voice, and scowled at me in surly fashion, but he said 'Good-night' and agreed with me that it was cold.

His voice was a surprise to me. It was soft and musical, with just a tinge of melancholy in it, and it was the voice of a man of culture – a voice altogether out of keeping with the squalid surroundings of the East End.

As he turned away, one of the police officers came out of the house he had been in, and walked a few paces into the darkness of the alley. 'Hello! What's this?' he cried, and then he called in startled tones to me to come along.

In the East End we are used to shocking sights, but the sight I saw made the blood in my veins turn to ice. At the end of the cul-de-sac, huddled against the wall, there was the body of a woman, and a pool of blood was streaming along the gutter from her body. It was clearly another of those terrible murders. I remembered the man I had seen, and I started after him as fast as I could run, but he was lost to sight in the dark labyrinth of the East End mean streets.

White's description of the suspected murderer was widely circulated. It was this description that allegedly suggested that the murderer was a Jewish medical student, who had taken this method of avenging himself on women of the class to which his victims belonged.

The mystery, however, that baffled the police more than anything was how the murderer and the victim managed to get into the alley under the eyes of the watching police. It was clear that the couple had not been in any of the houses, and they were not known to any of the residents. Therefore they must have passed into the alley from Whitechapel Road, and the two police officers were positive that in the four hours of their vigil not a soul had entered the alley. White had his own suspicions regarding the truth of this declaration, and his suspicions were shared by Sir Robert Anderson, who afterwards, in comparing notes with White, expressed the opinion that the murderer and his victim had entered the alley during the temporary absence of the two watching policemen. The men afterwards admitted that they had gone away for not more than a minute. It was a very short absence undoubtedly, but it was long enough to give the murderer time to walk into the alley with his victim.

Kosminski

'Theories!' exclaimed Chief Inspector Abberline when discussing the murders (this was to *Cassell's Saturday Journal* in May 1892). 'We were lost almost in theories; there were so many of them.' Eleven years later he expanded on this point to the *Pall Mall Gazette* by adding that the police 'have never believed all those stories about Jack the Ripper being dead, or that he was a lunatic, or anything of that kind'. What he did believe we don't precisely know, as apart from some odds and ends that survive the Scotland Yard papers are missing, presumed destroyed; and despite allegations, which have been denied (my own letter is dated February 1988), that the Home Office are sitting on secret files, all that is available would appear to be open for public inspection at the National Archives. The scale of the loss can be gauged by Abberline's own remarks that the police 'made no fewer than 1,600 sets of papers respecting our investigations' and that because of the desire of the East Enders to assist the police 'the number of statements made – all of them requiring to be recorded and searched into – was so great' that he himself almost broke down under the pressure. Although he doesn't say what he means by 'sets', it would be reasonable to interpret this word as meaning interviews. A figure of 1,600 interviews would still seem modest considering that at least a minimum of four murders were being investigated. Nor would this figure include the statements which were taken by the City police when investigating the Eddowes murder, of which nothing remains except some letters from the public; those are only a selection and are now deposited with the Corporation of the City of London Records Office.

The reporter from the *Pall Mall Gazette* had found Abberline surrounded by a sheaf of documents and newspaper cuttings relating to the case. Abberline never wrote his own account of the murders, and the reason for his discretion is to be found in a book of press cuttings, compiled by him, which I unearthed in the records of the Hampshire Genealogical Society. Interspersed throughout the cuttings are handwritten notations by Abberline. Irritatingly, there is nothing – not even press cuttings – about his two most interesting cases, the Whitechapel murders and the Cleveland Street scandal (a homosexual vice ring again involving the Duke of Clarence). But there is his explanation of why he never wrote his memoirs. It actually begins: 'Why I did not write my Reminiscences when I retired from the Metropolitan Police.' (His silence on those two cases has sometimes been interpreted as meaning that he was bribed to stay silent. There is no evidence for this. When he died in 1929 the value of his estate was £317 4s. 10d. His wife, who died only a matter of weeks after, left a personal estate of £32 17s. 3d. The gross value of her estate was £66 6s. 3d. There's no evidence here of any big pay-offs.)

The full explanation of the unwritten memoirs – which is even more irritating because of the hints of what he might have told – is as follows:

I think it is just as well to record here the reason why as from the various cuttings from the Newspapers as well as the many other matters that I

Commercial Street, Spitalfields. The Britannia public house ('Ringers') is on the corner of Dorset Street (bottom left). The Ten Bells public house is the corner building on the right.

Dorset Street looking towards Commercial Street. The woman on the left must be standing within a door or two of Annie Chapman's lodgings at 35 Dorset Street.

Mortuary photograph of Annie Chapman.

Annie and John Chapman taken c.1869.

Women outside a Spitalfields lodging house in Flower and Dean Street.

Double event: the murders of Eddowes and Stride.

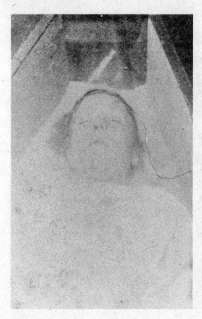

Mortuary photograph of Polly Nichols.

Mortuary photograph of Elizabeth 'Long Liz' Stride.

Berner Street, showing the entrance of Dutfield's Yard where Stride was murdered.

Mitre Square with Eddowes' body in situ.

Position of Eddowes' body as shown in a drawing made before removal.

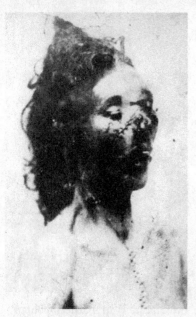
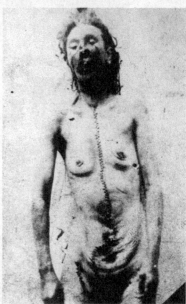

Mortuary photographs of Catherine Eddowes.

Ripper's corner, Mitre Square.

George Lusk, Whitechapel
Vigilance Committee.

Goulston Street – the Ripper's message was written on the jamb of the doorway.

Sir Charles Warren, Metropolitan Police Commissioner.

Major Henry Smith, Acting Commissioner, City of London Police.

Mary Kelly's room at 13 Miller's Court.

Mary Kelly's body. The heart was missing.

M.J. Druitt.

J.K. Stephen (front row left).

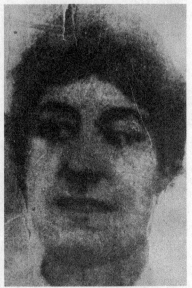

Annie Elizabeth Crook c.1886.

HRH The Duke of Clarence.

Sir William Gull.

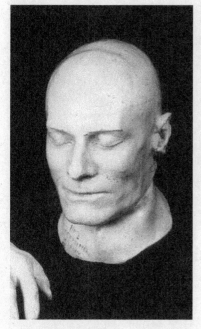

Death mask of Frederick Deeming.

Walter Sickert (1885).

Letter 'From hell' sent with a piece of kidney to Mr Lusk of the
Whitechapel Vigilance Committee.

Neil Cream.

George Chapman.

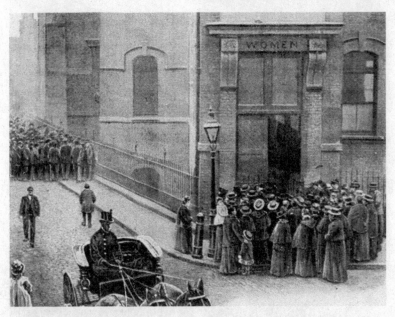

Providence Row Night Refuge (still standing). Mary Kelly allegedly stayed here for a short time.

Robert D'Onston Stephenson.

Dr Francis Tumblety.

Michael Ostrog.

James Maybrick.

Robert Anderson, Head of
Metropolitan Police CID.

Melville Leslie Macnaghten.

Detective Inspector Abberline.

A possible photograph of Abberline
(front row, first left). See foreword.

THE NEMESIS OF NEGLECT.

"THERE FLOATS A PHANTOM ON THE SLUM'S FOUL AIR,
    SHAPING, TO EYES WHICH HAVE THE GIFT OF SEEING,
INTO THE SPECTRE OF THAT LOATHLY LAIR.
    FACE IT—FOR VAIN IS FLEEING!
RED-HANDED, RUTHLESS, FURTIVE, UNERECT,
'TIS MURDEROUS CRIME—THE NEMESIS OF NEGLECT!"

The Nemesis of Neglect.

was called upon to investigate – that never became public property – it must be apparent that I would write many things that would be very interesting to read.

At the time I retired from the service the Authorities were very much opposed to retired Officers writing anything for the press as previously some retired officers had from time to time been very indiscreet in what they had caused to be published and to my knowledge had been called upon to explain their conduct and in fact they had been threatened with actions for libel.

Apart from that there is no doubt the fact that in describing what you did in detecting certain crimes you are putting the criminal classes on their guard and in some cases you may be absolutely telling them how to commit crime.

As an example in the Finger Print detection you find now the expert thief wears gloves.

Slightly less circumspect was Chief Inspector Donald Sutherland Swanson, who was the headquarters man between Anderson, as Assistant Commissioner head of CID, and the investigators on the ground. Abberline had been seconded from the Yard after the Nichols murder to co-ordinate the divisional investigations. Because of his willingness to give interviews he was wrongly credited with being in charge of the overall investigation.

Swanson's comments came to light in a copy of Anderson's *The Lighter Side of My Official Life*, which had once belonged to him and is now in the possession of his grandson. On page 138, after Anderson's statement that 'The only person who ever saw the murderer unhesitatingly identified the suspect the instant he was confronted with him; but he refused to give evidence against him,' Swanson had written, 'Because the suspect was *also a Jew* and also because his evidence would convict the suspect, and witness would be the means of murderer being hanged which he did not wish to be left on his mind. D.S.S.' He continued in the margin: 'and after this identification which suspect knew, no other murder of this kind took place in London.'

He added on one of the endpapers:

After the suspect had been identified at the Seaside Home where he had been sent by us with difficulty, in order to subject him to identification and he knew he was identified. On suspect's return to his brother's house in Whitechapel he was watched by police (City CID) by day and night. In a very short time the suspect with his hands tied behind his back, he was sent to Stepney Workhouse and then to Colney Hatch and died shortly afterwards – Kosminski was the suspect – D.S.S.

The book was a present, possibly from Abberline, and inscribed 'To Donald with every good wish from Fred'. The 'discreet indiscretions' (as Martin Fido has called them in the revised version of his book *The Crimes, Detection and Death of Jack the Ripper*) of Anderson's book were highlighted by the underlining of the words 'the traditions of my old department would suffer' following on from Anderson's reasons for not being more forthcoming about the Ripper's identity.

Fido's researches have unearthed more facts about Kosminski, who had been named by Macnaghten as one of three possible suspects. Until now there had been only this solitary reference to work on. In the Colney Hatch Hospital Admissions and Discharge Book to 1892 Fido found the following details: 'Aaron Kozminski, Hebrew hairdresser, admitted 7 January 1891, suffering from mania for 6 years, caused by self-abuse. His bodily state was fair; his main symptom was incoherence; he was not believed to be dangerous to himself or others, and he was discharged to Leavesden Asylum in 1894.' Leavesden was the Asylum for Imbeciles.

The case notes were fuller. His delusory 'instincts' let Kosminski believe that he knew what everyone world-wide was thinking or doing; they also commanded him not to accept food from other people. This led him to picking up and eating bread from the gutter. One of the places where he was seen doing this was on City police territory, in Carter Lane, one of the backstreets near St Paul's Cathedral. He wouldn't wash and wouldn't work and was alleged to have threatened his sister on one occasion with a knife. In January 1892 he attacked a hospital attendant with a chair. These incidents were in contrast to his normal apathy and inactivity, however. He was twenty-six years old when he was admitted to Colney Hatch Asylum on 6 February 1891. His trade was nominally that of a hairdresser. His next of kin was his brother Wolf (with whom he is supposed to have lived at 'Lion Square', Commercial Road, although no such place exists). He had been treated in the Mile End Old Town Workhouse Infirmary since July 1890 before being transferred to Colney Hatch. After his committal he became steadily more incoherent and withdrawn and was transferred to Leavesden as an incurable imbecile. He was still there when he died of gangrene in 1919.

Before discovering the entry for Aaron Kosminski, Fido had identified Macnaghten's suspect as one Nathan Kaminsky who, he argued, had been committed to Colney Hatch under the name of David Cohen, which, Fido was informed after the publication of his book, was a 'John Doe' for unpronounceable or misheard Jewish names. Cohen was not only the same age as Kaminsky but also, in Fido's opinion, the only East End Jewish lunatic whose committal and dates would explain the cessation of the murders. Fido further identifies Kaminsky with both Leather Apron and Anderson's mad Polish Jew. All that we know about Cohen is that he was twenty-three years old, had no known relatives, was extremely violent and had been brought to the Whitechapel Infirmary on 12 December 1888 after police had 'found him wandering at large and unable to take care of himself'. On 21 December he was sent to Colney Hatch, where he was force-fed, kept under restraint and put in a strait-jacket. He died a year later.

In Fido's opinion he is the only possible Jack the Ripper.

And that word 'possible' simply underlines the fact that yet again the identification with Jack the Ripper has not been proved. Clearly Swanson's Kosminksi and Fido's Kaminsky, a.k.a. David Cohen, don't match. They contradict one another at too many points. Bad hearing, bad memory, bad pronunciation and three people to prove one identity are just too much to take on board. To get round the complexities Fido argues that the Metropolitan and City police were each investigating a different man. The Met. hijacked the City's witness, Joseph Lawende, who saw Eddowes and a suspect together in Mitre Square. It was Lawende's description of the suspect – navy-coloured serge, red neckerchief, deerstalker cap and small, fair moustache – that the City police had circulated. When Lawende refused to confirm his identification of 'Cohen' (Fido ignores Lawende's own statement that apart from the clothes he would not know the man again) they had Cohen committed to the Whitechapel Infirmary.

The City police, meanwhile, had staked out Kosminski, who was eating out of the gutters, and found him to be harmless; he was still at large for a further three years after the Kelly murder before being committed by his family. Because of the rivalry between the two police forces, the Met. never let on that they had imprisoned their own suspect under a pseudonym, and when they referred in their memoirs to a 'young Polish Jew', the City thought that they were referring to the innocent Kosminski, and it was this unfair aspersion that provoked Smith's indignant outburst.

The truth is probably a lot less complex, but certainly Swanson's notes do raise some interesting questions. The central one is that of identification. Why did the suspect have to be taken to a seaside home for identification? My initial reaction was that this was done to get him away from the hot-house atmosphere of London, away from the press in particular, to somewhere quiet where he could be interviewed and, possibly, identified; but then I realized that this would have been too complex an operation and one that would quickly have been discovered as the witnesses were moved about. The correct explanation would seem to be that Kosminski was taken to the seaside home to be identified by someone who was convalescing and couldn't travel up to town, someone who had been taken sick or injured sometime after the Kelly murder, someone who was a male and a Jew. Fido argues that this was Lawende, but this now seems unlikely. According to Swanson, Kosminski was identified; but if so, why wasn't he charged? Why was he allowed to roam the streets for three more years? If we are to believe Fido, Swanson should have written 'Kaminsky' not 'Kosminski'. Or should it be 'Cohen'? Whoever it was, there was not the evidence to hold him or charge him with any of the murders.

Whatever the truth, Fido's theorizing does underline the point that these complex explanations were necessitated only by the shortage of original documentation. What is also often overlooked is that if the case had been solved, the investigators – that is Smith, Abberline, Anderson, Swanson, *et al.* – would not have been forced to try solving the case with hindsight and by contradicting one another in print. Similarly, too much weight can be given to the Macnaghten notes. These are often misinterpreted, and his three suspects – Druitt, Kosminski and Ostrog – are assumed to be the only ones. This is a misreading of what Macnaghten has said. He offers them up only as alternatives to Cutbush, says quite clearly that 'no shadow of proof could be thrown on any one' and goes on to name as possible suspects the three men, 'any one of whom would have been more likely than Cutbush to have committed this series of murders'. All three, as the notes make clear, were investigated (there is a reference to Druitt's family); if the notes are taken in conjunction with the rest of Macnaghten's statement, there was indeed not a shred of proof against Druitt, Kosminski or Ostrog.

Just to emphasise how much dissension there was in the upper ranks as to the Ripper's identity only Swanson and Anderson (who does not name him) suggest that it was Kosminski; Abberline and Godley believed that it was Chapman, while Macnaghten thought that it was Druitt.

Dr Stanley

In 1929 Leonard Matters published *The Mystery of Jack the Ripper*. In it he claimed that his book was based on the death-bed confession of an English doctor named Stanley that he was Jack the Ripper.

In his original introduction, Matters said that he had found the confession printed in Spanish in one of the journals in Buenos Aires where he had worked for some years on an English newspaper. In a revealing phrase Matters said that he had built up a story around that confession; and it is tempting to ask if his story did not come first and the facts, which were well researched and make up two-thirds of the book, come second. Certainly it is hard to escape from the conclusion that the Dr Stanley part of the book is fiction. Matters himself said that he could not vouch for the genuineness of the story but thought that it was entitled to some credence. He went on, 'That such a man of such a character and such a life story did really exist in 1888 it is beyond my hope to prove.' He said that a search of the records of the General Medical Council of Great Britain had failed to find anyone who could be identified with Dr Stanley, but went on to argue that only by accepting the existence of this elusive personality was it possible to delineate the true character of the Ripper.

His story was allegedly based 'on the recital of an anonymous surgeon in Buenos Aires who claimed to have been a student in London under the doctor, and to have been present when he died in the Argentine capital some thirty years ago'.

Matters begins by asking three questions. Why were all the Ripper's victims prostitutes? Why did the Ripper kill only in the East End? Why did the murders stop after that of Mary Kelly?

His conclusions were: that it was only among prostitutes the Ripper could find the woman he was looking for; that he knew that he would find her in the East End; and that the woman he was looking for was Mary Kelly.

Matters says that Dr Stanley's early career was an unbroken success. But his rapid fame as a brilliant young surgeon took a downward turn with the death of his wife when their son was only a few days old. This tragedy soured him and left him with a lasting contempt for his colleagues whose medical incompetence he blamed, to some extent, for her death. Gradually he withdrew into himself and lavished all his affection on the son, Herbert.

Matters quotes an anonymous contemporary who knew him at this time. (As he could not prove that Dr Stanley ever existed this was certainly a wonderful achievement!) 'X' was taken to the doctor's house in Portman Square and shown his collection of pathological specimens in the doctor's private museum. One of Dr Stanley's self-appointed tasks was a compilation of the pathological history of cancer. His only regret was that life was too short to allow him to complete it but this would be done by his son who, as the doctor believed, would one day 'be hailed as a saviour of humanity!'

'X' was led to speculate: 'There was no doubt Dr Stanley had centred all his hopes on that boy, and, looking at his museum, he saw in it not only the proof that he was right in his theory and surgical methods but that his son's future was wrapped up in his own victory over those he imagined to be his enemies.' 'X' also wondered about the effect it would have on Stanley if anything happened to his son. Undoubtedly the consequences would be tragic. And this, Matters says, is precisely what happened.

Herbert Stanley met Mary Kelly on boat race night of 1886. He was then a brilliant medical student and only twenty-one. They spent a week in Paris together before he discovered that she was diseased. This is the first big flaw in Matters's story. Kelly's post-mortem showed no trace of any such disease. Matters continues that the disease had taken firm hold on the boy before his father found out a few weeks later what had happened to him. For nearly two years they fought the disease with different cures before young Stanley died of its effects. By then the father knew the details of the short-lived affair with Kelly.

From the dramatic way he talks about it, one would suppose that young Stanley was the only person ever to have been afflicted with this disease, the name of which Matters modestly withholds from his readers. The following facts should be borne in mind to put the story into some perspective. According to Dr Henriques, in *Prostitution and Society Vol. 3*, about 50,000 people were treated anonymously for venereal diseases in the London hospitals in the middle of the nineteenth century. In the same period, about 20 per cent of the army was infected with the disease, as compared with today's figure of about 4 per cent. Most men seem to have accepted the risk as perfectly acceptable.

Both Donald McCormick and Robin Odell in their books make the point that venereal disease was a slow killer and that, if he had contracted it from Kelly, Herbert Stanley would not have died within so short a time as two years. But, as Odell points out, the main flaw in Matters's argument has always been that, according to the medical evidence, Kelly was not infected with venereal disease: the only disease that she was suffering from was alcoholism. But before jumping to the conclusion that she could not have passed on the disease to young Stanley, Odell cautioned:

too much faith should not, in all respect, be placed on Dr Phillips's remarks, for a woman can be a carrier of venereal disease without the disease itself being evident. Moreover, the causal organism of syphilis was not discovered until 1905, so that a doctor in 1888 could not have based his diagnosis solely on clinical evidence, which is especially difficult to establish in a woman (not to mention a case where the woman had been cut to pieces). If modern pathological examinations and blood-tests could have been made, they might well have shown that Kelly was a syphilitic.

The story goes on to describe Dr Stanley vowing to revenge himself on Kelly. This means scouring the East End for her. He spends a week or two to familiarize himself with the underworld and night life of London, creeping through alleys and back streets and learning how to dodge from one street to another without being seen. For his first encounter with a prostitute Stanley goes to Wardour Street where he knows that Kelly had once lived. To his dismay she is no longer there. He curses the woman now living in her old lodgings, and who, after she has listened to his tirade, slams her door and mutters, 'My God! I'm glad I'm not Marie. If I was that man would kill me. Somebody ought to tell Marie, but I don't know what's become of her.'

Clearly this is fiction.

In spite of his statement that he could not prove the existence of Dr Stanley, Matters neatly dovetails into his story the evidence of a Mrs North who describes her meeting with a man she thought was a doctor, a man of forty-five to forty-seven years of age, sinewy and strong, of tremendous force and will. 'His eyes were dark and glowed with fire,' says Matters. Dr Stanley subsequently learns that Kelly is living in the East End, and disguises his appearance. 'A change of attire; a slouching gait; a garbled form of English ... or an imitated foreign accent ...' At the same time he resolves to kill all the women whom he questions, it does not matter how many, so overwhelmingly strong is his desire for revenge. His first victim is Martha Tabram. Stanley panics and stabs her simultaneously with his surgical knife and triangular-shaped bayonet. Polly Nichols is his next victim and this time being calmer and more in control of himself he succumbs to another impulse and disembowels her for the specimen he wants for his surgical museum. He obtains further physiological specimens from Annie Chapman, Liz Stride and Catharine Eddowes who, before she is murdered, gives him the name and address of Kelly's lodgings. Here again there is a blending of fact and fiction, because the other name that Eddowes used was Kelly and it would have been easy for Stanley, if his story had been true, to have assumed that she was the woman he was looking for. Eventually Stanley, after keeping observation on Mary Kelly, overhears her say that her man has left her and that she'll be out on the streets unless someone pays her rent.

He follows her to Miller's Court and, awaiting his chance, creeps into her unlocked room. Shaking her awake he reveals his identity and gives her a chance to speak before he kills her. She has only time to scream 'Murder' before he uses the knife. His revenge is complete.

Afterwards Stanley wanders the world for ten years, apparently without his famous collection, and finally settles down in Buenos Aires. There he lives for some years and, recognizing a former pupil of his, writes to him when he eventually succumbs to cancer, the disease for which he had striven to find a cure. When the pupil arrives to see him Stanley tells him that he has only an hour or two to live. He confesses that he is Jack the Ripper and gives the visitor £100 to pay for a modest funeral and the rest to do with as he likes. He wants his visitor to promise to do something for him, but he dies before he can tell him what it is.

As a postscript to this story it is worth including Leonard Gribble's theory, put forward in an issue of *True Detective* (January 1973), in an article which he called 'Was Jack the Ripper a Black Magician?'

Once again, the story is about a doctor avenging himself on the East End prostitutes who had given his son the disease from which he had died in an asylum for the insane. Each of his victims is a blood sacrifice; but, on top of this, the murders are committed in such a way as to coincide with certain phases of the moon since the doctor can build up an occult pentagram to give himself immunity from discovery. In fact, there are six victims. Martha Tabram is the first. Her murder has an occult significance; apparently 3 × 13 is an occult formula which is why she was stabbed thirty-nine times. Stride, however, is not a victim proper. Because the Ripper didn't have time to complete his ritual slaying it was essential that he had to find a second victim quickly to make her death coincide with that particular phase of the moon. If he hadn't murdered Eddowes immediately afterwards the efficacy of the pentagram would have been broken.

Kelly's death and mutilation coincided with the final phase of the sacrificial period, which sealed the mystical pentagram and so brought the killings to an end.

George Chapman (Severin Antoniovich Klosowski)

George Chapman, whose real name was Severin Antoniovich Klosowski, was born on 14 December 1865 in the tiny Polish village of Nargornak. From December 1880 to October 1885 he was a surgical student in village practice. He completed his studies, which ended on 1 January 1886, with three months' practical surgery at the hospital in Praga. He then applied for, but failed to get the degree of junior surgeon. At most he seems to have been a *feldscher*, a hospital attendant or 'barber surgeon'. (This was a relic from the days when the professions of hairdressing and medicine were intertwined.) After a brief spell of military service he emigrated to England, arriving in 1888. His first known job was as a hairdresser's assistant in a shop in the High Street, Whitechapel. For some reason he was known as 'Ludwig' Klosowski (or Zagowski), which the English pronounced 'Schloski'.

Nothing is known in detail about Chapman's career in Whitechapel at this time, except that it coincided with the Whitechapel murders. Ex-Detective Sergeant Leeson, in his autobiography, *Lost London*, conveys some information that is relevant. He says that 'Chapman lived in Whitechapel, where he carried on a hairdresser's business in a sort of "dive" under a public-house at the corner of George Yard'. If true, then this has some significance as it was in George Yard buildings that Martha Tabram was stabbed to death. However, Leeson's statements must be treated with great caution, even when he is describing events with which he was intimately connected, such as the famous Siege of Sidney Street some years later. (In my book about this episode, I was able to check contemporary police documents and statements against his later statements in these memoirs. I found such alarming discrepancies between them that I decided *Lost London* was almost entirely untrustworthy.) In connection with this statement about Chapman, it should be borne in mind that Leeson did not join the Metropolitan Police until October 1890 and was not posted to Whitechapel until February 1891, and his statement must therefore be treated as second-hand evidence.

Fortunately we have the evidence of Abberline himself that Chapman lodged in George Yard. He had a shop in the basement of the White Hart public house, but as far as the records are concerned, he did not move there until 1890. Possibly there was some unrecorded period of temporary employment when Chapman was working and lodging there which prompted Abberline's statement. Officially at the time of the murders he was at 126 Cable Street but still within easy striking distance of the murder sites.

It is known that Klosowski changed jobs and went to work for a barber in West Green Road, South Tottenham, and that he subsequently bought his own shop in the High Road, Tottenham. He was a poor business man and, the shop failing, he was reduced once more to the status of barber's assistant. He worked for a barber in Shoreditch and then moved on to another shop in Leytonstone.

In 1889 he was introduced to one Lucy Baderski at the Polish Club in St John's Square, Clerkenwell. They had known each other for less than four or five weeks before they were married on August Bank Holiday, 1889. Klosowski, however, already had a wife whom he had left behind in Poland. She came to London and tried to oust her rival from his affections, and for a short time both women shared the same house with him. Eventually, Klosowski's legal wife realized the hopelessness of her situation and left. Afterwards he and Lucy Baderski went to live in Cable Street, close to the docks, before emigrating to America in 1890. In February 1891 Lucy left him because of his infidelities and returned to England alone.

According to Klosowski's story, he followed her in 1893

(although there is evidence to show that this happened a year earlier). The couple were reconciled, but only temporarily. Klosowski did not try to get custody of the two children of the marriage, probably because this would not have fitted in too well with the image that he liked to project of himself as a widower or bachelor.

At the end of 1893 he met one Annie Chapman (not to be confused with the Ripper's victim) and they lived together for about a year. After they broke up in December 1894 she found out that she was pregnant. He refused to help her, even to the extent of denying her a reference so that she could support herself and the child. The only legacy of this affair was that Klosowski borrowed from his discarded mistress the name of Chapman. This was to shake himself free of his tangled affairs which he did by suppressing totally the name of Klosowski. Years later, when he was questioned by the police, and asked if he was Klosowski, he replied: 'I don't know anything about the fellow.' The change of name, says H. L. Adam, in his introduction to the *Trial of George Chapman*, may have been inspired by other more sinister ambitions having 'for their primary purpose and *idée fixe* the pursuit, capture, and the destruction of women'.

He met his first victim when he was lodging with the Renton family in Leytonstone in 1895. Mary Renton's married name was Spink. Her husband was a railway porter who left her, taking their son with him, because she was an alcoholic. Chapman had changed his lodgings, and soon after the break-up of this marriage he and Mary Spink, a small blonde woman with short cropped hair, were seen about a lot together. Eventually they announced that they were getting married. This was a polite fiction, since each was still legally married. After they had set up house, Mary Spink had £250 advanced to her from a trust fund of about £600. A further £350 was advanced to her two years later, in 1897, only a short time before she died. Chapman and Mary leased a barber's shop in a poor part of Hastings but, because it was not very successful, they moved to a more affluent part of the town. Mrs Spink helped her husband by lathering and sometimes shaving the customers; she was popular with the customers and used to entertain them by playing the piano. These 'musical shaves' were very popular and the business prospered dramatically. In spite of this, Chapman gave it up within six months and returned to London as the landlord of the Prince of Wales tavern off City Road.

While in Hastings he had by no means neglected his casual love affairs. He purchased an ounce of tartar emetic from a local chemist. Back in London, Mrs Spink, who seldom suffered from anything but a hangover, began to experience severe vomiting and stomach pains. Gradually her health broke down under these attacks and she became very emaciated. Chapman was very solicitous for his wife's health and supervised the food and medicines that were given to her. She weakened steadily under these administrations and, on Christmas Day 1897, she died. The cause of her death was given as phthisis due to her emaciated condition.

A few months later he hired a new barmaid named Bessie Taylor, who was soon installed as the new but unmarried Mrs Chapman. Like her predecessor, she soon acquired the same haggard condition. To avoid arousing suspicion among the customers who had known his first wife, Chapman gave up the Prince of Wales tavern and moved to Bishop's Stortford where he took over The Grapes. While they were there, Bessie Taylor went into hospital for an operation. Afterwards Chapman became even more brutal to her, to the extent of threatening her with a revolver. They moved to London again where he leased the Monument Tavern in the Borough. He continued to ill-treat his wife. This aggravated her condition, and she became steadily thinner and more frail. None of the doctors who examined her realized that she was being slowly poisoned. On 14 February 1901 she died. Cause of death was given as 'exhaustion from vomiting and diarrhoea'.

Just a few months later Chapman met his final victim, a young woman named Maud Marsh, whom he hired as barmaid at the Monument Tavern. From a letter that was produced at his trial, it is clear that she held out against him for some time before moving in with him as Mrs Chapman No. 3. Her pathetic lie that they were husband and wife did not deceive her parents, who were suspicious of Chapman and never trusted him for one moment. Within a short time Maud began to suffer from the same pains and symptoms as had her predecessors. Solicitous as ever, Chapman insisted on preparing her food and medication himself. Mrs Marsh eventually suspected that her daughter was being poisoned and called in another doctor to examine her. His visit precipitated the final tragedy. Chapman gave his wife a final massive dose of poison and she died the next day. The local doctor, warned by telegram by Dr Grapel (who had examined her) that his patient was being poisoned, was too late to save her. He refused to issue a death certificate and Chapman's fate was sealed when the post-mortem showed traces of arsenic. He was arrested on 25 October 1902, the day of Edward VII's coronation. Only then was it discovered from his private papers that he was also Severin Klosowski. He was charged with the murder of Maud Marsh, and subsequently with the murders of Mary Spink and Bessie Taylor. Their bodies when exhumed were found to be in a remarkably good state of preservation, one of the surest indications of poisoning by arsenic.

Chapman's trial began on 16 March 1903 and lasted four days. His only friend, it seemed, was his Polish wife who begged to see him. This he refused to agree to. His defence counsel did not call for any new evidence or witnesses on his behalf. The only thing he would do was play for the jury's sympathy, by claiming that Chapman was a 'hated alien'. This line was unsuccessful, and the jury took only eleven minutes to bring in their verdict of guilty. He was hanged at Wandsworth prison on 7 April.

Chapman has always been a leading Ripper suspect. This can be attributed, in part, to H. L. Adam who, when he edited the *Trial of George Chapman*, was able to draw upon the knowledge of ex-Chief Inspector Godley who had not only arrested Chapman but had worked with Inspector Abberline on the Ripper investigation. Godley is clearly the source for Adam's statement that Abberline thought that Chapman and the Ripper were one and the same person; when Godley made his arrest Abberline told him, 'You've got Jack the Ripper at last!'

The arguments in favour of Chapman being the Ripper can be briefly summarized as follows: that he may have been working in Whitechapel at the time and had the necessary surgical skill to have committed the killings and the mutilations both quickly and efficiently; that the description of the man who was seen with Kelly was – yet again! – an accurate description of Chapman himself; that the Americanisms such as 'boss' in some of the Ripper correspondence suggest an American background, which Chapman certainly had from his three-year sojourn there, although this carelessly overlooks the fact that he only acquired such a background two years after the murders; the callous joking of some of the Ripper correspondence, which was typical of his brutal humour; that the last murder was committed while Chapman was still in London and that the similar murders were committed in the immediate area of Jersey City which was where he opened his shop in America. This last point does not hold up, since a thorough search of contemporary records shows that the only murder which could be possibly referred to as such was that of 'Old Shakespeare', real name Carrie Brown, who was knifed and mutilated in New York in April 1891.

The case against Chapman's being the Ripper must necessarily hinge on the character of the Ripper himself, whoever he was. In an attempt to understand it, the following extract is taken from Krafft-Ebing's *Aberrations of Sexual Life*, edited by Dr Alexander Hartwich.

From the observations to be now recounted it emerges with utter clarity that the perverse urge in murders for pleasure does not solely aim at causing the victim pain and – most acute injury of all – death, but that the real meaning of the action consists in to a certain extent imitating, though perverted into a monstrous and ghastly form, the act of defloration. It is for this reason that an essential component of murders for pleasure is the employment of a sharp cutting weapon; the victim has to be pierced, slit, even chopped up. The correlation between pleasure-murder and defloration is further confirmed by the fact that the chief wounds are inflicted in the stomach region, and in many cases the fatal cuts run from the vagina into the abdomen. In boys an artificial vagina is even made in pleasure-murders.

Comparatively often the killing of the victim results from strangulation [my italics], that is to say, in the simplest manner, without any weapon being used, and certainly in some way linked with coitus, as before or after it, seldom as a substitute. But it would seem as if the said act usually failed to satisfy the murderer, so that afterwards the corpse is hacked to bits, in which connection it is especially the genitalia, and in the case of women also the internal genital organs, which are concerned. In an extremely grisly manner one can connect a fetishistic element too with this process of hacking up the victim, inasmuch as parts of the body – and here again it is particularly the genitals which are concerned – are removed, and in a certain degree made into a collection.

It is obvious that individuals as seriously psychopathic as the perverts in this group may also display the most diverse other sex-deviations, such as e.g. homosexuality, paedophily and fetishism. At the same time there is a high degree of hypersexuality and especially before and during the act.

The point that I am making here is that this is an instantly recognizable portrait of the kind of man we know that Jack the Ripper must have been.

But can we also say that is a portrait of George Chapman?

Clearly it is not. Coincidences such as Chapman living in Whitechapel at the time of the murders seem meaningless once the portrait of the sadistic murderer has emerged. Jack the Ripper could never have made the change from a murderer of this type to the coldly calculating wife-poisoner of Chapman's ilk. It is impossible to fit the two characters into the same frame, and on this ground alone Chapman should not be considered a candidate for the Ripper.

Dr Pedachenko

To understand Donald McCormick's *The Identity of Jack the Ripper* it is essential to know something of the Klosowski/Chapman theory, since the author uses it as a springboard for his own theory. His primary source material was the (unpublished) three-volume *Chronicles of Crime* by the graphologist Dr Dutton, already referred to in connection with the handwriting analyses of the Ripper correspondence (pp. 119–30). Unfortunately these 'chronicles' were either lost or destroyed after Dr Dutton's death in 1935, and when McCormick came to write his book, nearly twenty-seven years later, he was obliged to fall back on the notes which he had taken in 1932 and then forgotten about. McCormick described *Chronicles of Crime* as being 'not a single narrative, but rather a collection of impressions and theories which he noted at various periods'. Apart from the Ripper case, 'they covered a number of other interesting cases'. So it is fair to assume that McCormick has built his theory on the notes that he took of Dr Dutton's jottings. This is a major weakness of his book. The reader, if he is to have any confidence in these findings, has a right to expect an accurate recounting of facts that he can check. Unfortunately, where this is possible, McCormick often undermines the confidence of his readers. The most glaring example is in his retelling of the Siege of Sidney Street case, where he takes two well-documented incidents – the murder of three London policemen and the siege itself – and turns it into a single incident, although the events happened several miles apart and with nearly three weeks between them. He made the same mistake in *A History of the Russian Secret Service*, published in 1972, which he wrote under the pseudonym of Richard Deacon.

According to McCormick, Dr Dutton was friendly with Inspector Abberline who discussed this case with him on more than one occasion. From Inspector Godley's statement, although the genuineness of it has been challenged and may have been a H. L. Adam invention, we know that Abberline congratulated him on having caught the Ripper when he arrested Chapman in 1902. But, according to Dutton, he changed his mind – more than fourteen years after his original investigation, if Dutton is correct. McCormick goes on:

What finally convinced Abberline that he had made a mistake in thinking Klosowski was the Ripper was his discovery that the Polish barber-surgeon had a double in London and that this double, a Russian and also a barber-surgeon, sometimes posed as Klosowski for reasons which were not apparent . . . Could this be the same Russian surgeon hinted at by Sir Basil Thomson and others, the character named as Ostrog by Sir Melville Macnaghten? Or could it be the Russian named by William Le Queux as Dr Alexander Pedachenko?

As the story is rather complicated I shall break it down, as McCormick did, into the Russian and English sources.

Russian source. In 1923 the journalist and amateur spy, William Le Queux, published his autobiography, *Things I Know About Kings, Celebrities, and Crooks*. He was a name-dropper on a grand scale as can be readily judged from some of his chapter headings – 'What I Know about Kings'; 'Evenings with "Carmen Sylva", Queen of Roumania'; 'What the Sultan of Turkey told me'. In fact, he was a good high-society gossip columnist with a lot of readers, and there is probably truth in his claim that, after the murder of Rasputin, 'the Kerensky government handed to me, in confidence, a great quantity of documents which had been found in the safe in the cellar of his house, in order that I might write an account of the scoundrel's amazing career.' Among the papers was an incomplete manuscript called 'Great Russian Criminals' which, to his amazement, contained the truth about the Jack the

Ripper murders. Here is part of the extract that he copied before he returned the manuscript.

The true author of these atrocities was disclosed by a Russian wellknown in London, named Nideroest, a spy of our Secret Police, who was a member of the Jubilee Street Club, the Anarchist Centre in the East of London. One night in the club the identity of 'Jack the Ripper' was revealed to him by an old Russian Anarchist, Nicholas Zverieff. The mysterious assassin was Doctor Alexander Pedachenko, who had been on the staff of the Maternity Hospital at Tver, and lived on the second floor in the Millionnaya, but had gone to London, where he lived with his sister in Westmoreland Road, Walworth. From there he sallied forth at night, took an omnibus across London Bridge and walked to Whitechapel where he committed his secret crimes.

Alexander Pedachenko, according to Zverieff – whose record appears in the reports of the Secret Police – was aided by a friend of his named Levitski, and a young tailoress, called Winberg. The latter would approach the victim and hold her in conversation and Levitski kept watch for the police patrols, while the crimes and mutilations took place. Levitski, who had been born in London, wrote the warning postcards signed 'Jack the Ripper' to the Police and Press. It was through Levitski that Zverieff knew the truth.

Before giving the rest of the quotation, which is an explanation of the above, it is worth examining this statement in a little more detail, for every one of these facts comes from the man called Nideroest – even though he claims to be passing on the information given him by 'the old Russian Anarchist Zverieff'.

The only information that Le Queux gave about Nideroest's background was a single sentence that he had 'found out that a man named Nideroest was a member of the Jubilee Street Club and was known in connection with the Anarchist affray at Tottenham, and also with the Sidney Street affair'. When his book was published, *The Star* was quick to comment that he 'lets a large cat out of the bag when he reveals that the disclosure of the author of these atrocities originates with a Russian well known in London, named Nideroest, a spy in the Russian police ...'

Nideroest first hit the national headlines in January 1909 when he used a false name to get into the hospital where one of the Tottenham Outrage gunmen, who had shot two persons and wounded numerous others, was lying wounded. Nideroest did this by pretending to be his brother. He was arrested before he could get to the wounded man and there is a photograph of him in the *Daily Mirror* of 27 January 1909 being led away. In court next day Detective Inspector McCarthy said that he had known him for some years and that four years earlier he had concocted a bogus story about bombs being made in Whitechapel. He was not an anarchist but a casual journalist. Nideroest's only explanation for his behaviour was that he had gone to the hospital to work up a sensational interview and that it was only by pretending to be a relative that he could get in. The bench discharged him with a reprimand. It was this and the Sidney Street incident, after which Nideroest claimed to have helped the famous Peter the Painter escape from the house, that led Le Queux's reviewers – who were clearly well aware of the facts – to denounce Nideroest as an 'unscrupulous liar'.

The other and more important point, which McCormick omits to mention, is that in 1909 Nideroest was only twenty-four years old, as his photograph confirms. This means that he was three years old in 1888. So, whenever that interview with Zverieff took place, it must have been at least fifteen years after the Ripper murders. Indeed, one can pin it down even more accurately. According to Nideroest, the facts were given to him in the anarchist Jubilee Club. This club was not opened until 1906, and so it must have been after that date. McCormick, later on, offers further proof of Pedachenko's existence by quoting an extract from an *Ochrana Gazette* which he had been shown by a Russian exile, Prince Belloselski (who had been given this lithograph copy by Myednikov, former head of the Moscow Ochrana, the Secret Police). This gazette was a confidential Secret Police bulletin, issued twice a month to the heads of sections to keep them up to date on what was happening in revolutionary circles. McCormick quotes one of the items contained therein:

KONOVALOV, Vasilly, alias PEDACHENKO, Alexey, alias LUISKOVO, Andrey, formerly of Tver, is now officially declared to be dead. Any files or information concerning him from district sections should be sent to the Moscow Central District of Ochrana. Such information, photographs, or identification details as may still exist might refer to KONOVALOV, PEDACHENKO or LUISKOVO either individually or collectively. If documents held by you do not contain these names, they should also be examined for any information concerning a man, answering to the description of the above, who was wanted for the murder of a woman in Paris in 1886, of the murder of five women in the East Quarter of London in 1888 and again of the murder of a woman in Petrograd in 1891.

KONOVALOV's description is as follows: Born 1857 at Torshok, Tver. Height medium. Eyes, dark blue. Profession, junior surgeon. General description: usually wore black moustache, curled and waxed at ends. Heavy, black eyebrows. Broad-shouldered but slight build. Known to disguise himself as a woman on occasions and was arrested when in woman's clothes in Petrograd before his detention in the asylum where he died.

This document was dated January 1909, but the actual date of receipt most probably was in the latter half of the previous year. What makes a close examination of it so fascinating is that it is asking for – not giving – information about the wanted man. The authors are not even sure that any 'information, photographs, or identification details', exist. The names are the permutations under which they might find him; but if these failed to throw up any information then their files were to be searched for 'a man' answering the description and wanted for various murders. Even more astonishingly, they knew that he was arrested in Petrograd and that he died in an asylum. With this information available to them, why had they not been able to trace him? Why did they have to put out a general appeal for any existing photographs, information or identification details? The fact that they had not been able to find him strongly suggests that, between the two control dates of 1906 and 1908, Nideroest had fed back the story which he claimed had been told to him by Zverieff, and the Ochrana had published it in turn in the hope of finding some confirmatory evidence.

But if the records did not exist, then what is the explanation for the second half of Le Queux's extract from the 'Great Russian Criminals' manuscript:

The report of Nideroest's discovery amused our Secret Police greatly, for, as a matter of fact, they knew the whole details at the time, and had themselves actively aided and encouraged the crimes, in order to exhibit to the world certain defects of the English police system, there having been some misunderstanding and rivalry between our own police and the British. It was, indeed, for that reason that Pedachenko, the greatest and boldest of all Russian criminal lunatics, was encouraged to go to London and commit that series of atrocious crimes, in which agents of our police aided him.

Eventually at the orders of the Ministry of the Interior the Secret Police smuggled the assassin out of London, and as Count Luiskovo he landed at Ostend, and was conducted by a secret service agent to Moscow. While there he was, a few months later, caught red-handed attempting to murder and mutilate a woman named Vogak and was eventually sent to an asylum, where he died in 1908.

After the return to Russia of Levitski and the woman Winberg the Secret Police deemed it wise to suppress them, and they were therefore exiled to Yakutsk. Such are the actual facts of the 'Jack the Ripper Mystery' which still puzzles the whole world.

The opening sentence – that the police were greatly amused as they knew the details of Nideroest's discovery – is clearly not true. If they had known them, why should the Moscow Ochrana have appealed for information about a man who had been brought to Moscow by a secret service agent and some months later had been caught there attempting to murder and mutilate a woman? The question can be put even more simply: why should the Tsarist secret police not only find, but even doubt the existence of, one of their own men when the secret police of the Revolutionary Government that overthrew them were able to do so and to say just how 'amused' their predecessors had been by the incident? The answer that immediately springs to mind is that the Revolutionary police were discrediting their predecessors as much as possible and that they were faking extra evidence. In fact, Le Queux was the perfect 'fall-guy as well as propagandist for the new régime'.

The genuineness of the Rasputin papers is open to doubts on several counts. They were written in French which Rasputin, according to Prince Belloselski, 'was certainly not fluent enough in ... to dictate a narrative in that tongue. If he dictated this at all it must have been in Russian.' Once the doubts have been raised they harden into near certainty that the papers were faked, particularly when A. T. Vassilyev, who was the Tsarist police chief, states in his book, *The Ochrana*, that Rasputin's apartments were searched immediately after his death for compromising documents and that none were found. This is not to say that Le Queux did not receive any papers from the Kerensky government. Indeed, that he might have done so is confirmed by an independent source, C. W. Shepherd, whom Le Queux in his memoirs describes as editor of the Northern Newspaper Syndicate. 'Shep' ghosted three books for Le Queux and was highly amused when the publisher wrote to Le Queux after the receipt of one of these manuscripts, 'I see the old hand has not lost its cunning.' When I asked him if he had ever seen the Rasputin papers he told me that he had once had to make a flying visit to St Leonards or Hastings where Le Queux was then living (he could not recall the date) and while he was there, Le Queux had pointed out the Rasputin documents to him. He said: 'I saw them in a terrific-sized envelope, sealed and plastered with signs and codes and all sorts of things.' Unfortunately Le Queux never opened it in his presence.

The only reason for Le Queux to have been sent these papers was, as Prince Belloselski says, to help 'show up the Czarist Government in the worst light. Indeed, the only object for Kerensky to pass these documents on to Le Queux would have been for propaganda purposes.'

Le Queux must have realized that he was being used in this way. Although he was a money-spinner he was also a lavish spender and had to spend much of his time abroad to avoid his creditors. He was constantly hard up and yet, with this new evidence in front of him, he nowhere refers to it in his biography of Rasputin but chooses to wait five years before appending it as a sort of footnote in his autobiography. His only explanation for his startling decision is the rather lame excuse that he had only recently discovered that a doctor called Pedachenko actually did live in Tver.

One doubts him, just as one doubts the genuineness of the Rasputin papers. So what the Russian sources eventually boil down to is a collection of papers that came into existence only after 1906 – eighteen years at least after the murders; and the source for them was a well-known liar: Nideroest had been publicly proved to be one on more than one occasion.

They have to be dismissed from the case.

The only point not so far discussed with respect to these sources, is what possible reason the Russian secret police had for sending Pedachenko to England to commit these murders. This was allegedly done to show up the defects in the English police system. This is such a preposterous argument, however, that it cannot be taken seriously. McCormick suggests, slightly more plausibly, that Pedachenko was being used as an *agent provocateur* to discredit the anarchists who were using England as a base for their attacks on the Tsarist regime. He claims that Nideroest was a counter-espionage agent and that this was his role when he helped his colleague, the anarchist leader Peter the Painter (Peter Piatkow) to escape from the house in Sidney Street which was done with the connivance of the English police. This is to suggest, quite ludicrously, that the English police condoned the instigation of the Latvian anarchists' jewel robbery that led to the murder of three of their colleagues – among the worst crimes in English police history – and then let the real architect of it escape and let two men die in the siege itself. The chief argument against this theory is that the anarchists and other aliens were not expelled to their own country, even when they were implicated in such plots. Of the Sidney Street gang, eight were tried for murder and, with one exception – and her sentence was quashed on appeal – all were acquitted. None of them was expelled and, in the case of the woman who was found guilty, the jury made a specific request to the judge that she should not be deported. To underline this point, one of those involved, the only one who was not an anarchist, was sent back to Russia in 1917 as the Bolshevik delegate from London; after the October revolution he became deputy head of the Cheka! It was British policy to tolerate these political refugees who included such names as Lenin, Litvinoff and, for a very short time in 1907 for a Bolshevik conclave, Stalin.

None of them was expelled as an undesirable and yet Nideroest was just that. This fact stands squarely in the way of McCormick's theorizing: Nideroest was arrested in 1909 and expelled from the country in 1915.

British source. McCormick quotes an entry from Dr Dutton's diary of 1924:

Another theory on the Ripper. This time by William Le Queux in *Things I Know*. It is a great pity that he did not follow up what is a useful clue. By failing to do so, and by taking the Rasputin MS at its face value, he has only made a fool of himself. Further examination might have shown that Pedachenko was Klosowski's double. The fact that Pedachenko was a doctor at a Russian hospital is neither here nor there. What Le Queux should have found out was that Pedachenko worked as a barber-surgeon for a hairdresser named Delhaye in the Westmoreland Road, Walworth, in 1888.

McCormick found out that there was such a hairdresser as Dutton had described, but by itself this means little. He does not produce any evidence for Pedachenko's existence. Dr Dutton's source for his story was a Dr J. F. Williams, who told him that a Russian barber-surgeon named Pedachenko assisted him occasionally at St Saviour's Infirmary on an unpaid basis. Dr Williams believed that Pedachenko worked as a barber-surgeon in various establishments in south London and that he 'removed warts, treated skin diseases' – which is exactly what a *feldscher* might be expected to do.

Dutton also quotes the private evidence, again uncorroborated, of Wolff Levisohn, who was one of the prosecution witnesses at Chapman's trial. He had first met Chapman when he was working in High Street, Whitechapel, in 1888. At the time Levisohn knew Chapman as Ludwig Zagowski. They met from time to time up until 1890. At Chapman's trial Levisohn made one of the most damaging, and so far unquoted, statements against the whole Chapman/Ripper theory. He said: 'I talked to the accused about medicines, and he asked me if I could get him a certain medicine, but I said no, I did not want to get twelve years.' What did he mean? From such a remark the only inference that can be drawn is that Chapman was asking him to get a poison of some sort. It could not have been drugs, as it was not then a criminal offence to use them. As this request was made before 1890 it is a strong argument in favour of Chapman's having consistently stuck to the same method throughout his murderous career. It also makes one wonder whether he managed to get this substance from somewhere else and, if he did, who was his victim? Was there a murder of which we know nothing? Certainly such consistency of method is far more likely than the theory that he changed his nature from frenzied sadist with a knife to a cold, calculating poisoner.

Levisohn saw Chapman once again in 1894 or 1895, when the latter was working in Tottenham, and then lost sight of him until 1903, when he was tried. According to Dutton, however, Levisohn told Abberline at the time of the Whitechapel murders that 'he should look for a Russian who lived somewhere in Walworth, did a certain amount of illicit doctoring and attended barbers' shops to cut out warts and moles.' This tallies with Dr Williams's story. There was apparently some resemblance between Pedachenko and Chapman, so much so that, according to Dutton, 'Abberline for a long time thought that Pedachenko and Klosowski were one and the same person.' This, the evidence suggests, they surely were. We do not know when Chapman asked Levisohn to get him some poison, but if it was early on in their relationship, and if Chapman was confident as well as careless enough (as the evidence throughout his trial showed that he was) to have done so, then this would have been sufficient for Levisohn to give his tip to Abberline. True, the name he gave Abberline was 'Ludwig Zagowski', but it is just possible that – being a traveller in hairdressers' appliances – he had discovered that Chapman was working under an alias in the Walworth Road.

To sum up, the evidence from the British sources suggests that Pedachenko/Chapman was a single person and not two individuals as Dr Dutton maintains. Indeed the only person who tries to separate them is Dr Dutton. As McCormick says, 'Dutton's suggestion that "Klosowski" posed as his double, with the implication that the latter was Pedachenko, is not followed up by any explanation.' What Dutton has done is to blur some of the Chapman evidence and relate it to the Nideroest story and to documents that did not come into existence until nearly twenty years after the murder and possibly even later. It is significant, surely, that the reference to Pedachenko was not entered in his diary until 1923, which was the year following Le Queux's publication of *Things I Know*.

McCormick's book is highly readable but almost worthless as a research tool. Unfortunately, since first published in 1959, the book has become increasingly discredited. Sources cannot be checked, dialogue has been invented and the facts cannot be trusted.

Neill Cream

Dr Neill Cream is another famous murderer who has been suggested as Jack the Ripper. His chequered career of arson, blackmail, abortion and murder was finally brought to an end in 1892 when he was found guilty of the murder of four London prostitutes, whom he had picked up in the boroughs of Walworth and Lambeth (which led to his being called the Lambeth Poisoner) and poisoned with strychnine. On the scaffold he is said to have exclaimed: 'I am Jack the – ' just as the bolt was drawn. The hangman is said to have sworn that this was so. What makes the incident open to doubt is that among those who were present in their official capacity was the new Commissioner of the City of London Police, Henry Smith, who boasted many years afterwards in his autobiography that nobody knew more about the Ripper case than he did. Smith, it will be remembered, had several times clashed with Warren on the latter's handling of the case. The fact that Smith does not mention this incident is surely significant.

Far more damaging to Cream's claims, however, is that from November 1881 to July 1891 he was serving a life sentence for murder in the Illinois State Penitentiary at Joliet in America.

Donald Bell suggested a new Cream/Ripper theory in his article entitled 'Jack the Ripper – The Final Solution?' which appeared in *The Criminologist* (Vol. 9, No. 33, 1974).

Bell points out that racketeering and corruption flourished in the Chicago of the 1880s and argues that Cream might have bribed his way out of prison, or escaped. In corroboration, a major handwriting expert, Derek Davis, asserts that Cream's writing matches that in two of the Ripper letters.

Yet the evidence of the Governor of Illinois, the prosecuting attorney, contemporary newspapers, Cream's relatives, and Cream himself proves that he was not released until 1891.

There is further evidence of his continued imprisonment in a petition sent by Cream's solicitors to the Home Secretary while Cream was in Newgate Prison, shortly before his execution on 15 November 1892. This petition included a sworn affidavit from Thomas Davidson, an accountant-bookkeeper with Messrs John Ross & Co., Quebec. He stated:

That, as one of the executors under the will of the late William Cream, of Quebec, I found on the testator's death [1887] his eldest son, Dr. Thomas Neill Cream, a life prisoner in Joliet Prison, State of Illinois, USA, for complicity in murder. That being desirous of assuring myself as to his guilt or innocence I applied to the authorities connected with his trial and conviction for the evidence upon which such conviction was based and received such documentary evidence as convinced me of his innocence. That I then exerted every legitimate influence I could command to secure his liberation, and succeeded eventually in getting him released in the early part of the summer of 1891. That he came immediately to me in Quebec on being liberated, and that at my first interview with him I concluded he was unmistakably insane, and stated my conviction to his brother, Daniel Cream, in whose house he was stopping.

The other relevant affidavit was made by Jessie Cream, the sister-in-law in whose house Cream had stayed after his release. She said that Cream had been released from the Joliet Prison in Illinois on or about 29 July 1891. He had stayed with her family until he sailed for England in September 1891.

Besides these two affidavits, there are the facts that in December of 1890, Cream wrote from prison to Pinkerton's National Detective Agency, asking that someone be sent to see him and that on 12 June 1891, his life sentence was commuted to one of seventeen years, which, with time off for good behaviour, meant his release on 31 July 1891. The date of his pardon is confirmed by the Joliet *Daily News* of 13 June 1891.

Unless these facts are disproved – and Donald Bell does not disprove them – then suppositions about handwriting, similarity of appearance to Ripper suspects, and the multitude of other vague generalizations fall down and Cream is left a poisoner, which is what he was, and not Jack the Ripper.

There is a further theory, that he had a double and that they provided alibis for each other. Early in Cream's career he was defended on a charge of bigamy by Sir Edward Marshall Hall who advised him to plead guilty. Cream refused to do so and protested that he had been in prison in Australia at the time of the offences. His description was sent to the prison in Sydney where he claimed to have been, and the prison confirmed that a man of that description had been in prison at the times in question. Cream was released but was recognized again by Marshall Hall when he was tried on the charges of murder many years later. Marshall Hall's theory, according to his biographer Edward Marjoribanks in *The Life of Sir Edward Marshall Hall*, was that 'Neill Cream had a double in the underworld and they went by the same name and used each other's terms of imprisonment as alibis for each other.'

This has led to the suggestion that while Cream was serving his life sentence in America, his double was committing the Whitechapel murders. As the double had given Cream an alibi for the bigamy charge, Cream subsequently tried to repay the debt by shouting those last, interrupted words from the scaffold.

Duke of Clarence, Stephen, Gull and Sickert

In 1970 Dr Thomas Stowell caused something of a public sensation when he published, in *The Criminologist*, his 'A Solution' to the Jack the Ripper mystery. His source material was apparently the private papers of Sir William Gull who had been Physician Extraordinary to Queen Victoria. Throughout his article Stowell referred to the suspect only as 'S'. However, he dropped enough clues to show that he was pointing a finger at HRH Prince Albert Victor ('Eddy'), Duke of Clarence, the eldest son of the future King Edward VII. When asked to confirm or deny this interpretation, Stowell would do neither, apparently on the grounds that he did not want to embarrass the present Royal Family. Moreover, Stowell died within a few days of publishing his theory, and his notes were burned, unread by his distressed and mourning family.

It is hard to take Clarence seriously as a suspect. According to James Pope-Hennessy:

Even his nearest and dearest, who were naturally bent on making the best of poor Prince Eddy, could not bring themselves to use more positive terms. Prince Eddy was certainly dear and good, kind and considerate. He was also backward and utterly listless. He was self-indulgent and not punctual. He had been given no proper education, and as a result he was interested in nothing. He was as heedless and as aimless as a gleaming goldfish in a crystal bowl.

From childhood he had been handicapped by feeble health. At twenty-four years old he suffered from gout. He was attractive to women and preferred dissipation to work. Because of his long neck – 'a neck like a swan' was how the family described it – he was forced to wear excessively high starched collars which led to his nickname 'Collars-and-cuffs'. In a letter to Clarence's father the Prince of Wales, Viscount General Wolseley, who had lead the failed attempt in 1885 to rescue General Gordon beleaguered in Khartoum and later became C-in-C of the army, maintained that Clarence disliked the army (which he joined after leaving university), was immature for his age and his brain and thinking powers were described as maturing slowly – which was qualified in the same letter by the addition: 'some of our very best & ablest men have mentally matured with extreme slowness'. He was then twenty-seven years old, and died the following year.

Fortunately it was possible to verify from other sources that

Stowell had indeed been referring to Clarence, as was generally supposed. He had discussed his theory at various times with other people, among them the author Colin Wilson, who had met him in 1960 when he was writing a series of articles for the London *Evening Standard* called 'My Search for Jack the Ripper'. This research was to be the raw material for his masterly novel, *Ritual in the Dark*. Stowell invited Wilson to lunch and in the course of their conversation it became clear that he thought Wilson had reached the same conclusions as himself about the Ripper's identity. In fact, the 'clues' in Wilson's articles to which he attached so much significance were quotes from the newspapers of the time, which Stowell might easily have found out for himself. This illustration of the casualness of Stowell's research goes some way to explaining the not infrequent errors which he makes – a casualness that might be attributed to his age, however, for he was already in his seventies. Wilson found him a friendly and likeable man and for a long time was under the impression that Stowell was a surgeon, which is how he had introduced himself, although Wilson wondered from the way that his hands were shaking as he cut his steak just how much longer he would be able to continue operating.

Stowell's greatest discovery, or so he claimed, was that Clarence had not died in the great flu epidemic of 1892, as the history books stated, but in a private mental home near Sandringham, from 'softening of the brain' due to syphilis. If true, this information could not have come from the private papers of Sir William Gull, who died in 1890 at the age of seventy-three, two years *before* Clarence. Presumably, then, it came from some other source. It is lamentable, in view of the claim's startling nature, that this source was not identified.

Stowell is often wrong on small but important points of detail. For instance, he says that 'S' was forced to resign his commission when he was twenty-four – which Clarence never did – shortly after the raiding of a male brothel in Cleveland Street catering for aristocratic and wealthy homosexuals. Clarence is generally considered to have been one of its patrons because one of those involved was his personal equerry, who was forced to flee the country to avoid prosecution. In the publicity that inevitably followed these revelations, there was a newspaper smear which alleged that among those involved but not named was 'the highest in the land', which has always been taken as a direct reference to Clarence, but again without proof.

Whether Clarence was homosexual or not is open to doubt. As Michael Harrison says in his biography, *Clarence*, 'the destruction of Eddy's [Clarence's] correspondence, and the discreet silence maintained about his private activities, have made the task of assessing his character no easy one'. His homosexuality must remain 'not proven' and so too, without the benefit of Sir William Gull's papers, must Stowell's most damaging allegation that Clarence became infected with syphilis at one of the shore parties that he attended while on a visit to the West Indies. In time, this alleged syphilitic infection, so Stowell believed, sent him insane and led him to commit the Whitechapel murders.

Stowell alleged that the Royal Family definitely knew after the second murder, and possibly even after the first, that Clarence was the murderer. Within a few hours of the 'double event' murders on 30 September, Stowell goes on, Clarence was placed under restraint and shut away in a private mental home. Stowell's critics were quick to point out that Clarence was shooting in Scotland on those dates, and also that between 3–12 November, during which period Stowell would have him escaping from the asylum and committing the Miller's Court murder, he was at Sandringham taking part in his father's birthday celebrations. Clearly, if he was the madman that Stowell says he was, and if he was locked up once more after Miller's Court, it becomes impossible to explain why or how, immediately after these celebrations, Clarence should have been sent abroad as his father's personal representative to Denmark.

Stowell stressed the similarity in appearance between Clarence and some of the eye-witness descriptions of possible suspects, particularly of those wearing deerstalker hats, which he suggests that Clarence may have worn as a kind of ritual vestment. Certainly there was a startling similarity in appearance between Druitt and Clarence. Indeed, the resemblance between them is so overwhelming that the argument can go both ways, and is just as favourable to the Druitt theory as to Clarence. Clarence's skill in disembowelling prostitutes, Stowell continues, might have been acquired by his observing and learning the art of dressing deer (another reason for wearing a deerstalker) when he was out hunting, which might in turn also have stimulated his psychopathic rages.

Throughout Stowell's article the characters of 'S' and Clarence wheel about, like two moons through the heavens, occasionally overlapping sufficiently at the edges to show that there might be some common linkage but breaking away almost at once to reveal the internal contradictions of much of the evidence. Stowell says, for instance, that 'S' recovered sufficiently to go on a five-month cruise on which he was accompanied for part of the time by his parents. Clarence did, in fact, go as far as Port Said with the Prince and Princess of Wales when he made a journey to India in 1889. In the following year he was formally installed as the Duke of Clarence and Avondale, yet, according to Stowell, Sir William Gull, who was treating him, told his father while he was away that his son was dying of syphilis of the brain. Paresis (softening of the brain) is usually reckoned to appear fifteen to twenty years from the time of infection, symptoms being manifest for two to three years before death. Obviously there can be no absolute time scale for such a disease; some venerologists put the earliest time for the onset of paresis at ten years after infection but the general rule is fifteen. Clarence was a victim of the great flu epidemic that swept through Europe in 1892 and he died of pneumonia on 14 January 1892, aged twenty-eight. If he had caught the pox in the West Indies in 1879, and died as a result of it in 1892 (and there is no evidence to show that he did) then Stowell's theory is possible – just.

*

Clearly the evidence is thin indeed for supposing that Clarence was Jack the Ripper, and yet he plays an equally prominent role in at least two other theories. The first was aired in Michael Harrison's biography of Clarence, which examined the question of whether or not he was Jack the Ripper. Harrison concluded that he was not, but was convinced that the Ripper was somebody close enough to Clarence to have been confused with him. Harrison's researches convinced him that Stowell's 'S' was Clarence's tutor at Cambridge, James Kenneth Stephen, with whom he believes Clarence had a homosexual relationship, not necessarily a physical one, and that the murders were committed by Stephen out of a twisted desire for revenge because of the gradual cessation of this relationship.

Stephen's father was Sir James Fitzjames Stephen, the judge who is remembered nowadays for his mishandling of the Maybrick trial in 1889 (see page 253). It was so gross that he had to be given police protection from an outraged public. He was forced to retire from the Bench in 1891 because of the brain disease which had been gradually creeping up on him. Within a year of his retirement his son died in an asylum for the insane. Cause of death, so the medical certificate stated, was a mania lasting two and a half months, the persistent refusal of food for twenty days, and exhaustion.

According to one of his contemporaries, Stephen had 'added to his father's powers and force of intellect a cultivated taste in the delicacies of scholarship. He was no mere bookworm, but a man with a natural bent towards dainty and exquisite language in prose and verse.' (After which it comes as no surprise to learn that his cousins were Vanessa Bell and Virginia Woolf.) In 1883 he was chosen to be Clarence's tutor at Cambridge, where the Duke was sent for two years. University was regarded more as some kind of finishing school than as a place to improve his mind, which a former tutor had once described as 'abnormally dormant'. According to Harrison there was a sexual scandal of some kind between tutor and pupil, but there seems to be little evidence of it. The accusation seems chiefly to be based on Harrison's interpretation of the old rugby song, 'They Called the Bastard Stephen', which he thinks refers to Stephen and Clarence.

At the end of his time at Cambridge, on 17 June 1885, Clarence was gazetted to the 10th Hussars, and the relationship with Stephen, whatever it was, gradually petered out.

Two years later Stephen had an accident that resulted in serious brain damage. According to Quentin Bell, the nature of the accident was not definitely known, but family tradition has it 'that he was struck by some projection from a moving train'. Harrison, however, claims that while Stephen was out riding near Felixstowe his horse shied and backed him into the moving vane of a windmill. After treatment he made what seemed to be a perfect recovery. Only much later was it realized that the brain had been permanently damaged and that he was slowly going mad.

Quentin Bell says in his biography of Virginia Woolf:

One day he rushed upstairs to the nursery at 22 Hyde Park Gate, drew the blade from a sword stick and plunged it into the bread. On another occasion he carried Virginia [Woolf] and her mother off to his room in De Vere Gardens; Virginia was to pose for him. He had decided that he was a painter – a painter of genius. He was in a state of high euphoria and painted away like a man possessed, as indeed he was. He would drive up in a hansom cab to Hyde Park Gate – a hansom in which he had been driving about all day in a state of insane excitement. On another occasion he appeared at breakfast and announced, as though it were an amusing incident, that the doctors had told him that he would either die or go completely mad.

Harrison says that it was after his tragic accident that Stephen became Sir William Gull's patient. This was apparently after Gull had suffered his first stroke in 1887. At the time of his accident, Stephen had been a fellow of his college and a barrister, looking ahead to an excellent career. Now, like Clarence, he lacked concentration, vacillating between one interest and another, but with bouts of lucidity in between. He told his father that he intended to be a professional man of letters, and published a weekly journal called *The Reflector* which ran for only a matter of weeks before folding for lack of support. His father had to settle its debts. Possibly with a view to curbing some of his son's excesses, his father appointed him to a Clerkship of Assizes on the South Wales circuit, one of his reasons being that this would give him some practical experience of life at the Bar. In fact, Stephen's illness and other absences effectively prevented his taking up his duties and in 1890 he resigned. In 1891, still under treatment, he published a pamphlet defending the compulsory study of Greek at the universities, and brought out two slim volumes of poetry, *Lapsus Calami* and *Quo Musa Tendis*. As Harrison points out in his analysis of these poems, Stephen shows both his parvenu snobbery as well as his pathological hatred of women, one of whom he suggests in a poem should be 'done away with, killed, or ploughed'.

Later the same year he was committed to a mental asylum where he stayed until the following year, 1892, when he died on 3 February.

What evidence then is there for Harrison's theory that Stephen was the Ripper? His explanations are elaborate, ingenious and often amusing; but they cannot be taken too seriously. Harrison argues that the inevitable termination of the homosexual relationship which might have existed between the two men aggravated Stephen's jealousy and made him look for ways of revenging himself on Clarence. But why, one asks, should the brutal murder of five unknown East End prostitutes upset the heir to the throne? Harrison argues that Clarence may have been pressured by the Royal Family to curtail his friendship with Stephen. If so, then Stephen may have been offering up some kind of blood sacrifice.

★

There is the fact that the first (Smith) was 'offered up' on the Feast of the Great Mother, a savage deity whose temples were served castrated priests who, after their ritual castration, dressed as women. There is also the fact that the tenth and last 'offering' (Coles) was made on the 13 February, the Ides of February, the Roman Feast of Terminalia in honour of Terminus, patron of limits, boundaries, treaties, and *endings*. It was customary, though forbidden by King Numa Pompilius, who had established the feast, to *offer blood sacrifices* – usually a young lamb or pig. Unless it is the wildest coincidence, the 'sacrifice' that the classical scholar, Stephen, offered to Terminus on the morning of the Ides of February, 1891, bore a name which made her markedly suitable as a victim – Coles: Latin *coleus*, from Greek χολεος, 'a sheath', which in Latin is 'vagina'. It was in this same year that J. K. Stephen published his very able pamphlet, *Living Languages*, in defence of the compulsory study of Greek at the universities.

Another of Harrison's arguments is that one of Stephen's poems, called 'Air; Kaphoozelum', suggests that when Stephen wrote it he was thinking of the ribald verses which were as familiar then as they are today to anyone who takes part in a pub crawl or plays any sport, and whose chorus runs:

> Hi ho, Kaphoozelum,
> Kaphoozelum, Kaphoozelum,
> Hi ho, Kaphoozelum, The Harlot of Jerusalem.

The villain of this song killed ten harlots, and Harrison suggests that Stephen did the same, his other five victims being Emma Smith (who said that she was stabbed by five men!), Alice McKenzie, Frances Coles, Mellett or Davis (murdered 28/29 December 1888) and Annie Farmer. In order to get the arithmetic right, Stride and Eddowes are perversely counted as one victim. Annie Farmer is also included when, in fact, she was not murdered at all. According to *The Times* report of 22 November:

Considerable excitement was caused throughout the East End yesterday morning by a report that another woman had been brutally murdered and mutilated in a common lodging-house in George Street, Spitalfields, and in consequence of the reticence of the police authorities all sorts of rumours prevailed. Although it was soon ascertained that there had been no murder, it was said that an attempt had been made to murder the woman of the class to which the other unfortunate creatures belong by cutting her throat, and the excitement in the neighbourhood for some time was intense.

The victim of this last occurrence fortunately is but slightly injured and was at once able to furnish the detectives with a full description of her assailant. Her name is Annie Farmer and she is a woman of about forty years of age who lately resided with her husband but on account of her dissolute habits was separated from him. On Monday night the woman had no money and, being unable to obtain any, walked the streets until about half-past seven yesterday morning. At that time she got into conversation in Commercial Street with a man she describes as about thirty-six years old, about five feet six inches in height, with a dark moustache and wearing a shabby black diagonal suit and hard felt hat. He treated her to several drinks until she became partially intoxicated. At his suggestion they went to the common lodging-house, 19 George Street, and paid the deputy eight pence for a bed. That was about eight o'clock and nothing was heard to cause alarm or suspicion until half-past nine, when screams were heard proceeding from the room occupied by the man and Farmer. Some men who were in the kitchen of the house at the time rushed upstairs and met the woman coming down. She was partially undressed and was bleeding from a wound in the throat. She was asked what the matter was and simply said, 'He's done it,' at the same time pointing to the door leading into the street. The men rushed outside but saw no one except a man in charge of a horse and cart.

The sequel was reported the next day.

The man who committed the assault on Annie Farmer on Wednesday morning has not yet been captured. It is now believed that the wound to Farmer's throat was not made with a sharp instrument; also that the quarrel arose between the pair respecting money, as when the woman was at the police station some coins were found concealed in her mouth. The authorities appeared to be satisfied that the man has no connection with the recent murders.

Clearly the woman had faked the attack to divert attention from the robbery. When she was caught she tried to bluff it out and pretend that she had been attacked. The fact that the police took her to the station and not to hospital suggests that they knew quite clearly what she was up too. They must have done, to have caught her with the coins in her mouth.

But the weightiest argument against such elaborate conjecturing is that nowhere does Harrison make a point-by-point comparison of Stephen and Stowell's 'S' to see if they were the same person. He had done so with Clarence. Had he done it in Stephen's case he would have seen at once that they could not be one and the same man. Stephen never went on a world cruise, was never commissioned in the army, for example.

Yet Harrison insists that there is a scarcity of factual evidence, and that the case against Stephen must therefore be argued from internal evidence.

He makes two final points. First, that there is some similarity between Stephen's handwriting and that in the two Ripper letters beginning 'From Hell' and 'Dear Boss', which he reproduces. He finds a striking similarity, indeed, between the forming of the letter 'K' in the letters and the initial 'K' of Stephen's Christian name in signature. The other point he makes is that there is stylistic similarity between Stephen's poetry and the verse of some of the anonymous Ripper letters. The main objection to these points is that very little reliance can be placed on a handwriting comparison. The handwriting of the German murderer Peter Kürten, who was known as the Düsseldorf Ripper because of the way that he imitated his notorious predecessor, changed completely after each murder, so much so, indeed, that he used to point out to his wife the newspaper reproductions of anonymous letters that he wrote to the police, so confident was he that she would never recognize them – nor did she, which would seem to deny Harrison the support of even this flimsy strut.

A full rebuttal of Harrison's handwriting analysis was made by Thomas J. Mann in the Journal of the World Association of Document Examiners (*WADE Journal*, Vol. 2, No. 1, June 1975), Chicago, Illinois. Mann believes that only the Lusk letter is likely to be genuine and his extremely detailed analysis is based on that. It complements the analysis of C. M. Macleod (p. 129-30).

Dealing with the Lusk letter first, Mann says that the handwriting is the result of finger movement, giving very little freedom, rather than whole arm or forearm movement. It is the type of movement used by semi-literate individuals unskilled with the pen and to whom writing is not a familiar process. This does not prove that the writer had a poor educational background. The important question that has to be asked is whether it is the disguised handwriting of an educated person or the natural script of someone who was semi-literate?

Disguised handwriting has to be drawn slowly or else, with speed, the writer's natural idiosyncrasies will show through. The only way to disguise these is to control the pen strokes by writing slowly; but then this itself produces tell-tale signs. In the Lusk letter there are indications of unusually slow writing but many more signs of normal, unconscious speed. Mann thinks that the letter was written at a slower than average speed, which the heavy pressure on the nib tends to indicate. Nor is there the hesitation characteristic of deliberate disguise. Everything considered, the evidence does not support the hypothesis of disguised handwriting; what it does support is the hypothesis of a semi-literate penman.

Certain idiosyncrasies of the writer are a peculiar clockwise arc on the tail of letters. A normal tail would be counterclockwise. Then there are the numerous ink blots which give the letter its messy appearance. Most of them start on the left-hand side of the letter, which suggests that the writer may have redipped his pen at the beginning of each line. This is not true of every line but it does suggest that a more experienced penman would have avoided these large refill blots. With other evidence they indicate that the writer was neither very skilful with the pen nor concerned with clarity and legibility, and that he was not concentrating on the manner of his writing.

There are other indications of semi-literacy. The words 'tother' 'prasarved' and 'Mishter', the last two apparently phonetic misspellings, possibly indicate an English dialect. But since 'knif ' and 'whil' are not phonetic misspellings the writer must have had enough education to know that the silent *k* and *h* were part of the words. More interesting is the word 'women' which should read 'woman' – unless of course he was referring to the double murder, and if so, did he mean to say 'one of the women'? The layout of the letter suggests a copybook training but the omission of the date and the inclusion of the word 'signed' suggests that he did not learn his lessons well.

Mann is highly critical of Harrison's arguments for Stephen's guilt – especially his ready acceptance of 'thirty-four attested letters' written by the murderer. This is a reference to Donald McCormick's Dr Dutton, who had asserted that this number were in the same handwriting. Mann comments that nowhere do Dutton, McCormick or Harrison give any proof of the similarity of two letters, let alone thirty-four.

Mann then makes his own detailed comparisons – twenty-six in all – between the Lusk letter and specimens of Stephen's handwriting falling on either side of the 1888 date. The overwhelming evidence is that the two do not match; and if the author of the Lusk letter was indeed Jack the Ripper, then J. K. Stephen was not that man.

The other name which frequently crops up in these theories is that of Sir William Gull, who first came to public notice in 1871 when he successfully treated the Prince of Wales for typhoid fever. Queen Victoria was so grateful for his 'great services' to the

Crown that she rewarded him the following year by creating him Baronet and Physician Extraordinary to the Queen, in addition to his existing title of Physician in Ordinary to the Prince of Wales and to the Royal Family generally.

Stowell says that Gull was seen more than once in Whitechapel on the night of a murder and suggests that he may have been there for the express purpose of certifying the murderer insane. Who saw him there, one asks? Stowell was quoting from Gull's own papers, so are we to assume that the doctor was watching himself? And if 'S' was insane and Gull was treating him, why should the latter wait in Whitechapel to catch him when he could have done so much more easily and with far less fuss in his own consulting rooms? One can hardly believe that it was necessary to catch 'S' in the act of murder to prove his insanity.

Stowell quotes a story about the medium R. J. Lees, a spiritualist who, according to Fred Archer in his book *Ghost Detectives*, used to hold seances for Queen Victoria. Apparently Lees had three visions of the coming murders. On the first occasion he claimed to have seen the murder committed. He described the murderer as wearing a dark tweed suit and a light-coloured overcoat, which he used to cover up his bloodstained shirt. Lees was apparently so shaken by this experience that he went abroad – only to bump into the murderer on his return while boarding a London omnibus at Shepherd's Bush. His wife who was with him and who seems to have had a refreshing degree of scepticism only laughed at him when he pointed out the man as Jack the Ripper, as did also a policeman whom Lees tried to persuade to arrest the man. While they were arguing the man jumped into a cab and drove away.

The police apparently took Lees's story a little more seriously when, without knowing that they had received a letter threatening to clip the next victim's ears off, he told them he had seen in another vision that the ears were mutilated. This apparently convinced them that his powers were genuine, and they took him seriously when he told them of a third vision, this time of

Kelly's death. They allegedly used him as a human bloodhound, after the body had been found, in an attempt to trace the murderer's flight from Miller's Court. He took them to a fashionable house in the West End belonging to a highly reputable physician. Under questioning, the doctor's wife told them that her husband had 'sudden manias for inflicting pain'. On one occasion she had caught him torturing the cat, and on another brutally beating their son. She had noticed that her husband's absences from home coincided with the murders.

The doctor, when questioned, admitted to sudden losses of memory. He had found bloodstains on his shirt and on another occasion scratches on his face which he could not account for. When his wardrobe was searched the tweed suit and light overcoat which Lees had seen in his first vision were found among his clothes. The doctor wanted to kill himself when he realized what he had done. Instead, a specially formed commission on lunacy found him to be insane and he was committed to an asylum where he died many years later.

There are several variants of this story but the general outline is the same in each. Stowell went on to speculate as to whether the house that Lees had gone to was Gull's at 74 Brook Street. His own variant of this story had been told to him by Gull's daughter who said that her mother had been subjected at the time of the murders to a cross-examination by a medium and asked a lot of impertinent questions. Sir William Gull who came downstairs while she was being questioned admitted that he had had losses of memory since a slight stroke in 1887 and on one occasion had discovered blood on his shirt. Stowell speculated that all this might have been a deliberate attempt on Gull's part to divert suspicion from Clarence, although one would have thought that this was carrying self-sacrifice a little too far, especially when there was every chance of the murders continuing.

Medically, the slight stroke that Gull had in 1887 was the first attack of severe paralysis. Although he recovered from it, its effects were serious enough to prohibit him from further medical practice. Taken with the fact that he was seventy years old at this time, this is surely enough to cast doubts on the story of his roaming about Whitechapel trying to catch his patient. There is enough internal evidence in the story to show that the doctor referred to could not possibly have been Gull. According to Lees, the wife complained that she had caught her husband brutally beating their small son; Gull's son was by this time a barrister, and so could hardly have been the child referred to. Finally, Gull did not die in a lunatic asylum. He died at home on 29 January 1890, after a third stroke which left him speechless.

However, in spite of these doubts, Gull played an even more sinister role in the story told by Joseph Sickert who claimed to be the natural son of the Victorian artist Walter Sickert but whose real name was Gorman. This story had its first public airing when the Jack the Ripper crimes were investigated by television's fictional detectives Barlow and Watt in the BBC television series, *Jack the Ripper*. This in turn became the springboard for Stephen Knight's *Jack the Ripper: The Final Solution*.

Unfortunately, it isn't.

Knight and Sickert collaborated on the book. They alleged that Walter Sickert was deeply implicated in the murders although they do try to soften the blow by saying that he was probably acting under duress. Knight goes so far as to suggest that his theory resolves the ambiguity of Stowell's 'S' which, so he says, stands for 'Sickert'. The fact that the details fit the artist even less than the prince pales into insignificance at the revelation that there was not one Jack the Ripper but three! The other two are supposedly Sir William Gull and a coachman, John Netley.

The motive for the murders is the alleged marriage of the Duke of Clarence to a Roman Catholic. There is no proof that such a marriage took place nor has one been alleged until now. No matter, this does not stop Knight from alleging that Clarence was a regular visitor to Sickert's studio at 15 Cleveland Street nor that it was on these visits that he met and fell in love with Annie Elizabeth Crook who worked at a tobacconist's shop near by.

She became his mistress, so the story goes, and subsequently his wife. The affair supposedly had to be kept secret because with the amount of anti-Catholic feeling that then existed the announcement of such a marriage might have shaken the foundations of the throne itself. Sickert and Mary Kelly are supposed to have witnessed the marriage. A daughter, Alice Margaret, was born to the couple on 18 April 1885. Such a birth did occur, but whether Clarence was the father is impossible to prove; the father's name was left blank on the birth certificate.

The happiness of the couple was apparently short-lived. Again in the story, in April 1888 Clarence and Annie Crook were abducted from Cleveland Street by government officials. Sickert was returning to his studio and was an eyewitness to this. They were taken away in separate carriages and never saw each other again. Annie was detained for four months in Guy's Hospital where she was operated upon by Sir William Gull who destroyed her memory in some devilish manner. She was never the same again. She spent the rest of her life drifting in and out of work-houses and other such institutions, and died in 1920.

Meanwhile, reverting back to 1888, Mary Kelly, knowing that as an eyewitness to the marriage she might be in danger, was in hiding in the East End. There she fell in with Nichols, Chapman and Stride and with their help tried to blackmail the authorities into buying her silence. The plan misfired and Sir William Gull was charged with the extraordinary job of silencing them. His unlikely accomplices, so Knight alleges, were Queen Victoria, the Prime Minister Lord Salisbury, the Freemasons, Sir Charles Warren, Sir Robert Anderson, Inspector Abberline and a host of minor walking-on parts. Have we left anyone out? I don't think so. Even Oscar Wilde gets a mention.

Using the same facts that were supplied to Simon Wood and myself by Alan Neate, the former Record Keeper of the Greater London Records Office, it is astonishing to see how selective Knight was with his material. The papers in question relate to the

Crook family – Sarah, Annie and Alice. Seen in their proper context, a totally different picture of the family emerges. It is worth going into in detail as little of this material has been published before. Most surprising of all was the deletion from Knight's story of Sarah Ann Crook, the mother of Annie and the grandmother of Alice. She doesn't even get a mention and yet the greater part of the material supplied by Alan Neate relates to her.

She was born on 31 August 1838, according to Poor Law entries, at 22 Great Marylebone Street. We don't know her maiden name, only that her parents were born in Berwick-upon-Tweed. There was also a sister who was living at 8 Carlisle Street, Soho Square in 1895. Sarah was twenty-four when she had a daughter, Annie Elizabeth Crook. This child was not the rustic heroine of Knight's imagination. He wrote: 'She was of Scottish descent, and had wound her way to London from her country village in the Midlands, her rustic imagination brimming with visions of fortune in the big city.' The fact is that Annie Crook was born in north London on 10 October 1862; her birthplace is given alternatively as St Marylebone Infirmary and St Pancras. Even had she been born in Berwick, she would not have been of Scottish descent, for Berwick has been the northernmost town of England since 1462, the last time it changed hands with the Scots. It is doubtful whether either mother or daughter ever strayed much beyond the adjacent districts of St Marylebone, St Pancras and Holborn. According to a Board of Guardians deposition dated 18 December 1913, Sarah was legally settled in the parish of St James Westminster, which is where she had lived at 18 Portland Street (now D'Arblay Street), Carnaby Street and elsewhere for about forty years, up to 1902. When this deposition was made Sarah was living in Tooting Bec Hospital.

The surname Crook belonged to William Crook, whom Sarah is stated to have married (there is conflicting evidence) in 1863, a year after Annie's birth. Whether the child was illegitimate, whether the child was his or someone else's, we don't know. Nor do we know if he was the father of Sarah's second daughter, of whom we likewise know very little.

William Crook is listed variously as being a cabinet-maker, piano-maker and french polisher. On 13 May 1882 husband and wife were destitute. They were given outdoor relief by the St Pancras Relieving Officer of meat and bread to the value of 1s. 5d. Their past addresses were 24 Francis Street for seven months, Howland Street, for three months, and others at Saville Street, St Marylebone, Hanson Street and Whitfield Street. Sarah suffered from epilepsy, and because of this an order was made to admit her to the workhouse; but someone has written across the Relieving Officer's report, 'Didn't come'. Apart from the specific references to her destitution, the epilepsy, getting worse as she grew older, was the probable reason why she spent so much time without her husband in the workhouses and infirmaries. The same argument applies to Annie, who was also epileptic, until hemiplegia, paralysis of one side of the body, led to her continual confinement from 1903 onwards. The likelihood that the epilepsy was inherited is a more pragmatic explanation than Knight's suggestion that it was induced by a brain operation performed by Sir William Gull.

On 5 June 1891 Sarah's fits and destitution were the cause of her being taken to the Relieving Officer by police. She earned money by working as a charlady, as did Annie, now aged eighteen. Sarah and William were then living at 16 Upper Rathbone Place. Six months later William was apparently living with Sarah's second daughter, now Mrs Jackson, at 9 Phoenix Street and Sarah herself at 21 Great George Street. William died in the St Pancras Infirmary on 4 December 1891 aged sixty-one. Cause of death was given as 'Prostatic obstruction, cystitis consecutive Bright's disease'.

On 12 October 1895 Sarah was admitted to the St Pancras Workhouse for causes given as hysteria and alcohol. A month later she was in the Poland Street Workhouse having been homeless for two nights. She was then fifty-seven. She gave previous addresses at 11 Pancras Street (now Capper Street), for three weeks, 23 Carnaby Street, for ten months, and Devonshire Street (now Boswell Street), Holborn, for six months.

Annie Crook surfaces into this twilight world when her daughter Alice, Sarah's granddaughter, was born on 18 April 1885. As we have seen, the space for the father's name was left blank on the birth certificate. Knight's argument is that the father was Clarence. However, far more questions are posed by the entry on Alice's marriage certificate – she married in July 1918 when she was thirty-one – where her father's name is given as 'William Crook (deceased) – General labourer'. Two questions spring to mind immediately: was this done to conceal the stigma of her illegitimacy or was there an incestuous relationship between her mother and grandfather? Alternatively, if there was such a relationship, need it have been incestuous given that William Crook is said on one document not to have married Sarah until a year after Annie's birth and so may not have been her father? Could this explain why he and Sarah were living at separate addresses when he died? Either way, the marriage certificate is a fatal blow to the Clarence theory.

On 22 January 1889, just over two months after the Kelly murder, Annie and the four-year-old Alice were destitute and brought to the Endell Street Workhouse. Their last address was

The birth certificate of Alice Crook in which the name and
surname of her father is left blank

The marriage certificate of Alice Crook in which William Crook
is shown as her father

9 Pitt Street (later renamed Scala Street), Tottenham Court Road. They left the next morning before the visit of the Assistant Relieving Officer. It's worth noting as a rebuttal to Knight's theory that there was no attempt at concealment nor was any attempt made to detain them although we are supposed to believe that at this particular moment they were being hunted down by Sir William Gull's mad coachman John Netley.

In fairness to Knight it is worth adding that he suggested to Alan Neate that Annie may have used the surnames Maitland or Macklin, which points to concealment, but this was for the 156 days she was allegedly in Guy's Hospital after her abduction.

One name that Annie definitely did use was Greenwood (or Greenaud, which is the other alternative given). On 8 December 1895 her mother Sarah was taken from Bow Street police station to Bear Yard Infirmary as she had had a series of epileptic seizures aggravated by drink. Her relatives were given as the sister living in Soho Square and Annie Crook or Greenwood living at 91 Wild House and then at 1 Stephen Street, Tottenham Court Road. She subsequently lived at 23 Carnaby Street using the same surname. This suggests either a marriage or a common-law relationship – almost certainly the latter, as she drops the surname two years later. On 19 May 1897 Sarah was taken to Charing Cross Hospital suffering from a scalp wound. She had been found by police on the Dials (presumably Seven Dials) and had probably injured herself through an epileptic or drunken fall. Annie's address on this occasion is given as Mrs Greenwood, Room 91, Sardinia Dwellings, Drury Lane. Ten days later, when Sarah is in the Poland Street Workhouse because she is homeless and cannot be moved because of sore feet, Annie's address has been struck through, as has her surname Greenwood; in place of the address has been inserted, 25 Ward Westminster Union (the term Ward in this context meaning a district of the borough and not a hospital ward) and Crook substituted for Greenwood. Sarah had five days at the Poland Street Workhouse; a note on the form explains 'Appl. sent to Cleveland Street a few weeks back, but took her own discharge, not liking the food.'

On 29 April 1894 Alice, now nine years old, spent one day in the Endell Street Workhouse because she was destitute and her mother a prisoner (we don't know why or for how long). She was discharged 'to Northaw', an establishment which cannot be identified with certainty but which may possibly have been a charitable home called 'Mrs Kidston's Convalescent Home for Destitute Children' at that place.

Eight years later, on 26 August 1902, Alice, aged seventeen, applied to St Pancras parish (No. 7 Ward) for relief. She had measles and the form also noted that she was 'Stone deaf '. This was a permanent handicap, though whether she was born deaf or it was the result of childhood illness, we don't know. She was given meat 1s. and milk 6d. Under 'Occupation' the space is left blank, though possibly she may have been a charwoman like her mother and grandmother. A note says that the grandmother (now sixty-four) kept the three of them in food. They were then living together at 5 Pancras Street (later renamed Capper Street), Tottenham Court Road. They had one room for which the rent of 3s. per week was paid by a friend (Greenwood?). At this particular time four weeks' rent was due. There is no suggestion here of Sickert supporting the girl.

Six months later they were still at the same address. Annie was the only one who appeared to be working. She was then a casual hand at Crosse & Blackwell. Five weeks' rent was due. On 7

February 1903 Annie's epilepsy was so bad (presumably she was having fits) that the police were called and they in turn summoned a doctor at 2.30 a.m. She was admitted to the St Pancras Workhouse. On 28 October she applied for relief but appeared to be so ill that she was sent back to Pancras Street and told to wait until the workhouse conveyance called for her that evening.

Although there is only one recorded gap of three months (see table on page 241) and a break in the records of seven years (the records for Hendon Infirmary – now Colindale Hospital – are missing), it seems almost certain that the rest of Annie's life was spent in workhouses and infirmaries. Her admission record for 15 November 1904 mentions paralysis. Her death certificate in 1920 specifically mentions hemiplegia, paralysis of one side of the body. Medically it is possible that an aneurysm caused the epilepsy and subsequently burst to produce the hemiplegia. Another explanation for the arterial degeneration is syphilis, which might have resulted if she had ever earned money as a prostitute as so many women were forced to do in similar circumstances; a conviction for prostitution might explain her imprisonment in 1894. Whatever the reason, her partial paralysis does suggest some mobility which might have led to her temporary discharge from hospital on 7 August 1906. Clearly there was a deterioration. Three months later she was readmitted to hospital where the worsening condition confined her for the rest of her life. Alice was admitted to the Poland Street Workhouse on 11 October 1905. The cause of her distress was given as her deafness and a bad foot. Eight years later, when she was admitted with her grandmother to the Endell Street Workhouse, both women were described as market porteresses with Messrs Deaton, Covent Garden. Sarah was then seventy-five years old. She died on 18 November 1916 in Caterham Mental Hospital.

Annie died four years later in the Lunacy Observation Ward of the workhouse at 367 Fulham Road where she had been moved to four days before from the Fulham Road Infirmary (later St Stephen's Hospital).

Case notes dated 12 March 1913 had stated that Annie had 'spells of amentia. Is an epileptic.' Amentia is defined as absence of intellect; idiocy. Seven years later the notes for her last four days show that she was insane. For 20 February 1920 they read, 'Confused – sometimes noisy & hilarious, at other times almost stuporous – has delusions that she is being tortured – takes no interest in her surroundings.'

The end came on 23 February 1920: 'Sudden attack of cardiac failure which ended in death at 12.40 a.m.' Next of kin was given as a daughter, Mrs Gorman, of 195 Drummond Street, Hampstead. This was Alice, who two years earlier had married William Gorman, aged forty-five, a fish curer, and was the mother of Joseph 'Sickert' Gorman, the source of Knight's story.

Long before the end of Knight's book, one is asking over and over again, 'Where's the evidence?' The answer, of course, is that there isn't any. He has skilfully woven his story and tells it well; but where he can be checked, using the same documents, he falls down badly.

Let us begin with Sickert's studio at 15 Cleveland Street. There is no evidence that he ever had a studio in Cleveland Street, although he did have one at the same number in Fitzroy Street, only a short way away – but not until 1917. Knight quotes a great deal from Marjory Lilly's *Sickert, The Painter and his Circle*, which is where I suspect he got the numbering from. Allegedly, when Clarence and Annie Crook were abducted at the same time in April 1888, 'two men in brown tweed' went into the studio and brought out Clarence while a 'fat man and a woman' went into Annie's basement at No. 6 and brought her struggling to the street. They were then driven off in separate directions. It's a nice piece of fiction. Using the same directory and rate books yields the information that No. 15 and its neighbours were pulled down in 1887 to make way for three Middlesex Hospital establishments: the Trained Nurses Institute, the Residential College and the Medical School. Had the abduction taken place in April 1888 then there must have been a lot of surprised nurses or workmen looking on.

As far as 6 Cleveland Street is concerned, Alice's birth certificate confirms that Annie was living there when she was born in 1885. The ground-floor shop was run by John Pugh, hairdresser, and the electoral register shows James Hinton and Charles Horne also living at this address. Annie wasn't shown, since at this time women didn't have the vote. Knight argues that Annie was still living there when she was abducted in April 1888. She must have been living elsewhere between those dates for in that period Nos. 4 to 14 were pulled down and replaced with a block of flats called Cleveland Residences. According to the rate book for 1888, there was an Elizabeth Cook living in the basement of No. 6. According to Knight, he had been told by Joseph Sickert that Crook was often rendered as Cook (there is no evidence for this in the workhouse records), and this was the information he was looking for. Unfortunately for Knight, Elizabeth Cook was still living there in 1893, so clearly the two women were not the same. Further proof that Elizabeth Cook is not Annie Elizabeth Crook is that when Annie and Alice were admitted to the Endell Street Workhouse on 22 January 1889 their last address was given as '9 Pitt Street, Tottenham Court Road'.

So her abduction could not have taken place, either.

The next major stumbling block is Annie Crook's alleged Roman Catholicism. All the evidence actually points the other way, to the uncomfortable fact that she was a Protestant. Her daughter was baptized into the same faith and, even more damning, her admission entries into the various workhouses, infirmaries and hospitals make the same point.

The only discrepancy relates not to her but to Alice. When she was married, at St Aloysius's Chapel, St Pancras in 1918, it was 'according to the Rites and Ceremonies of the Roman Catholics', which suggests that if Alice was not a late convert, she had adopted her husband's faith on marriage. But even supposing that Annie had been Catholic there is still no reason why this so-called 'threat' to the throne had to be done away with by such bloody means. The Royal Marriages Act was – and still is – operative. Any such marriage between Clarence and her could have been set aside as illegal because not only was Clarence under twenty-five at the time but also he had married without the Queen's consent. The Act had been specifically designed by George III to stop his sons from entering into marriages of which he disapproved; he had used it to nullify the marriage of Augustus, Duke of Sussex, even though a second son had been born in lawful wedlock. It has been binding on the Royal Family ever since. Even without it, the authorities could have used the Act of Settlement (1700), which is still in force, and which expressly debars anyone who marries a Roman Catholic from 'inheriting the Crown'.

Knight's original trio of murderers is Gull, Netley and Sir Robert Anderson, head of CID, who is supposedly acting as a look-out. However, to resolve the inconsistencies in the story, as Knight himself admits, Sickert is substituted for Anderson. He becomes the third man, although his role is never clearly defined.

What value then can be placed on Sickert's claim that he once lived in the same lodgings as Jack the Ripper (see p. 163)? If he knew the truth about Clarence's marriage and his affair with Annie – which must have lasted from 1884, when Alice was conceived, to 1889, the time of the Cleveland Street scandal – why did he draw this red herring over the trail and why, if he knew the truth, was he himself never silenced?

Equally involved are the Freemasons who fear that they too will be toppled if the throne falls. Salisbury, Gull, Warren, Anderson and so on, *ad infinitum*, are Freemasons. Nobody is left out. They are all involved in the sordid cover-up of putting down five Whitechapel whores. The murders are carried out according to Masonic formula, hence the disembowellings and fearful mutilations. Nichols, Chapman and Stride are lured into the coach, driven by Netley, and fed poisoned grapes by Sir William Gull who subsequently mutilates them. Their bodies are later dumped in the streets which explains the lack of sightings, awkward times and few traces of blood at the murder scenes. Eddowes, who also used the surname Kelly, is (so the theory has it) murdered in mistake for Mary Kelly.

The book becomes more and more frustrating as one searches for hard facts.

Lord Salisbury, the Prime Minister, whom Knight accuses of being a leading conspirator, was not a Mason although the second Marquess and one of his sons were. Salisbury himself did not join (*Freemason*, 29 August 1903).

Knight expects the reader to take a great deal on trust but gives nothing himself. Compare his treatment of two men – John Netley and Dr Benjamin Howard.

His documentary proof for Netley's existence rests on three newspaper cuttings dated 1888, 1892 and 1903. The first refers to an unnamed hansom cab driver, the second to a man called Nickley who tried to drown himself, and the last to a horse-van driver, John Netley, who was killed in an accident near the Clarence Gate into Regent's Park (this seems to be Knight's sole justification for assuming him to be the same man). There is no proof that these three incidents were linked, or that Nickley and Netley were the same man. For the sake of the story we have to assume that they are.

But look what happens to Dr Howard.

According to the Chicago *Sunday Times-Herald* of 28 April 1895, Dr Howard was one of twelve London physicians who had sat as a court of medical inquiry and as a commission in lunacy upon a brother physician who had been responsible for the murders. The piece was headed 'Capture of Jack the Ripper'. Knight spends three-and-a-half pages proving to his satisfaction, if not to ours, that the unnamed physician referred to was Sir William Gull. While the book was still in proof, Richard Whittington-Egan published *A Casebook on Jack the Ripper*. By chance he had found in a London bookshop a letter from Dr Howard, angrily denying the story. The letter was dated 26 January 1896 and had been sent to the editor and publisher of

The People newspaper. He had been abroad and had only learned of the story on his return.

Understandably, he was furious. Knight calmly pooh-poohs his denial and says that he could hardly admit to having broken Masonic secrets and that the existence of such a letter is not surprising.

As far as Walter Sickert himself is concerned, Knight makes a great deal out of his eternal fascination with the mystery of Jack the Ripper. Having accused him of being directly involved in the murders, he cites in evidence Sickert's apparent preoccupation with a red handkerchief which he wore about his throat when working and which Knight alleges he wore on the night of the murders. What isn't mentioned is that this happened twenty years after the murders, in 1917, and was no more than a prop to help his thinking as he worked. He had many such props. Marjorie Lilly, whom Knight is quoting, describing this incident with the red handkerchief, says that:

he had two fervent crazes at the moment, crime and the princes of the Church; crime personified by Jack the Ripper, the Church by Anthony Trollope. Thus, we had the robber's lair, illumined solely by the bull's-eye lantern; when he was reading Trollope we had the Dean's bedroom, complete with iron bedstead, quilt and bookcase. The ecclesiastical flavour so congenial to him was somewhat marred by the red Bill Sykes handkerchief dangling from the bedpost; but the presence of this incongruous article in the Dean's bedroom was not a passing whim; it was an important factor in the process of creating his picture, a lifeline to guide the train of his thought, as necessary as the napkin which Mozart used to fold into points which met each other when he too was composing. Sickert was working now on one of his Camden Town murders and while he was reliving the scene he would assume the part of a ruffian, knotting the handkerchief loosely round his neck, pulling a cap over his eyes and lighting his lantern. Immobile, sunk deep in his chair, lost in the long shadows of that vast room, he would meditate for hours on his problem. When the handkerchief had served its immediate purpose it was tied to any doorknob or peg that came handy to stimulate his imagination further, to keep the pot boiling.

Knight further quotes Marjorie Lilly as saying that Sickert would have 'Ripper periods' in which he would dress up like the murderer and 'walk about like that for weeks on end. He would turn down the lights in his studio and literally be Jack the Ripper in word and mood.' But, again according to Lilly, Sickert 'had his Burns days, his Byron days, his Whistler days, his Degas days, his Napoleon days, his Dr Johnson days and many other days . . .' Osbert Sitwell makes the point, which helps to explain the above, that the artist is often his own model; it's cheaper for one thing, and with the aid of 'beards, coats, hats and the rest, it was possible at the same time to vary the person before him in the mirror'. It was a practice that Sickert had adopted from an artist friend who kept on the pegs in his studio 'the various disguises he wore when posing for the characters in his own drawings'.

Sitwell had one other piece of information that Knight missed. One of the stories Knight tells is of Lord Salisbury, the leading conspirator, visiting the artist's studio and paying him £500 for a picture for which he might have received only £3. When Sickert told the story to Osbert Sitwell he told it about an artist whom Sitwell calls Vollon. In the Joseph Sickert story, as told to Knight, the painter allegedly said that the incident really related to him. This caused Knight to speculate that the money was really payment for Sickert's part in the murders and for making the plan work. Had Knight gone on to read Sitwell's *Noble Essences* instead of confining himself to the introduction to *A Free House!* he would have learned that Sitwell had subsequently checked on the incident with the Marchioness of Salisbury and found that the painting by A. Vallon (not Vollon) was still at Hatfield and still showing the family group that Salisbury had asked the artist to include and for which he had paid the £500.

Whoops, there goes another 'fact'.

Whichever way you look, there is not a shred of evidence to

back up Knight's theory; there's absolutely nothing to connect either the Crook family or Walter Sickert (other than his curiosity about them) with the Jack the Ripper murders.

What, then, would he accept as evidence? Ironically, in the end, not even the public statements of his source Joseph Sickert.

Knight's book was originally published in 1976. Two years later, in the *Sunday Times* (18 June 1978), Sickert confessed: 'It was a hoax; I made it all up.' He went on to say that his part of the story was 'a whopping fib'. The only part he stuck to was that concerning his mother's parentage. The part about Jack the Ripper was pure invention. He said: 'As an artist I found it easy to paint Jack the Ripper into the story I had been told about Prince Albert Victor and my grandmother by my father when I was six years old' (in the book he was about fourteen). Sickert added that he had decided to confess because things had got out of hand. 'I want to clear the name of my father. I didn't think that much harm would come from it at the time because I thought the story was just going to appear in a local paper. As far as I am concerned Jack can go back to the Ripperologists.'

On 2 July 1978 Knight replied that he was not surprised that Sickert had now tried to denounce his book. He had threatened to do so after Knight had told him that his father, Walter Sickert, had been directly involved in the killings. He felt that by making the monstrous statement that he was the son of a man personally involved in the murders, he had betrayed him. He had begged Knight not to publish his findings about his father but when Knight refused, Sickert had said that he would find some way of exonerating him even if it meant denying the whole story. Knight says that he had been prepared for this and before showing him the last chapter had secured a signed statement that he had recounted his father's original story with complete accuracy.

Sarah Ann Crook (grandmother)

Periods spent in Workhouses and Infirmaries. Bracketed dates indicate consecutive periods of refuge.

St Marylebone Workhouse	19–21.8.80
St Pancras Workhouse	14.5.82 (1 day)
St Giles Workhouse, Endell St	5–12.6.91
	15–17.5.92
Poland Street Workhouse	13.8.95–9.9.95
St Pancras Workhouse	{12–24.10.95
Poland Street Workhouse	{25–28.10.95
	2–23.11.95
St Giles Workhouse, Endell St	8.12.95 (1 day)
	4–14.5.96
Strand Union Workhouse, Edmonton	10.10.96 (1 day)
Poland Street Workhouse	27.11.96–14.1.97
Strand Union Workhouse, Edmonton	19.1–13.3.97
	{20.3–27.4.97
Poland Street Workhouse	{28–29.4.97
Cleveland Street Infirmary	{29.4–18.5.97
St Giles Workhouse, Endell Street	{19–23.5.97
Poland Street Workhouse	29–31.5.97
St Giles Workhouse, Endell Street	28.5–9.6.98
	13–15.6.98
	29.10–2.11.98
Strand Union Workhouse, Bear Yard	{24–26.11.98
Strand Union Workhouse, Edmonton	{26.11.98–29.3.99★
Poland Street Workhouse	26.3–12.4.99
Strand Union Workhouse, Bear Yard	{14–15.4.99
Strand Union Workhouse, Edmonton	{15.4–6.6.99
St Pancras Workhouse	27.6–17.7.99
Strand Union Workhouse, Bear Yard	{28–29.9.99
Cleveland Street Infirmary	{29.9–25.10.99
Strand Union Workhouse, Bear Yard	{25.10.99 (1 day)

Strand Union Workhouse, Edmonton	{25.10.99–28.2.00
Cleveland Street Infirmary	3.3–19.6.00
Poland Street Workhouse	4.4–5.6.01
Strand Union Workhouse, Edmonton	{27.7–1.8.01
Cleveland Street Infirmary	{1.8–9.9.01
Hendon Infirmary	{9.9–14.12.01
Cleveland Street Infirmary	{22.12.01–26.2.02
Poland Street Workhouse	{26.2–5.4.02
	2.12.04–27.3.05
	11–12.4.05
	14.4–15.5.05
	{23.10.05 (1 day)
Cleveland Street Infirmary	{23.10–3.11.05
Poland Street Workhouse	{3.11.05–31.1.06
	2–5.2.06
	8–9.3.06
	11.3–9.4.06
	11–13.4.06
Strand Union Workhouse, Bear Yard	{16.4.06 (1 day)
Cleveland Street Infirmary	{16–25.4.06
Poland Street Workhouse	{25–30.4.06
Cleveland Street Infirmary	{9–22.5.06
Strand Union Workhouse, Bear Yard	{22.5.06 (1 day)
Poland Street Workhouse	15.11.06–30.1.07
	(With Annie and Alice. See dates)
Poland Street Workhouse	13.2–28.3.07
	5.10–9.12.07
	19.8–7.9.08
	16–17.9.08
	28.10–16.11.08
	15.3–12.5.09
St Giles Workhouse, Endell Street	29.4–14.5.13
	(With Alice. See dates)
	{12.6.13 (1 day)
Cleveland Street Infirmary	{12–25.6.13

St Giles Workhouse, Endell Street	30.6–1.7.13
Cleveland Street Infirmary	{1.7.13–?
St Giles Workhouse, Endell Street	{17–20.10.13
	{21.10–29.11.13
Tooting Bec Mental Hospital	{29.1–16.12.13
Caterham Mental Hospital	{16.12.13–18.11.16 (Dead)
(now St Lawrence's Hospital)	

* *There is possibly an error in date of discharge in view of the overlap with next entry*

Much as Knight didn't want to believe him, Sickert was telling the truth – the whole thing was a hoax. All the evidence confirms it.

At the beginning of his book Knight placed a quotation from *Twelfth Night*: 'here comes my noble gull-catcher' which, I have always assumed, was a compliment to himself for having provided, as he thought, the final solution. Clearly he didn't and the kindest thing that can be said about Knight and this particular piece of research is that he was (forgive the pun) gullible.

The extremes to which the Clarence theorists can go is best exemplified by Frank Spiering's *Prince Jack*. The author attempts to justify his bizarre creation by stating in the introduction that the book 'is mainly a reconstruction of what *I* feel did happen, based on everything I read, officially and unofficially'. His only original source of fresh material was the location, so he claimed, of a copy of Gull's notes 'bound in an ancient portfolio' and kept in the New York Academy of Medicine. Presumably it was from these that he was able to describe Gull's hypnosis of Clarence and his watching horrified 'as Eddy showed him how he slit the woman's throat'. From this examination Gull allegedly discovered the 'latent cause' of Eddy's demented state. The syphilis had thrust him into fits of fantastic rage. Violence was the outpouring of his pain.

Annie Elizabeth Crook (mother)

Periods spent in Workhouses and Infirmaries. Bracketed dates indicate consecutive periods of refuge.

St Marylebone Workhouse	18.4–6.5.85
	(With Alice)
St Giles Workhouse, Endell Street	22.1.89 (1 day)
	(With Alice)
St Pancras Workhouse	7–23.2.03
	12–27.3.03
St Pancras Infirmary	{28.10–12.11.03
St Pancras Workhouse	{13.11.03–13.5.04
Highgate Hospital (hemiplegia)	{13.5–11.11.04
St Pancras Workhouse	11–14.11.04
Poland Street Workhouse	{14.11.04–7.8.06
	13.11.06–3.4.07
	{(With Alice and Sarah. See dates)
Cleveland Street Infirmary	{3.4–11.6.07
Hendon Infirmary	{11.6–31.10.07
Cleveland Street Infirmary	{31.10.07–12.3.13
Hendon Infirmary	{12.3.13–?
Fulham Road Infirmary	{18–19.2.20
(now St Stephen's Hospital)	

Note: Both Annie and Alice also received out-relief from the St Pancras Board of Guardians between 1902 and 1903

Alice Margaret Crook (daughter)

Periods spent in Workhouses and Infirmaries. Bracketed dates indicate consecutive periods of refuge.

St Marylebone Workhouse	18.4.85–6.5.85
	(With Annie)

St Giles Workhouse, Endell Street	22.1.89 (1 day)
	(With Annie)
	29—30.4.94
St Pancras Infirmary	1—5.9.04
Poland Street Workhouse	{10—11.10.05
Cleveland Street Infirmary	{11—20.10.05
Poland Street Workhouse	{20—21.10.05
	{22—26.11.06
	{(With Annie and Sarah. See dates)
Cleveland Street Infirmary	{26—29.11.06
Hendon Infirmary	{29.11—4.12.06
Poland Street Infirmary	{4.12.06—28.1.07
St Giles Workhouse, Endell Street	{29—30.4.13
	(With Sarah. See dates)

Note: Both Alice and Annie also received out-relief from the St Pancras Board of Guardians between 1902 and 1903

The book has never had a British publication. This may be partly due to the faulty research and to the style, which the American reviewer, Dale L. Walker, described as 'concocted, Grade Z fiction':

Through the darkness he watched her lean against the wooden fence and begin to pull up her skirts. Eddy removed his coat, revealing the leather butcher's apron tied around his waist. She stared at him in a second, obviously trying to make out what he was up to. Playfully at first, he reached to her throat, grabbing the red bandanna. Then he let his knife slide out of the newspaper.

The woman gave a sudden grunt, and in terror began to push at him. As she tried to shove him away, with one hand clutching the bandanna, Eddy dropped the knife and hit her in the face with all his might.

She reeled back against the fence. He hit her a second time. Twisting the bandanna knot tighter, it seemed to take several minutes before her choking stopped. Then she suddenly sank backward.

Picking up the knife and levelling it at her throat, he hacked back and forth twice until the blade touched bone.

He could feel her wet blood all over his hands as he lay her down near the steps where there was more light. Tearing open the collar of her dress, he drove the knife into her chest, revealing her heart and lungs and then with another thrust he ripped open her stomach.

Spiering took exception to Walker's description of his book. Writing some weeks later to the newspaper in which the review was printed, he made the astonishing claim – not in his book – that 'the Gull papers contained the confession of Victoria's grandson, HRH Prince Albert Victor Christian Edward, the Duke of Clarence and Avondale, whom the Royal Physician was treating for syphilis. They detail the Prince's account of the sordid murders he committed in Whitechapel and his motivation for these murders.'

The thought that such a shattering confession might exist prompted Walker and myself to write to the New York Academy of Medicine in an attempt to locate these papers. In both instances the result was the same. A reply to my letter from the librarian dated 13 January 1986 stated that all of the material available for researchers is catalogued:

None of the entries in our catalogue for works by or about Sir William Gull contain the material referred to by Mr Spiering. In a library the size and age of ours, it is possible that a set of notes bound with a larger work or other works could have gone unnoticed by our cataloguers, but it is highly unlikely. Mr Spiering was never able to remember or reconstruct the catalogue entry he submitted for retrieval from our stacks and in which he allegedly found the notes by Gull. Thorough searches by staff also proved fruitless.

Losing possession of a document such as this – if it existed – is on a par with some of Spiering's other research. A full page plate of Sir Charles Warren is in fact a portrait of Sir Hector Macdonald, a contemporary British Army officer serving in the Sudan. The mistake was repeated in the paperback edition, even though it had been pointed out to him.

In 1978 Spiering challenged the present Queen to open the Royal archives on the Duke of Clarence, offering to stop impending publication of his book if she held a press conference and revealed what she knew about her 'great uncle's acts of murder and his own extraordinary death'. (The book suggests that Lord Salisbury, possibly with the connivance of Clarence's father the Prince of Wales, determined that he should be done away with and had him killed with a morphine overdose.) A Buckingham Palace spokesman said that his allegations were not sufficiently serious to warrant a special statement from the Queen, but the archives would be opened to Mr Spiering and he could examine them, as had other researchers.

Spiering's reaction to the offer – 'I don't want to see any files' – led to the inevitable conclusion that his challenge had been made to publicize his book.

Spiering failed to substantiate any of his allegations. In 1980 he was completing an article on Gull's notes and his discovery of them. It never appeared.

Grade Z Fiction?

Walter Sickert

Ripper and Royalty has been the perfect combination for the sensation seekers despite the ridicule that has been heaped upon the resulting theories. A comic book, with the Duke of Clarence as Jack the Ripper fighting Dracula for the love of Mary Kelly, had to be either a high or low point in Ripperana, depending upon your perspective. Sickert's name has continued to be bandied about as a suspect ever since Knight involved him in his trio or quartet of killers. A more determined effort than Knight's to put Sickert into the frame, was made in 2002 by the American crime novelist Patricia Cornwell, who pointed an accusing finger in *Portrait of a Killer – Jack the Ripper – Case Closed*, which of course it is not. Nothing in her book can point to that self-satisfying conclusion. Cornwell had already been pre-empted by Jean Overton Fuller's *Sickert and the Ripper Crimes* which was published in 1990 and which, as the title suggests, points to Sickert being the Ripper, but with an equal lack of evidence, some of it clearly picked up from the Knight–Gorman–Sickert theory, to substantiate the charge. Cornwell makes no acknowledgement to this work except for the book's title in the paperback bibliography.

Cornwell, having seen sinister undertones in some of his paintings, believes that Sickert was a psychopath, a fraud, that he may have murdered as many as twenty to forty people before he died in 1942, and that he continued to kill until he was burnt out. He was also one of the leading artists of the day. Many of his paintings hang in national collections.

Sickert's supposed motive for the murders is that he had a penile fistula which left him as a child emotionally and physically scarred. The evidence for this is a throwaway statement by a relative by marriage based on family hearsay. The reality is that the hospital where he was treated dealt with anal and not penile fistulas and, even if true, it certainly does not seem to have affected his subsequent affairs and three marriages. Sickert later declared that the operation had completely cured his problem. Nonetheless, Cornwell insists that it was a penile fistula and that his treatment at home and at hospital, and the resulting sexual failures, were part explanation for the Whitechapel murders. (Overton Fuller remarkably thought that seeing the first stage production of *Dr Jekyll and Mr Hyde* in August 1888 might have triggered something latent within him and brought forth the Mr Hyde side of his character.)

Cornwell's research involved DNA technology. One

complication was that none of the artist's DNA was available for comparison. When he died, he was cremated. There are no family members alive or known from whom DNA could be taken. There is no evidence for Joseph 'Sickert' Gorman's claim that he was Sickert's son; he was thirteen years old when the artist died, which means that Sickert had sired him at the unlikely age of sixty-nine.

DNA is passed down from both parents. Cornwell usefully makes a comparison with an egg; the nuclear DNA, passed down from both parents, would be found in the yolk and the mitochondrial DNA would be found in the egg white. Mitochondrial DNA was found on the Dr Openshaw letter; an Ellen Sickert letter; an envelope from a Walter Sickert letter; a stamp from a Walter Sickert letter; and a Ripper envelope that tests positive for blood but is so degraded that it might not be human. There is no way of knowing who any of this DNA belonged to. Statistically this mitochondrial sample excludes 99 per cent of the contemporary Victorian population which means that, with an estimated national population of more than forty million people, this DNA sequence could have been found in more than four hundred thousand persons. It has to be repeatedly stressed that there is no Sickert DNA for Cornwell's comparison. There is no proven connection between Sickert and the Ripper letters. Even a sample of commonplace stationery cannot make this link, although Cornwell struggles to make one. But, for a moment, let us assume that there was and that Sickert could be proved to have written this letter. So what if he did? It no more makes him Jack the Ripper than Tom Bulling, the journalist Best or his provincial colleague, or George Bernard Shaw, or any one of the hundreds who wrote such letters.

Cornwell's research was focused in part on the clutch of Jack the Ripper letters in the National Archives at Kew and the London Metropolitan Archives. What survives is only a fraction of what was known to exist. Those in the London Metropolitan Archives I rescued from an otherwise empty cupboard in the cellar basement of City police headquarters. The fact that many of the letters were missing their envelopes was entirely due to the fact that over the years the stamp collectors within the force had removed them, because they wanted the stamps for their collections. This made a precise dating of some of the letters impossible.

Cornwell became convinced, contrary to all logic and without any evidence to support her claim, that most, if not all of the public correspondence had been written by Sickert in a disguised hand. When I asked her at a Readers and Writers Roadshow publicizing her book, whether she had actually looked at the claims by the journalist called Best that he and a provincial colleague had written some of it, she said that she had not. Nor, in her book, does she even consider the possibility that Thomas Bulling was the author of the letter to the Central News Agency giving the name Jack the Ripper.

She finds further evidence of Sickert's so-called guilt in the series of paintings known as *The Camden Town Murder*. This was a commonplace murder in 1907 of a prostitute named Emily Dimmock. The woman's throat had been cut, but there were no other mutilations, which did not stop the newspapers from making Ripper comparisons. There was a newspaper story some years later that Sickert – who had moved into the area two years earlier – had seen the body before its removal to the mortuary. Cornwell's inference throughout is that he was the murderer and that he was back in business after a gap of nearly twenty years. Nowhere in her discussion of the case does she mention that a young artist named Robert Wood had been tried for the killing and acquitted.

The *Murder* series is a collection of paintings and drawings showing nude women, generally sprawling in different poses on beds, with a clothed man either standing or sitting close by. When they were exhibited one magazine described Sickert as an art anarchist 'representing the extremes of revolutionary modernity'. The increasing commercial activity of the art world meant that the artist had to sell himself in order to market his pictures, he must be a 'picturesque figure . . . or must have genius for self-advertisement before he can hope to be attractive to the public mind'. Sickert certainly knew about self-advertisement. He had been a professional actor before he was an artist. Contemporaries other than Osbert Sitwell have described how he liked dressing up as 'a cook, a raffish dandy, a Seven Dials swell, a book-maker, a solicitor, or an artist even'. His role-playing as Jack the Ripper, his claim that he had lodged in the same room as the murderer (one of his paintings is called 'Jack the Ripper's bedroom'), even that he had pencilled the name of the murderer into a book which was subsequently lost, were ways of advertising the *Murder* works by association with the Ripper murders.

The splayed position of the nude in 'L'affaire' may contain visual references to the Ripper murders since Kelly and Eddowes were found in the same position with legs splayed and heads turned to one side. Judith Walkowitz has argued that there was a domestic re-enactment of the Ripper drama between husbands and wives. Magistrates received many applications with regard to threats used by husbands against wives, such as 'I'll Whitechapel you'. It may be that it is this sick re-enactment during an argument about the rent that the works capture, which explains the lack of murders actually taking place in the pictures.

Cornwell tries to argue that the Camden paintings are further evidence that Sickert must have been Jack the Ripper, as only the murderer, apart from the investigators, would have known how the bodies had been left. Unfortunately descriptions had already been published in *The Lancet*, which Sickert, with his fascination for the subject, may have read or, as is much more likely, had seen in the book *Vacher l'eventreur et les crimes sadiques* which was published in France in 1899. Joseph Vacher was known as the French Ripper who confessed to the murder, mutilation and rape of eleven people. He was guillotined in 1898. The importance of this book is that the section on the Ripper murders published, for the very first time, the mortuary photographs of Eddowes and one of Kelly. As a regular visitor to France, and with his strong interest in the subject, almost certainly Sickert would have bought a copy of this book, which would explain the similarities of the poses, his ability to describe the mutilations and why, if he were the trophy hunter that Cornwell suggests, there are no paintings based on the Nichols, Chapman and Stride murders. That there are none is almost direct confirmation of the fact that the *Murder* paintings were based on the photographs in the Vacher book. It would also explain the dating of the paintings, which were done between 1907 and 1912. He links the Ripper murders to the Camden Town murder in order to sell them.

Cornwell is very selective in her evidence. One of her constant mantras is that she can't prove that Sickert did the murders but then no one else can prove that he did not. This is an outrageous statement. It is up to her to prove that he was the Ripper and not for other people to prove that he was not. Richard Shone, in a lengthy review in the *Spectator*, showed that there was ample evidence for Sickert being away on holiday in France at the time of the murders; this was dismissed with a throw-away remark that he could have made a swift Channel crossing to return and commit them.

By the end of her book, Cornwell herself seems to weary of the chase. Much of her evidence degenerates into personal statements with no hard facts behind them. Nothing she says comes close to offering a solution.

James Maybrick

In March 1982 a man calling himself Michael Williams telephoned the literary agent Doreen Montgomery asking if she would care to see Jack the Ripper's diary, which he was convinced was the real thing. The caller's real name was Michael Barrett. The diary was a scrapbook, hardbound in black cloth, with seven bands of gold foil across the two-inch spine. The first forty-eight pages had been cut out, with seventeen blank pages at the end; in between were sixty-three handwritten pages of the 'diary'. A small fragment of what was believed to be the torn edge of a photograph was lodged in the binding, which suggested that the cut out pages had had photographs mounted on them.

The writer was alleged to be a Liverpool businessman, James Maybrick, whose wife Florence was accused of murdering him with arsenic in 1889. She was convicted and sentenced to be hanged but was reprieved and the sentence commuted to penal servitude for life. She was released after serving fifteen years and died in America in 1941.

Everything about Shirley Harrison's book *The Diary of Jack the Ripper* has proved controversial. Its origins have been muddied from the beginning. It was said to have been found under the floorboards of Battlecrease House, Maybrick's home, when repairs were being carried out. Barrett would say that he had been given it by a drinking friend, Tony Devereux, later that he had forged it and later still that it had been forged by his wife, Anne. Two years later Anne Barrett, reverting to her maiden name of Graham after breaking up from Mike, would say that the diary had been a family hand-down from her father, and that, to preserve her anonymity, she had given it to Devereux to give to her husband whom she hoped would use it as the basis for a novel. She had done it in this way to stop her husband from pestering her family with questions. Her father would say that he had seen the diary in 1943 and was given it by his stepmother in 1950.

The book itself is genuinely old but whether late Victorian, or even Edwardian, is open to question. The major problem that has to be faced is: when did the ink go on the paper? Was the ink itself genuine? One of the experts hired to give a date to the diary's composition discovered in the ink a synthetic dye called nigrosine which, he said in his report, had been in use only since the 1940s and that the ink did not date from 1889 but post-1945. Subsequent research, however, showed that the ink had been commercially patented in 1867 and was in general use by the 1870s. According to one specialist, although the diary had passed a range of tests, a modern forgery could not be ruled out as 'someone just might have been able to synthesise a convincing ink or located a bottle of ink of sufficient age that was still usable (although these seem to be quite rare)'. A qualification that was made throughout these and subsequent tests on the diary was that further testing was essential to establish authenticity. Financial restraints, so its backers claimed, were a hindrance to the full testing needed.

According to Mike Barrett, he had bought the ink from the Bluecoat Chambers Art Shop, Liverpool. The owner suggested that it was possibly an ink supplied by Diamine, a Liverpool firm, which was almost identical to that used in Victorian times. Any expert would know that it was modern. Analysis of the diary's ink showed that it contained chloroacetamide, a preservative first marketed in 1974.

More potentially damaging to the genuineness of the diary was the discovery of a ladies' watch, an 18-carat gold Lancaster Verity hallmarked 1846, which had supposedly belonged to Maybrick, with the words 'I am Jack J. Maybrick' scratched across the centre together with the five Ripper victims' initials about the edge. Such a convenient discovery at this time immediately invited comparisons with the Ireland forgeries of the eighteenth century when William Ireland, to convince doubters of the genuineness of his Shakespeare manuscripts, immediately produced chair, candlestick and a host of other objects to vouch for their authenticity. Robert Smith, Shirley Harrison's literary agent, thought that the signature on the watch was similar to Maybrick's own signature. Writing one's normal signature on the strip of a plastic credit card is difficult enough; to scratch a normal signature on the inside of a ladies' watch plus a confession 'I am Jack' and the initials of the five victims is a feat worthy of admiration.

Dr Turgoose, at the Manchester Institute of Science and

Technology, using a scanning electron microscope to examine the inside of the watch, thought that the engravings might date back ten years, and possibly much longer but could not rule out the possibility of forgery as he could not conclusively prove the age of the engravings. 'They could have been produced recently,' he said, and 'deliberately artificially aged by polishing, but this would have been a complex multi-stage process, using a variety of different tools, with intermediate polishing or artificial wearing stages.' Another expert said that the engravings were of some considerable age and privately (why privately?), they could date to 1888 or 1889. Again there was the proviso that more work needed to be done to pinpoint their age.

Given that the estimated value of the diary if genuine was reckoned to be £4,000,000 it is astonishing that what might have been the clinching tests on it and the watch were never carried out.

But the biggest problem facing the investigators was that the handwriting of the diary did not match the writing and signature in Maybrick's will or on his marriage certificate. Nor does it match a lengthy inscription, in a Bible given by Maybrick to his mistress, published in Anne Graham's book. Handwriting comparisons were made by Sue Ironmonger, a member of the World Association of Document Examiners. She believes that an individual's handwriting is as revealing as fingerprints. 'It doesn't matter if a person is young or old, or switches from their right to left hand after an accident. The style may appear to change but, in fact, the components of every individual's handwriting remain consistent.' She could not link the diary with the Maybrick will, the Dear Boss letter and other Ripper letters in the National Archives. She is in no doubt that the diary was not written by James Maybrick.

Further evidence of Maybrick's supposed guilt was said to have been found in the Mary Kelly photograph. Bloodstains on the wall beside the bed (Dr Bond says 'arterial blood was found on the wall in splashes close to where the woman's head must have been lying') supposedly show the letters FM (Florence Maybrick). However, one of these 'letters' is partly obscured and, it has been argued, could have been the letter 'J' for 'James Maybrick'. This, frankly, is wishful thinking. Such letters, had they been visible, must have been equally visible not only to the police and doctors but to the inquest jury who visited the room. The journalist accompanying the jury describes how the inspector, 'holding a candle stuck in a bottle, stood at the head of the filthy, bloodstained bed, and repeated the horrible details with appalling minuteness. He indicated with one hand the bloodstains on the wall, and pointed with the other to the pools which had ebbed out to the mattress.' The fact that nobody mentions such letters is clear evidence that they did not exist. Reading letters into the bloodstains is like reading faces in the clouds; we are fooled, as Hamlet would say, to the top of our bent.

The diary is not a diary in the conventional sense with days and dates. It is a series of entries to which the reader must give his or her own chronology. This, I have always thought, was the cleverest part of the forger's skill as any 'wrong' interpretation or misattribution could always be explained away as reader error.

There is no hard evidence to link the persona of Maybrick, the Ripper and the writer of the diary. They remain separate entities despite the arguments of the diary's supporters to meld them together into one recognizable identity. *The Ripper Diary: The Inside Story*, published only in 2003, is a useful synthesis of the ten years of investigation into it. After weighing up all the evidence the authors were forced to conclude: 'Despite the many tests by experts in ink, handwriting and paper, for all the weighty opinions of historians, psychologists and authorities on the Ripper, not to mention the best efforts of Scotland Yard detectives, journalists and private investigators, over the last decade, we are no nearer knowing the true origins of this most controversial of documents.'

Robert Donston Stephenson

Self-styled Doctor Roslyn D'Onston.

According to Melvin Harris, author of *Jack the Ripper: The Bloody Truth*, *The Ripper File*, and *The True Face of Jack the Ripper*, here is the only suspect who has the right profile for being Jack the Ripper.

Robert Donston Stephenson was born in 1841 in Sculcoates in Yorkshire. His father was a mill-owner and co-proprietor of a manufacturing company. Stephenson had a good education, possibly in Munich, although he was subsequently to claim that he had medical degrees based on studies in France and the United States. In 1859 he briefly joined Garibaldi's army in the struggle towards a united Italy, inflating his age by four years, and gained the rank of lieutenant. As a boy he had always been fascinated by occult science and in 1860 was introduced to the writer Bulwer Lytton who initiated him into the hermetic Lodge of Alexandria. He was a pupil of Lytton's and came to know all the practices of the 'forbidden art' of Black Magic. In 1861 family pressure forced him to take a post, almost a sinecure, with the customs service in Hull, a job from which he was eventually fired. In the next few years he travelled widely in Asia and America, acquiring knowledge of magical practices, before heading for London and possibly living on some small family allowance supplemented by freelance journalism. He dropped the family name of Stephenson except on those occassions when he was forced to use it.

D'Onston was living in Whitechapel at the time of the Ripper murders. He was forty-seven years old. In appearance, at this time, he was 5 ft. 10 ins., of sallow complexion with a heavy, mouse-coloured moustache waxed and turned up at the ends, brown hair turning grey and of a military appearance. The person giving the description said that he was not a drunkard 'but a regular soaker – can drink from 8 o'clock in the morning until closing time but keep a clear head'.

On 26 July 1888 he booked in as a private patient, registered as neurosthenic, at the London Hospital in Whitechapel. As a private patient, it is argued, he would not have had the same restrictions placed on him as would other patients and so could freely move about the hospital and the extensive grounds which would have given him cover on his nocturnal prowlings. If he was Jack the Ripper then the first killing in Buck's Row would have been literally just across the street from the hospital, a walk of no more than three or four minutes. He would have been ideally placed to commit the other murders. The Ripper's killing ground was a walk of no more than thirteen to fifteen minutes across from west to east, between Buck's Row and Mitre Square, and about the same walking distance, north to south between Hanbury Street and Berner Street.

D'Onston's motives for the murders can only be guessed at. Harris suggests *inter alia,* the allure of the unknown, but argues too for a black magic/sexual motive involving ritual killing. A partial answer to the question of motive had been supplied by D'Onston himself in an article he wrote for W.T. Stead's *Pall Mall Gazette* of 1 December 1888 headed 'Who is the Whitechapel Demon? (By One Who Thinks He Knows)'. He puts the view that there was a distinct motive for the killings and mutilations, and that is that they were necessary to provide the substances essential to a black magic evocation of evil spirits and demons. Essential to some of its workings were substances which could 'only be obtained by means of the most appalling crimes, of which murder and mutilation of the dead are the least heinous. Among them are strips of the skin of a suicide, nails from a murderer's gallows, candles made from human fat . . . and a preparation made from a certain portion of the body of a *harlot.* This last point is insisted upon as essential.' The certain portion necessary was the uterus. The murdered were laid out in the form of a calvary cross.

In D'Onston's possession, one story goes, was a box containing five ties, each one stiffened, it was believed, with the congealed blood of the Ripper's victims. D'Onston, when boasting that he knew Jack the Ripper, explained that when the killer took away the missing organs from his victims, he tucked them into the space between his shirt and his tie.

The first four murders were apparently 'taunt and display' killings; being indoors, the murderer could afford to linger over the Kelly killing.

In November 1888, D'Onston asked Stead for money to hunt down the Ripper. Not surprisingly, as D'Onston was still in hospital, Stead refused. D'Onston remained in the London Hospital until 7 December 1888, having had a rest cure of 134 days. On leaving hospital D'Onston, living in a common lodging house near St Martin's Lane, met George Marsh, an amateur detective, who had himself been trying to hunt down the Ripper. They met two or three times a week and discussed the murders. D'Onston explained how the murders were committed. The killer, he said, was a woman hater and to get himself into a sufficient state of arousal would 'bugger' her and, with his right hand, cut her throat at the same time while holding on with the left. He told Marsh that the Ripper was Dr Davies, who had been a house physician at the London Hospital and lived in the locality of the murders. The two men drew up an agreement to share the reward that was being offered when they had procured the conviction of the doctor. In this agreement D'Onston is referred to as 'Dr R. D'O Stephenson (also known as "Sudden Death")'. The latter was a gambling term.

Marsh's statement was made on Christmas Eve 1888. On Boxing Day D'Onston went to Scotland Yard and made a five-page statement explaining why he thought that Dr Davies was the killer. One night he had seen him act out the killing on an imaginary woman and after learning from Stead that the last victim had been sodomized wondered how Dr Davies knew.

There must have been a follow-up inquiry from the police but, if so, the documentation has been lost. Certainly no action was taken against Dr Davies.

Inspector Roots, who wrote the covering report on D'Onston's statement, added that he was someone that he had known for twenty years. He was a Bohemian, drank heavily and carried drugs with him to sober him up and stave off delirium tremens. Recurring bouts of illness led to D'Onston's gradual decline. He converted to Christianity and worked for eleven years on a book, *The Patristic Gospels*. He died in Islington Infirmary on 9 October 1916.

D'Onston's illness, the alcoholism and the drugs that he had to take to stave off the delirium tremens would surely have incapacitated him from committing the Ripper murders. Having said that, W. T. Stead suspected him of the murders. He was not the only one. The police thought so too. He was arrested once on suspicion, although there is no surviving documentation to this effect. But supposing that he was the murderer, how to explain his mistakes? Why, for example, should he say that the Goulston Street graffiti was on the wall above the body of Catharine Eddowes in Mitre Square? Were such mistakes deliberate to convince people that although he had knowledge of the murders the mistakes proved he could not be the murderer? Or was it something less sinister? Inserting himself into the story may have been his way of being considered an authority on the murders and as a way of getting more work from his freelance journalism or borrowing money, as he had tried to do with Stead. As a private patient in the London Hospital, he would have been in a slightly more privileged position than the average patient to be aware of the stories and rumours that were current. He is not deliberately making mistakes to persuade people that he is not the Ripper. This is why he gets details wrong. He is recycling gossip. Either alternative has to be considered.

D'Onston is an interesting suspect chiefly because of where he was at the time of the murders. He is on the Ripper's killing ground, he has the medical knowledge to commit the murders and mutilations; he has to be seen as one of the more heavyweight suspects.

Michael Ostrog

Ostrog's name appears in the *Police Gazette* of 26 October 1888. His aliases are given as Bertrand Ashley, Claude Clayton and Dr Grant. At least another twenty were used, including Stanistan Sublinksy and John Sobieski. He was described as a Polish Jew, age fifty-five, height 5 ft. 11 ins. with corporal punishment marks on his back (presumably from a birching or flogging), dark brown hair, scars on the right shin and right thumb, two large moles on the right shoulder and one on the back of the neck. He was generally dressed in a semi-clerical suit. He served numerous terms of imprisonment, the earliest recorded in 1863 and the last in 1904. He did nine years of a ten-year sentence, given in 1874, and was released on licence in August 1883. In 1887 he was sentenced at the Old Bailey to six months' hard labour for larceny. Additional police information was that he was a surgeon by profession and a desperate man.

Ostrog was a confidence trickster and sneak thief. He does not come into the category of a major criminal. The sums and property involved seem to be very small – a gold watch from a barmaid, two valuable books from an Eton schoolmaster – but this should not minimize the fact that he was a dangerous man. He was in possession of a loaded eight-chambered revolver when he escaped over a roof from the police in West London. In Burton-on-Trent he was already a prisoner when in the police station he pulled his revolver on the arresting officer who managed to grab him by the wrist and turn the muzzle back on him. Some of his behaviour shows obvious signs of insanity, which is what he pleaded in September 1887 when he received his Old Bailey sentence. A doctor told the court that he was only shamming but before the end of the month Ostrog was transferred from Wandsworth Prison to the Surrey Pauper Lunatic Asylum suffering from mania, cause unknown. He was described as recovered when discharged on licence on 10 March 1888, but failed to report to the asylum.

The police tried to trace him through the *Police Gazette* in October 1888 but it was not until 17 April 1891 that he was traced and brought before the Bow Street magistrates and committed to a workhouse where he was certified insane. Two years later he was diagnosed as recovered and resumed his career of small-time thieving with occasional bouts of imprisonment, sometimes with hard labour. He eventually disappears from the records in 1904. His place and date of death are not known.

Ostrog can be dismissed as a suspect. New research shows that, unknown to Scotland Yard, at the time of the Ripper murders in 1888 he was in custody in France, where in November he began a two-year sentence.

Joseph Barnett

Suggested as a suspect by Bruce Paley in his book *Jack the Ripper: The Simple Truth.*

Barnett was a London-born Irishman, thirty years old, a licensed porter at Billingsgate Fish Market. He and the Miller's Court victim Mary Kelly were together for eighteen months. He had picked her up in Commercial Street and they began living together the next day. Their relationship was a mixture of violent quarrels and comfortable times. When she was not drinking Kelly was a nice and pleasant person. When drunk, she underwent a personality change and became very abusive. In appearance, she was about twenty-six years old of fair complexion, with light hair and attractive features. She would sometimes wear a black silk dress and often a black jacket which made her look shabbily genteel. The night of her murder she was wearing a linsey frock and a red crossover shawl. Neighbours said that she kept herself apart and rarely associated with them. Possibly this was through Barnett's influence. His money was keeping her off the streets although she still seems to have stayed in contact with old friends. Barnett possibly played up to her sense of difference. He alone referred to her as Marie Jeanette Kelly, presumably a reference to time she had spent in France. To everyone else she was plain Mary Kelly.

The couple moved into Room 13, Miller's Court, 26 Dorset Street eight or nine months before the murder. In the court there were six houses let out in tenements, mostly to women, the rooms being numbered. On entering the court from Dorset Street, there were two doors on the right-hand side. The first door led to the upper floors of Number 26. It had seven rooms. The first floor front, facing Dorset Street, was over a shed or warehouse, with large doors, which was used for the storage of costermonger barrows. Until a few weeks before it was the nightly refuge of homeless persons who went there for shelter; according to a *Daily Telegraph* report one of those had been Catharine Eddowes. The second door opened into Kelly's room, which was at the back of the house, and about fifteen feet square. Dorset Street itself, although only a short thoroughfare was made up principally of common lodging houses. The officially registered number of beds for the street was about six hundred but the number of residents is said to have been about fifteen hundred. Nine doors down, at No. 35, and on the same side of the street as No. 26, was Crossingham's lodging house from which Annie Chapman had been ejected on the night she was murdered two months before Kelly. At the top and bottom of the street there were public houses, the Britannia, known as 'Ringers' after the surname of the couple who managed it, on the corner with Commercial Street, was just across the road from Hawksmoor's Christchurch and the Ten Bells.

According to Paley, the deaths of Emma Smith and Martha Tabram may have provoked a strong reaction in Kelly; she may even have known them and possibly there was a sense of relief that she was no longer working the streets. But at this point, for reasons not known, Barnett lost his job at the fish market where he had worked for the past ten years. His earnings became irregular. He worked in the fruit market where he sold oranges.

The rent for their room, which was in Mary Kelly's name, was four shillings a week. According to his evidence to the coroner's court, when she died they were twenty-nine shillings in arrears. His money had kept Kelly off the streets but as the tensions mounted between them the temptation for Kelly to turn again to prostitution must have been overwhelming. Paley believes it was at this point that Barnett decided to turn murderer to terrorize Kelly into staying off the streets. He would read her the newspaper accounts of the murders, and wrote the Jack the Ripper letters to the press to guarantee their publication and to fuel her terror still further. In this he seems to have been successful, but the lodging debt mounted and Kelly, tiring both of her confinement and possibly of Barnett himself, turned once more to prostitution. She brought matters to a head by bringing another prostitute to share their meagre room of only fifteen feet square. It seems likely that the cramped space must have forced the three of them to share the bed as well. After two or three days, Barnett could tolerate the situation no longer. He and his 'wife' had a violent quarrel and Barnett moved out of Miller's Court and into a lodging house in New Street, next door to Bishopsgate police station.

According to Barnett he was playing whist in his lodging house until 12.30 a.m. on the morning of the murder. Paley believes that he subsequently went back to Miller's Court to reason with Kelly, to beg her to take him back and give up prostitution. Kelly, we know, had been drinking for most of the day and evening and another violent quarrel resulted, possibly there were taunts of Barnett's sexual and financial inadequacies, and it ended in her death and brutal mutilation. (On a personal note, I remember talking to Tony Mancini who was tried for the murder of Violette Kaye in 1933 for the Brighton Trunk murder. He was acquitted of the murder but years later admitted to it. I asked him what was the breaking point which provoked him to kill Violet. He said she was drunk, they quarrelled and throwing herself back on the bed with legs in the air and opening wide she gestured and said, 'That's what you're here for.' That was Mancini's breaking point. If Paley is correct, possibly something similar may have happened to Barnett.)

Barnett was detained for four hours of questioning by Inspector Abberline later that afternoon, and his clothes examined for bloodstains, before being released. Clearly the police were satisfied that he was not involved in Mary Kelly's death.

Others have agreed with Paley that Barnett was Kelly's murderer, but not with his scenario. The general agreement is that Barnett murdered Kelly after a violent quarrel and then, to make her death look like a Ripper killing, mutilated the body in the way that he thought from the press reports the other four bodies may have been mutilated. The possibility is that the Kelly killing had nothing to do with Jack the Ripper.

Dr Francis J. Tumblety

Tumblety has to be the most important suspect to surface in the past two decades. Completely missed by other authors, he surfaced in a 1913 letter by Chief Inspector J. G. Littlechild to George R. Sims, writer of perhaps the most famous and definitive Victorian ballad, 'It was Christmas Day in the Workhouse'. This letter eventually came into the possession of Stewart Evans, owner of possibly the largest collection of Ripperana in the world. It is a key document in every sense. Written by somebody who was at the heart of the investigation, it names the author(s) of the original Jack the Ripper letter to the Central News Agency and names Dr Tumblety as the man suspected to have been the Ripper.

Quack doctor, charlatan and misogynist, the Irish–American Francis Tumblety was born in 1833 in Ireland. The family moved to Rochester, New York when he was quite young and as a teenager Tumblety sold books (this seems to have been a euphemism for pornography) and papers on the canal boats plying between Rochester and Buffalo. He disappeared about the age of seventeen and when he returned home ten years later was as a 'great physician'. For somebody who had been described as 'utterly devoid of education' only a decade before, this might have been a striking achievement, except that his qualification was non-existent. His medical training had been acquired in a hospital in Rochester. In appearance he was a walking advertisement for his quackery. His flamboyance, his eccentric dress (including on occasions plumes, medals and big spurs), his white horse and the greyhounds and other dogs that followed him, attracted the customers. His profits from the medicines that he peddled, such as the 'Tumblety Pimple Destroyer' and 'Dr Morse's Indian Root Pills', brought him a good living and occasional brushes with the law. One patient died from his atrocious malpractice and there was an accusation of attempting to procure an abortion for a prostitute. Several times he escaped from towns just one step ahead of the law. He was not always so lucky. He was arrested and temporarily imprisoned for three weeks on suspicion of being involved in President Lincoln's assassination. It was in this Washington period that his hatred of women was made evident. At an all-male, chiefly military, dinner party he savagely denounced all women, especially prostitutes, 'cattle' was one of his epithets, before showing his guests into a room where one side was filled with large wardrobe-size display cases containing anatomical specimens; over half of them contained uteri from 'every class of woman'. His explanation for his extreme misogyny was that he had once been married and that he discovered only after their marriage that his wife was a prostitute who was still plying her trade.

In the late 1860s he came to England for the first time. According to Chief Inspector Littlechild he 'was at one time a frequent visitor to London and on these occasions constantly brought under the notice of the police, there being a large dossier concerning him at Scotland Yard. Although a "Sycopathia [*sic*] Sexualis" subject he was not known as a sadist (which the murderer unquestionably was) but his feelings towards women were remarkable and bitter in the extreme, a fact on record.'

The authors Evans and Gainey believe that on reaching London during a visit in June 1888, instead of staying in hotels as formerly he took up lodgings at 22 Batty Street, off Commercial Road, which was adjacent to Berner Street where Stride was killed. This, they believe, was his base when he killed Nichols, Chapman and Eddowes. According to newspaper reports the German landlady heard her American lodger return home early on Sunday, 30 September, the morning of the Stride– Eddowes murders, and later that day found that the shirt he had asked her to wash was wet with blood on the cuffs and part of the sleeves. As Evans and Gainey speculate that the Stride killing was a non-Ripper murder the blood-staining has to refer to the Eddowes killing. The landlady reported her suspicions to the police and they staked out the house hoping the lodger would return, which he never did. There were variants of this story in the newspapers. All of this is speculation.

In October 1888 Scotland Yard asked the San Francisco police to send specimens of Tumblety's handwriting, which they had offered to forward. They repeated the request on 22 November, asking that they should be forwarded immediately. On 7 November, two days before the Kelly murder, Tumblety had been arrested on charges of gross indecency with four named men. The date when one of these offences was alleged to have taken place was 31 August, the day of the Polly Nichols murder. He was remanded on bail of around £300 but, once released, jumped bail and fled to France. On 24 November, using an alias, he boarded a French steamer for the seven-day crossing to America. A report had already been published in the *New York Times* that he had been arrested on suspicion of involvement in the Whitechapel murders, but it was later said that, not having enough evidence to hold him for the murder charges, the police had arrested him for these lesser offences.

What then is the evidence for Tumblety being the Ripper?

Littlechild says he was 'amongst the suspects, and to my mind a very likely one'. Not *the* suspect, is what he is saying, but a possibility along with a number of others. According to Inspector Byrnes, who had Tumblety under surveillance after his arrival back in New York, there was no proof of the doctor's complicity in the Whitechapel murders and the offences for which he was wanted were not extraditable. He was also under surveillance by an English detective. It is hard to see why he was there if there was not the evidence to extradite Tumblety. Possibly he was hoping that the doctor would cross over the Canadian border to Montreal where he had an office. Once there he could have been arrested for the gross indecency offences, as English law applied in Canada, and extradited back to Britain.

Even more puzzling is Littlechild's assertion that after leaving France, Tumblety was never heard of again. The police surveillance must have been lax because on 5 December 1888 a workman saw him leave the house where he was staying (Tumblety was showing 'a great deal of nervousness', constantly glancing over his shoulder) and, making his way down the street, caught an uptown bus. According to one newspaper, people who knew him best thought that he was going to some quiet country town where he could rest until the excitement died down. Almost certainly this is what he did, because only a few months later he published a booklet he had written in the intervening period, *Dr. Francis Tumblety – Sketch of the Life of the Gifted, Eccentric and World Famed Physician*, attacking the 'reptile press' for the infamous slanders made against him yet skilfully evading all mention of his arrest and the charges alleged against him. Why, one asks, when Littlechild was so highly placed, and if Tumblety was such an important suspect, why did he not know any of this, even when he was writing to George R. Sims in 1913, ten years after the quack doctor's death?

Physically and in age Tumblety does not match any witness descriptions of the killer. He was fifty-five years old at the time of the murders. The man seen talking to Annie Chapman was around forty. This suspect was seen only from behind. Other witnesses speak of a man between twenty-eight and thirty-seven years old. In height Tumblety was 5 ft. 10 ins. Witnesses put the man's height between 5 ft. 3 ins. and 5 ft. 9 ins.

For the last ten years of his life, Tumblety lived with an elderly niece in Rochester, New York. Her house was both his home and his office. Clearly, with his whereabouts known and no attempt at concealment, if any evidence could have been brought against him for the Whitechapel murders it would have been. He died on 28 May 1903.

Frederick Deeming

Frederick Bailey Deeming killed his first wife and four children in 1891. Before emigrating to Australia with wife number two, he had disposed of their bodies under the kitchen floor of their home in Dinham Villa, Rainhill, near Liverpool. His second wife was murdered within a month of their landing in Australia. She was buried under the bedroom floor of the house near Melbourne. Deeming's prospective third wife was already on her way to meet him when the body of wife number two was discovered. He was arrested, and executed on 23 May 1892. In prison he claimed to be Jack the Ripper but this was mere boasting, since he had been in prison at the time of the Whitechapel murders. After his execution a plaster death mask was forwarded to New Scotland Yard, apparently because of the persistence of these rumours, and for many years it was pointed out to visitors as the death mask of Jack the Ripper; it is now in the famous Black Museum. This has helped to perpetuate the myth, which was also reinforced by the following piece of doggerel verse:

> On the twenty-third of May,
> Frederick Deeming passed away;
> On the scaffold he did say –

'Ta-ra-da-boom-di-ay!'
'Ta-ra-da-boom-di-ay!'
This is a happy day, An East End holiday,
The Ripper's gone away.

The Slaughterman

In *Jack the Ripper in Fact and Fiction*, Robin Odell suggests that the killer was a Jewish *shochet*, or ritual slaughterman, who was never caught or identified. In doing so, he makes the perfectly valid point that a current preoccupation with identifying the Ripper has sometimes led to exaggerated accounts of the murders and to a lack of interest in the murderer's probable motives and character.

In Whitechapel in 1888 there was a Jewish abattoir in Aldgate High Street where the slaughtering of animals regularly took place and where there must have been many *shochet* to cope with the demands of the expanding immigrant population. Possibly the *shochet* in question may have been a refugee from Eastern Europe who fled to America in the great wave of persecutions following the anti-Jewish decrees of the early 1880s. He may have stayed there for just one or two years before moving on to Britain and finally settling in London. This temporary residence in America might help to explain some of the obvious Americanisms in some of the Ripper letters, for example 'Boss'. Such expertise in slaughtering would explain why the police, in at least two of the murders, were baffled by the lack of blood. Odell attributes this to the manner in which the victims were handled – he compares it to the way in which the Japanese kicked away the trunks of the people they had just beheaded – so as to prevent the murderer's clothes from becoming bloodstained. Unfortunately, he completely omits to suggest that the victims might first have been strangled. Any blood would then seep onto the ground and be soaked up by the victim's clothes, which, the police reports confirm, is what actually happened.

In explaining his theory, Odell begins by quoting Dr G. Sequeira, the police surgeon who examined Eddowes, to the effect that the killer was no stranger to the knife. *Shochets* had considerable expertise with the knife – as they showed when performing the *shechitah*, or ritual slaughtering, which was 'designed to drain the meat of blood which was sacred to God'. In the abattoir the animal was prepared for slaughter by hobbling its legs with ropes and 'casting' its throat for the knife, which was long-bladed and carefully honed to give a razor-sharp edge. To comply with Talmudic law it had to be free of any nicks or blemishes, since to kill with an imperfect weapon would invalidate the slaughtering and the meat would be forbidden to Jews. The blade was tested by being drawn backwards and forwards across the index finger of the other hand and when the *shochet* was satisfied that the blade complied with the religious law he would give the benediction and draw the razor-sharp knife across the prescribed area of the animal's throat. A quick forward and backward stroke, and the work was done, the throat cut through to the bone. Death was immediate, and as the *shochet* stepped back the animal's life-blood gushed to the ground from the severed arteries and veins. Having done this, the *shochet* had to make a post-mortem examination, or *bedikah*, of the animal. First he had to make sure that the throat had been cut correctly and that the windpipe and gullet had both been severed. Next, he had to make an incision in the chest and examine the heart and lungs for injury or disease. A third incision was then made in the abdomen so that the stomach, intestines, kidneys and internal organs could be similarly examined. If there was any sign of disease or injury the meat was *trefah*, or forbidden; if not, the meat was marked kosher, or fit.

Some anatomical knowledge and a degree of skill were clearly necessary to remove these and other parts of the body, as prescribed by Jewish law, and, as Odell remarks, 'if there were any doubts about equating the elementary anatomical knowledge displayed by Jack the Ripper with the skill of a slaughterman,

surely these must now be dispelled.' Clearly, the *shochet*'s expertise
would account for the skilful butchering of his victims.

This may be so, but such expertise was not confined to a
shochet. Judging by the following letter, written by a contemporary
of the Ripper to the harassed police, it would have been possessed
by any good professional butcher. The letter is interesting and
worth quoting at length. Although it shows how a *shochet* may
have worked – assuming for the moment that Odell's theory is
correct – at the same time it disposes of his argument that an
ordinary butcher or slaughterman would not have had the
literacy to write the one or two genuine Ripper letters.

The writer was R. Hull, of 4 Bloomfield Road, Bow. The
letter is dated 8 October 1888:

From the age of 14 years till past 30, I was a butcher so that I can speak
with some authority. Doctors, I think, but little know how terribly
dextrous a good slaughterman is with his knife. There has been nothing
done yet to any of these poor women that an expert butcher could not do
almost in the dark. It is not known perhaps to the medical fraternity that
a slaughterman is a dexter handed man. Consequently Doctors are misled.
And as to the time taken by the murderer to do the most difficult deed
done as yet, I think it would be reduced to about one third of the time
stated by them if done by a practical man, which according to their own
evidence it must be or some one connected with their own craft. I cannot
think that inexperienced men could do it. I have never seen the inside of
a human being, but, I presume there is little difference between such and a
sheep or pig. I could when in the trade, kill and dress 4 or 5 sheep in one
hour. Then as to the blood, do not be misled, if done by a butcher he will
not have any or very little upon his person. I have many a time gone into
the slaughterhouse and killed several sheep or lambs and scarcely soiled
my clothes, that is when the weather has been fine and the skins have
been dry. It likewise occurs to me, that if done by a butcher he would
know his work too well to attempt to cut the throat of his victim whilst
standing up, but when they have laid down for an immoral purpose, then
with one hand over the mouth and the thumb under the chin, then with,

what is known in the trade as a Sticking knife, which is a terrible weapon in the hands of a strong butcher, in the twinkling of an eye he has cut the throat, then turning the head on one side, like he would a sheep, the body would bleed out whilst he did the rest of his work, from which the blood would flow. The only fear of making a mess would be the breaking [of] a gut or intestine and that would not be done by one knowing his business. The slaughterman's knives consist of a set of three; the Sticking knife which is about 6 or 8 inches long in the blade, with a thick back to keep it from bending whilst severing the Pith or Spinal cord. The next is a Dressing knife, a little shorter and wider than the Siding knife, which is a longer one than either of the others, curved at the end so that it shall not go through the hides. This knife is only used just for one particular work in dressing beasts. They all have wooden handles rivetted through the tang of the blade.

A *shochet* was a minor cleric, a person of high respectability and some education, and possessing a deep religious faith. Although he would be of some standing in the community, it is unlikely that his income would have been much greater than that of the lower-class elements among whom he lived and worked. His dark clothes and black frock coat would have given him the slightly shabby and faded respectability that matches some of the descriptions of Ripper suspects. Because he was such a familiar figure, and a person to be trusted, this might explain why the victims were willing to trust themselves to go with him and were temporarily lulled into a sense of false security. Odell points out that a well-dressed stranger might have worked his charm on one or two occasions; but that he should continue to do so goes against all common sense. Yet this is precisely what did happen many years later when the Boston Strangler was terrorizing that city; it went against all the rules that he should have been able to persuade these women to open their doors to him, a perfect stranger, especially when their doors had been reinforced with locks and chains for the very purpose of keeping him out. How much easier it must have been in London's East End for the

Ripper to have persuaded women to go with him when they were starving, cold and ill, desperately in need of the few pence that he would give them for some food and perhaps even shelter.

Odell's theory is that the Ripper was possibly a psychopath suffering from some sort of religious mania: 'A ritual slaughterman steeped in Old Testament law might have felt some religious justification for killing prostitutes.' He draws a colourful picture of this man's background and mental state:

Lurking behind the respected character of the ritual slaughterman was the mind of a sexual sadist tormented with hideous desires. The tiger's heart was filled with cunning, premeditation, and fiendish delight in the perverted and these were the tools of his ambition. His distorted mind drove him to seek gratification for blood-lust in a manner that mirrored his professional ability. Jack the Ripper did not commit those terrible crimes because he was a slaughterman. He killed because he was a psychopath, but inevitably his perversions drew strength from his training and skill as a slaughterman.

Remorse was an alien feeling to the Ripper, for his mind was filled with an overpowering appetite that only death could end. In his twisted way he could claim, too, a sense of religious justification in clearing the East End streets of harlots. In such ways do wretched prostitutes become the butt of the sexual psychopath's inadequacy. Incapable of normal sexual relations, and inferior to the task of seduction, these perverts often seek the easy acceptance of prostitutes, and then in a cruel travesty of morals claim justification for killing them.

Unfortunately, it is impossible to agree with his final assertion that of all the potential murderers in London in 1888, the hypothetical *shochet* alone possessed all the requirements of motive, method and opportunity to murder prostitutes in the East End. The methods have already been discussed, and as we have seen, an ordinary butcher had precisely the same expertise and could wield a knife with equal dexterity. Motive and opportunity are even more easily disposed of: a similar case could equally easily be made against any unknown living in the East End at that time, and would be just as difficult to disprove. If the Ripper did strangle his victims – and the evidence suggests that he did – then Odell's theory falls to the ground. It is only by agreeing with Odell's argument totally and uncritically that we can accept it. Unfortunately, the facts are too few to do this.

In explanation of the Ripper's ceasing his activity after Miller's Court, Odell suggests that he was discovered by his own people who may have dealt with him according to their own brand of justice in preference to having him before the English courts. This would have effectively countered any of the outbreaks of anti-Semitism that Sir Charles Warren had feared might lead to rioting in the East End and which had prompted him to rub out the message on the wall. According to Sir Robert Anderson in his memoirs, *The Lighter Side of my Official Life*, the Ripper was a Polish Jew and it was 'a remarkable fact that people of that class in the East End will not give up one of their number to Gentile Justice'.

After the 'double event' which involved them for the first time, the City police didn't overlook the possibility that the Ripper might be a Jewish slaughterman. Replying to one correspondent who suggested that as 'Hebrew Butchers are special Adepts at Cutting the Throats of Animals and avoiding the force of Blood wouldn't it be worth While to ask the Inspectors of Slaughter Houses to take quiet observation of any Man using the Knife with the Left Hand,' Henry Smith answered, instructing a secretary on the back of the letter in red ink: 'Thank him for the suggestion and say we have accounted for the times of all the butchers and slaughterers.'

Smith pragmatically gave a set of *shochets*' knives to the City police surgeon, Dr Gordon Brown, to see if they could have been used in the murders. His report was that such knives could not have been used because of their curved ends. This information was given to the *Jewish Chronicle* to counter the rumours that the murderer was a Jew.

Perhaps the last word on this particular theory should be left to the anonymous scribbler who wrote:

> I'm not a butcher,
> I'm not a Yid, Nor yet a foreign skipper,
> But I'm your own light-hearted friend,
> Yours truly Jack the Ripper.

Jill the Ripper

William Stewart in his book set himself a more modest objective. He didn't try to prove the Ripper's identity but only the class of person that he might have been. He began by asking four questions: (1) what sort of person was it that could move about at night without arousing the suspicions of his own household or of other people that he might have met? (2) who could walk through the streets in bloodstained clothing without arousing too much comment? (3) who would have had the elementary knowledge and skill to have committed the mutilations? and (4) who could have been found by the body and yet given a satisfactory alibi for being there?

At first glance, the solution would seem to be a policeman. The only objection to this might be a low score under (3) – but even this could be overcome if it is remembered that most policemen were ex-army men with enough overseas experience of war to have given them a working knowledge of slaughtering, of both animals and men, and the treating of wounds. However, Stewart's choice was for a woman who was or had been a midwife. Such a woman might also have been an abortionist. Stewart postulates that she might have been betrayed by a married woman she had tried to help and sent to prison; as a result, this was her way of revenging herself on her own sex.

Stewart argued that such a woman would have had the theoretical knowledge for committing the mutilations. She could have moved about the streets at night without arousing suspicion, and she would have had the confidence of her victims. Her bloodstained clothing could have been explained away by a difficult birth or from her examination of one of the victims to see if she was alive. Alternatively, the clothes of the period would have enabled her to turn her skirts and cloak inside out to conceal the bloodstains.

Stewart makes a great deal of the point about bloodstained clothing, but he never seems to have considered the possibility of strangulation. He always assumes that the murderer must have walked away bespattered with blood. The nearest he comes to recognizing that something such as this could have happened is when he says that the murderer 'would have been easily able to almost instantly produce unconsciousness, particularly in persons given to drink, by a method frequently used on patients in these days by midwives who practised among the extremely poor'. This remark is never explained, but presumably he is suggesting that midwives partly throttled their patients by exerting half-pressure on the pressure points.

His main premise that the Ripper was a woman was based on Kelly being three months' pregnant (which she was not) and so, as a young woman in danger of being evicted, she wanted to terminate her pregnancy. He suggests that the midwife/abortionist was called and once inside Miller's Court seized her opportunity and killed Kelly as she was lying helplessly on the bed. Afterwards she burned her bloody clothing in the grate and escaped, wearing Kelly's clothing. The chief objections to this line of argument are that Kelly's clothes were left behind and that the only clothing destroyed, judging from the ashes in the grate, were the shirts, petticoat and bonnet belonging to Mrs Harvey (whom Stewart does not mention). Certainly if bloodstained clothing had been burned in the grate it would not have given off enough heat to melt the spout of the kettle, as actually happened. Stewart's theory is an attractive one if only because it would explain the sighting of Kelly – in fact, the midwife in disguise – at 8 a.m., a few hours after Kelly's death. Stewart's secondary points are to underline his main contention that the murderer was a woman. He says that Nichols's bonnet must have been given to her as she would not buy a hat and leave herself without the money for the bed. He ignores the fact that nowhere is there any evidence to suggest that Nichols bought the hat herself. Her exact words were: 'I'll soon get my doss money, see what a jolly bonnet I've got now.' From this Stewart deduces that the donor was not a man – since if it had been she would have boasted of the fact – but a woman.

The chief flaw in the whole theory is that once again, with the exception of Kelly, none of the women are known to have been pregnant. In fact, in view of their age (most of them were in their forties), living hard and drinking hard, it would have been surprising if they were. Stride certainly was not, and it is equally doubtful that Chapman could have been, particularly after the beating, including a kick in the stomach, which had put her in the infirmary for several days.

Stewart's theory was updated in a series of articles written for the *Sun* newspaper in 1972 by ex-Detective Chief Superintendent Arthur Butler of New Scotland Yard. He claimed that the murders were committed by an abortionist who had been living somewhere in the Brick Lane area and that four out of the seven victims (he includes Emma Smith and Martha Tabram) died because of bungled abortions and had not been murdered at all. In fact, he said, the mutilations were an attempt to conceal her mistakes. Two of the other three victims were murdered because they knew too much, he claimed, and the third, Long Liz Stride, was not a Ripper victim at all.

Butler's source for this theory was unconfirmed gossip. None of his sources is given, except for a reference to nephews of people who were living in the area at the time, and it is difficult to judge, without knowing more of the facts, what value to attribute to his statements. However, he begins by saying that

Emma Smith was murdered by the abortionist and her accomplice because she tried to blackmail them for more cash, as apparently she had done in the past. He complicates the story slightly by giving Emma a partner with the unlikely name of Fingers Freddy who, among other things, was a street conjuror. Freddy disappears, possibly into the Thames, says Butler, soon after Emma is murdered by the abortionist's accomplice. Butler has ignored Smith's own evidence that she had been attacked by four men, as well as the testimony of the witnesses who took her to hospital. Instead he paints a harrowing death-bed scene with a constable sitting by her bedside waiting for any other clues that she might give him as to the identity of her attackers. Apparently Butler was unaware of the fact that Smith had been dead and in her coffin for three days before the police were told about the original assault, and then only because the inquest was to take place.

Martha Tabram was similarly murdered, according to Butler, because she knew too much about the abortionist's activities. Allegedly a friend of hers named Rosie Lee went to the abortionist on the Bank Holiday Monday for her pregnancy to be terminated. Later, when Tabram called back for her, she was told that Rosie had been treated and had left. When Martha still could not find her friend after several hours of searching she went back to the abortionist and had a flaming row with her, the inference once again being that the abortionist had bungled her work. (Since Rosie had apparently disappeared without trace, it is surprising that the abortionist, having once found a foolproof method of disposing of unwanted bodies, did not use the same method for her other 'failures'.) Martha Tabram, said Butler, was killed the same night to stop her from talking.

Butler goes on to say that although he has no evidence that Polly Nichols was ever pregnant he knows (but does not give his source) that she had visited an abortionist twice in the previous two years.

Apart from murdering Smith and Tabram and possibly Fingers Freddy, the abortionist's accomplice comes in useful for removing the bodies in a pram and dumping them in the street.

Annie Chapman was apparently trundled through the streets like this, which, says Butler, accounts for a handkerchief being tied around her neck in order to stop her almost severed head from dropping off completely.

Butler objected to Stride being included as a Ripper victim on two grounds: first, that the throat was cut from left to right, which is in the opposite manner to the other victims (though without knowing the respective positions of murderer and victim this is hardly a valid point); and second, that he would not have killed Eddowes if he had murdered Stride because of the hue and cry that was going on in Berner Street. This assertion seems to display a complete lack of understanding of the nature of the sadistic murderer.

His final points about Kelly's death are much the same as those that were made by Stewart.

To sum up, without knowing the precise nature of Butler's sources it is impossible to know just how much credence can be attached to his theory, which must be dismissed as unsupported conjecture.

8. Gaslight Ghouls

In 1973 the Bubble Theatre Company was touring the London boroughs with *The Jack the Ripper Show*. It was one of several plays that the actors had scripted themselves and performed in two molecular-shaped tents which they pitched in the local park, or on any open space.

To get the full flavour you had to go on a wet and windy night, as I did. Wooden folding chairs stood in rows around the stage, which was in the middle of the tent. The stage itself was a simple platform about two feet high. There was no scenery. As the audience came into the tent they were met by the cast who were in period costume and full make-up and singing music-hall songs to the accompaniment of a jangling piano. Everyone was given a cup of wine upon entering. As I knew some of the cast I was given two (which lulled a sneaking suspicion that all was not well when they isolated me in a gangway seat on the front row).

The play is about the Sharp family of Victorian strolling players. Since there are only four of them they have obvious difficulties when playing Shakespeare: their bowdlerized productions are known as 'Sharp's Short Shakespeare Shows'. The son suggests that instead of Shakespeare they perform a 'Jack the Ripper' show. A stranger whom they spot lurking outside the tent is hired to play the Ripper. (While he was waiting for his cue, this actor was kept busy chasing off the local kids who kept peering through the canvas and racing round the tent, shrieking and whooping, like Indians around a wagon train.)

The stranger is – naturally – Jack the Ripper!

For the new 'production', the play within the play, the title is changed to the much more dramatic 'Sharp's Short Shocker'.

An equally dramatic change comes over the cast. The son, in particular, wears make-up, pouts, leers and grimaces with as much verve as the master of ceremonies in *Cabaret*.

The highlight of the second half is a parade of Ripper suspects. First is the mad Russian with a waist-length ginger beard concealing the hammer and sickle tattooed on his chest. Second is Montague Druitt who changes his identikit as frequently as he changes his hat, from a deerstalker to a bowler and back again. Third is the Duke of Clarence – one of the girls in pink tights, top hat, black underwear and a cardboard moustache. Fourth . . . but there was no fourth.

At this point I knew why I had been put in the front row. Before I could move, a large number 4 was dropped on to my shoulders and I was yanked on to the stage. There were cheers and shouts as the audience was asked to show by their applause if they thought that I was Jack the Ripper. Naturally they did. All I could do was bow and accept the prize which was presented to me on a covered tray – a glass of tomato juice.

Mistakenly, I thought they had finished with me. They had not.

Just before the end of the show, Jack the Ripper ran away! As the show could not end without him, and the audience had already indicated that they thought that I was the Ripper, I was forced back on to the stage again to take his place on the gallows. After I had been 'tried' and protested my innocence – which nobody believed! – I was 'hanged'.

From which you may gather that any resemblance between this and the real-life murders was purely coincidental.

Why such a series of murders should have inspired a literature and culture all of its own is one of the more puzzling aspects of the crimes. Alexander Kelly and David Sharp's *Jack the Ripper: A Bibliography and Review of the Literature* (1995) lists 923 books and articles that have been published on the subject. The number is now easily in excess of one thousand. Denis Meikle's *Jack the Ripper: The Murders and the Movies* (2002) is a study of more than fifty film and television series episodes that have been inspired by the murders. The interest shows no signs of abating. Four magazines – *Ripperologist, Ripperana, The Journal of the Whitechapel Society* and *Ripper Notes* – are devoted almost exclusively to the subject and there is an expanding website. A partial explanation of this phenomenon might be that because there has never been a universally accepted solution, everyone is free to add their own ending to the story. It doesn't matter if it flies in the face of reason – which it frequently does; the point is that the explanation is credible to the person offering it. Better still, the unities of time, place and action can be ignored. Just updating Kelly and Sharp's *Bibliography* will illustrate the point perfectly. Stories have since been written of the Ripper fleeing to the American West, where he carries on his old habits by murdering dance-hall girls, local Indians and Mr Lusk. He has murdered his way through the galaxy to lodge as an evil force in the computers of the Starship *Enterprise* and been chased through time by H. G. Wells to modern-day San Francisco; he has danced and sung his way across innumerable stages; he has gone several rounds with Sherlock Holmes; he has become a class weapon in more recent political interpretations; and – the ultimate – as mad Brigadier-General Jack D. Ripper he has brought Armageddon to Stanley Kubrick's *Dr Strangelove, or How I Learned to Stop Worrying and Love the Bomb*.

He has been resurrected vampire-style from a coping stone of London Bridge, and as the mad Earl of Gurney in Peter Barnes's *The Ruling Class*, who believed himself to be both Jesus Christ *and* Jack the Ripper!

Jack has been hanged in fishermen's nets, burned, has died in an electrified pond (*The Night Stalker*), been stabbed in revenge by American Indians and nuked himself (as well as the rest of the world). He has been a duo and a trio of killers. Retribution has not always followed. He has been elevated to the peerage, had a sex change which turned him into Jane the Ripper (*Night Heat*), taken holy orders to become a nun of Calais (*The Great Victorian Mystery*), eloped with poisoner Adelaide Bartlett, transmogrified into Umbrella Jack for the centenary and in a complete role reversal become Sherlock 'Jack the Ripper' Holmes.

Jack's comic-book potentialities have been seized on by a number of authors, most notably by Alan Moore and Eddie Campbell with their blockbuster *From Hell*, on which the Johnny Depp film was based. The royalty link was continued in a four-part *Blood of the Innocent* which had Prince Eddy battling it out with Dracula who threatens England with a vampire reign of terror, up to the throne itself, because Prince Eddy has killed the woman he loves, Mary Kelly. Another royal note was struck with the three-part *Spring-Heel Jack. Revenge of the Ripper* when Prince Eddy returns to twentieth-century London and introduces himself at a film premiere to Princess Diana by pulling out a knife and asking her to share 'a few bits of your Royal innards with me'. Even Batman has been recruited: in *Gotham by Gaslight* Bruce Wayne was framed for the Jack the Ripper murders. Less well known was the identity of Jack Hack in the Swedish comic *Fantomen*. The story *The Phantom as Sherlock* has the Phantom – normal dress tights, trunks and mask – becoming a Sherlock

Holmes look-alike, to catch Jack Hack whose real name is . . . Rumbelow. The writer's explanation was that he had got so much from this book that he gave Jack Hack my name as a sort of thank-you!

Such an overview of the subject helps one to see that, broadly speaking, the fictional treatments can be broken down into four main categories.

Sensationalism

This first really needs no amplification. A cursory glance at the contemporary illustrated magazines and a lot of the literature since should be sufficient to make the point. What is surprising is just how quickly the public seized on the dramatic possibilities. First in the queue was J. F. Brewer who capitalized on Eddowes's murder within a matter of weeks by publishing a piece of nonsense called *The Curse Upon Mitre Square A.D. 1530–1888*. Eddowes, so the story ran, had been murdered on the exact spot where the high altar of Holy Trinity priory had once stood and where Brother Martin still hovered over the scene of the crime he had committed centuries before when, insane with passion, a dozen times he had gashed the face of the woman who had plotted to bring disgrace upon the monastery. 'With a demon's fury the monk then threw down the corpse and trod it out of very recognition. He spat upon the mutilated face and, with his remaining strength, he ripped the body open and cast the entrails about.' Horrors! It was his sister he had killed. In despair Brother Martin turned his knife upon himself. The monks tried to burn the blood from the altar stones but the spot was cursed. Over the centuries, every night between midnight and 1 a.m., a dark young man in the garb of a monk would appear and point to the spot, uttering strange prophecies of terrible events that would occur there.

In what must be a classic example of bad taste the pamphlet in which this tale appeared carried only one advert on the red ink wrapper of its back page: 'Warner's Safe Cure for Kidney and Liver Disease'.

In the immediate aftermath of the murders a showman had offered to rent Kelly's room for a month, and another to buy the furniture. Possibly he was successful because four months later, in February 1889, there was a report that a music-hall was presenting an entertainment, possibly a sketch, about the Ripper and Mary Kelly.

In Finland in 1892 Adolf Paul published what was possibly the first piece of Ripper fiction. This was a collection of short stories in Swedish called *Uppskäraren* (*The Ripper*). Few copies of the book exist (one is in the Royal Library in Stockholm) as it was suppressed by the Russian censor – we do not know why. The basic plot is that Paul visits Berlin and, while he is there, he collides with the Ripper who is running away from yet another murder and causes him to drop his diary. The book is badly written and it is possibly the author's attempt to explain away the murders through the Ripper's sex drive that gave offence, and may have been the reason for the book's suppression.

Desmond Coke's *The Bending of a Twig* (1906) has been described as

an extreme illustration of the whole school career of the hero being influenced, and partly destroyed through reading a queer selection of school stories, provided by a well-meaning mother, consisting of Hughes's *Tom Brown's Schooldays* (1857), Farrar's *Eric* (1859), Kipling's *Stalky* (1899), Vachell's *The Hill* (1905), and a probably fictitious story ironically subtitled *A Tale of Real Life* in which the headmaster turns out to be Jack the Ripper.

Neither was the theatre to be found lacking. In 1910 there was almost unbelievably, a one-act comedy. Of far greater significance, however, was the work of the German playwright Frank

Wedekind who was struggling with the writing of his play *Lulu*. This was within just four years of the last Ripper murder. Not until 1895 was the manuscript entitled *Pandora's Box* submitted to his publisher who was afraid of the legal repercussions stemming from the murder of the lead character Lulu by Jack the Ripper. This forced Wedekind to divide his play into two parts, *The Earth Spirit* (1895) and *Pandora's Box* (1902), now known collectively as *The Lulu Plays*. These became the basis for two twentieth century masterpieces, the film *Pandora's Box* starring the legendary silent screen actress Louise Brooks (1929), and Alban Berg's opera *Lulu* (1937). Berg described Lulu as 'a glowing fireball, singeing everything that comes into contact with her'. Two husbands die, she shoots her lover, is sent to prison and, on her release, becomes a prostitute. Lulu is a predator and in a world of predators it is her fate to fall victim to the male of the species. Both she and her lesbian admirer are stabbed to death by Jack the Ripper. The play *Lulu* by Peter Barnes from the same sources had its premiere in 1970.

In 1975 the Ripper was more of the voyeur in a Swedish porn movie, *Musfallan* (*The Mousetrap*). 'Mus' in Swedish is a colloquialism for the vagina. The film's mousetrap was a seduction chamber. The brothel madam was played by Diana Dors.

At this point the term 'sensationalism' requires further qualification. This is a purely arbitrary categorization, but in the sensationalist treatment of the murders Jack the Ripper is an eponymous individual, a human shell without character or identity, a shrouded knife-wielding demon. He is the caped figure walking through the nineteenth-century fog with the Gladstone bag by his side. Berg's Ripper is the top end of the market. At the other extreme are books such as Robert Bloch's *The Night of the Ripper*, which it is hard to believe came from the author of the excellent story 'Yours Truly, Jack the Ripper', which subsequently became a television play introduced on American television by Boris Karloff. *The Night of the Ripper* mentions the usual suspects and practically everyone else – or so it seems – who was living at the time, including Bernard Shaw and the Elephant Man; Oscar Wilde exonerates the Duke of Clarence while Conan Doyle identifies London Hospital probationer nurse Eva Sloane as one half of a murderous Jack the Ripper duo (she strangles, he stabs). Dr Pedachenko is the other half but (no playing fair with the reader here) he doesn't appear until page 220 of a 252-page book. What the book lacks in suspense it makes up for with nastiness by spicing the beginning of each chapter with totally gratuitous examples of sadism culled from all ages and countries. None of these have any relevance whatsoever to the book. As in Ellery Queen's *Sherlock Holmes Versus Jack the Ripper*, a burning house provides the author with his exit. Pedachenko breaks his neck, Eva is spiked on some railings, and what the flames don't destroy (the Ripper knives, Kelly's foetus and the duo's disguises) good old dyspeptic Inspector Abberline of the Yard covers up.

Fire again destroys yet conceals from the public the Ripper's true identity, an ex-Scotland Yard detective, in Lyndsay Faye's *Dust and Shadow* (Simon and Schuster, 2009). No surprise then, that fire once more is a useful plot resolution in *The Autobiography of Jack the Ripper* by James Carnac (Bantam Press, 2012). This is supposedly a memoir written in the 1920s and which has only recently surfaced. Paul Begg gives an analysis of the possible genuineness of the work, which has facsimiles of some of the typewritten pages, and attempts to explain some of the text's contradictions. Unfortunately the most detailed murder is Stride's which is nonsense when compared with factual and detailed documentation that we know about her last hours. This is a novel we are dealing with and not a genuine autobiography. Fire, so useful in these novelisations, is used yet again to bring about a plot resolution. Carnac is killed in a gas explosion which reduces him to some charred remains. Happily for readers, he has just completed his autobiography.

Identification

In this second category the best-known story is Mrs Belloc Lowndes' 'The Lodger', which has had numerous derivatives. The story originated at a dinner party when she overheard one of the guests telling another that his mother's butler and cook, who were husband and wife and took in lodgers, believed that they had let one of their rooms to Jack the Ripper. This snatch of conversation inspired her tale, which was published in *McClure's Magazine* in January 1911. She did not get one favourable review. She mournfully complained that for the American edition she hadn't been able to find 'even one sentence of tepid approval'. Gradually, however, public opinion swung in her favour, so much so that two or three years later the reviewers were perversely complaining that each of her new books was a disappointment, and why didn't she write a new 'Lodger'.

By 1923 the sixpenny edition alone had sold more than half a million copies. It was turned into a stage play called *Who is He?*, and then into a silent movie directed by the 26-year-old Alfred Hitchcock, who helped to adapt the story. Today it is hailed as the first true Hitchcock-style movie. The star was England's leading matinée idol, Ivor Novello, but because of his following the storyline had to be changed to show that he was not the murderer and commercial interests dictated that his innocence be spelled out in big letters. Hitchcock would have liked Novello to have been the murderer, but the change was probably for the better since, as Hitchcock says, a cinema audience finds it easier to identify with an innocent man who is wrongly accused than with a guilty man on the run. There is a greater sense of danger.

When the film was first shown to the distributors they hated it. They thought it too heavy and Germanic. Bookings made on the strength of Novello's reputation were cancelled and it was put back on the shelves. Several weeks later they had second thoughts and showed it to the trade, which went into ecstasies and hailed it as the most important British film to date. It was a smash hit with critics and public alike.

The effect for which it is chiefly remembered is a shot 'through' the ceiling of the lodger pacing backwards and forwards and making the chandelier in the room below move with him. Hitchcock achieved this by shooting from below through a ceiling of plate glass an inch thick. He had to do it this way because the film was silent; if he had been doing it with sound, he would just have shot the swaying chandelier.

The fiction which most consistently goes for a solution, and therefore an identification, is that in which Sherlock Holmes is pitted against the Ripper. Although Conan Doyle never wrote anything even remotely similar, he did tell a reporter for the Portsmouth *Evening News* (4 July 1894) how he thought Holmes might have tracked the murderer. Doyle said that he remembered going to the Black Museum and looking at the letter which was purported to have come from the Ripper:

It was written in red ink in a clerky hand. I tried to think how Holmes might have deduced the writer of that letter. The most obvious point was that the letter was written by someone who had been in America. It began 'Dear Boss' and contained the phrase, 'fix it up', and several others which are not usual with Britishers. Then we have the quality of the paper and the handwriting, which indicate that the letters were not written by a toiler. It was good paper, and a round, easy, clerky hand. He was, therefore, a man accustomed to the use of a pen.

Having determined that much, we cannot avoid the inference that there must be somewhere letters which this man had written over his own name, or documents or accounts that could be readily traced to him. Oddly enough, the police did not, as far as I know, think of that, and so they failed to accomplish anything. Holmes's plan would have been to reproduce the letters in facsimile and on each plate indicate briefly the peculiarities of the handwriting. Then publish these facsimiles in the leading newspapers of Great Britain and America, and in connection with them offer a reward to anyone who could show a letter or any specimen of the same handwriting. Such a course would have enlisted millions of people as detectives in the case.

In fact this was one of the methods that Conan Doyle used in the real-life Edalji case but without the sort of success that Holmes might have expected. Perversely, Doyle's Edinburgh tutor, Dr Joseph Bell, who was the model for Holmes, claimed to have solved the Jack the Ripper mystery (*Tit Bits*, 24 October 1911). Bell explained how he and a friend with an analytical turn of mind similar to his own set out to investigate. He told a reporter: 'When two men set out to find a golf-ball in the "rough" they expected to come on it where the straight lines marked in their mind's eye to it from their original positions crossed. In the same way, when two men made investigations on a crime mystery, where their researches intersected, as it were, gave an important result.' In line with these principles Dr Bell and his friend made independent investigations and placed their conclusions in sealed envelopes which they eventually exchanged. Both envelopes contained a certain name. They gave this name to the police and soon afterwards the murders came to an end – or so Bell claimed.

The Holmes stories usually depend upon the recovery of an unpublished Dr Watson manuscript. Ellery Queen's *A Study in Terror* (published in Britain in 1966 as *Sherlock Holmes Versus Jack the Ripper*) is one such book. It is an interlocking story of past and present events. The main narrative is Dr Watson's unpublished account of the case; the sub-plot concerns the giving of Watson's manuscript to Ellery Queen so that he can investigate and clear the name of the man whom Watson wrongly identified as the Ripper. The sub-plot was discarded, as was Ellery Queen's solution, when a film version was made in 1965: Dr Watson's 'false' ending made for a simpler and much better story. One reason why the book is so unsatisfactory is the denouement in which six of the principal characters are killed, murdered or commit suicide in a little over four pages. One impales himself on his swordstick; four more are burned to death; and the sixth is stabbed by somebody *pretending* to be Jack the Ripper.

The unpublished Watson manuscript in Michael Dibdin's novel *The Last Sherlock Holmes Story* is considered a 'criminological time bomb' with its disclosure that Holmes, tired of being the people's champion, goes over to the opposition. He turns the murders into a contest of skill between himself and the police, and he runs greater and greater risks to prove in the end he can be the perfect killer just as he is the perfect detective. This book probably contains the most bizarre scene in the Holmes canon, with Dr Watson spying on Holmes who hums 'La donna é mobile' as he skins and hangs pieces of Mary Kelly from the picture rail. Others have theorized elsewhere that one of the unrecorded Ripper victims was Mrs Watson whom Holmes murdered so that his lover, Dr Watson, would return to him and their old life at 221B Baker Street!

In Geoffrey A. Landis's novelette, *The Singular Habit of Wasps*, Holmes is once again found to be mutilating the Ripper's victims except that the Ripper is an invention of the press and the women have been infected by some alien from another planet who has been forced to crash-land on earth. Holmes's justification for killing and mutilating the Whitechapel women is that they are already dead, living dead, and he is destroying the large purplish-white eggs, each containing a monstrous coiled shape, with which they have been impregnated. The alien has taken possession of an earthling's body and when finally challenged and brought down with bullets and set on fire Holmes and Watson could see 'that where a man's generative organs would have been was a pulsing, wickedly barbed ovipositor with a knife-sharp end writhing blindly in the flames'. As they watch the death throes, 'it bulged and contracted, and an egg, slick and purple, oozed forth'.

As new suspects are regularly added to the Ripper canon it is always interesting to see their first appearance in fiction. In 1998, three years after Stewart Evans and Paul Gainey had resurrected Dr

Tumblety as a Jack the Ripper, he is fictionally masterminding some outrage on behalf of the Fenian brotherhood in Barrie Roberts's *Sherlock Holmes and the Royal Flush*. The year is 1887, Queen Victoria's Jubilee Year, and a performance of Buffalo Bill Cody's Wild West Show is held at Windsor Castle. Tumblety's men are to attack and murder the Prince of Wales and the four kings riding inside a stagecoach (the Royal flush of the title is four kings and an ace). Only the two cowboys riding shotgun on the roof, Holmes and Watson in disguise, can save them from assassination.

After such role reversal it comes as no surprise to find Professor Moriarty in John Gardner's *The Revenge of Moriarty* detecting Montague Druitt as the Ripper and faking his (Druitt's) suicide to bring an end to the case because of the police activity which is ruining the running of his East End empire. Other Holmesian characters have also had a hand in catching the Ripper. Holmes's mysterious brother Mycroft is well to the fore in Ray Walsh's *The Mycroft Memorandum*, and there is *The Adventures of Inspector Lestrade* by M. J. Trow. Once again there are walk-on parts for Oscar Wilde and Conan Doyle, plus Lord Alfred Douglas and even an infant Agatha Christie.

Sociology and Politics

Recent stage productions have fallen into the sociological and political categories. Writers have tried to use the murders to explain the issues of the day, which has meant less preoccupation with the Ripper himself and more focus on Whitechapel working life. Unfortunately this has generally meant a music-hall setting with noisy cockneys and crowds of women with their hands forever on their hips hollering and shouting, plus a lot of good-humoured audience participation – and ultimately little point to the evening's proceedings. When *Ripper* (1973) was performed by the Half Moon Theatre Company, each of the murders was committed by a different and sometimes unnamed suspect. For instance, the body of Polly Nichols was wheeled on by a woman (a backstreet abortionist? Jill the Ripper?) and tipped onto the stage. By switching murderers the play was able to illuminate different facets of Victorian society, moving from a rich man's viewpoint to an immigrant's, from a working man's to a criminal's. Characters included some rather crude stereotypes, such as the stupid policeman, the greedy capitalist and the worthy trade unionist. The last scene was somewhat numbing. After Kelly had gone into her bedroom with Pedachenko, one wall was removed and a carcass of meat, spotlit from above, was hacked about by a man in a butcher's straw hat and apron who then tried to offer chops and kidneys to the audience. The play concluded with the cast doing a slow-time 'Knees Up Mother Brown'.

A music-hall setting also provided the dramatic framework when *Jack the Ripper* opened in London's West End the following year. This production provided a musical reconstruction of the murders, set in a music-hall and surrounding streets, as performed by the inhabitants of Whitechapel. Montague Druitt was portrayed as an avenging angel from Toynbee Hall, founded by the Revd Barnett as the People's University. The best number was probably 'Ripper's Going To Get You If You Don't Watch Out'. The show has proved popular, especially in Sweden and with amateur groups.

More recent musicals have been *The Reward of Cruelty* (Taylor and Watson); Christopher George and Erik Sitbon's *Jack the Musical*; *Jack the Ripper* (originally *The Lodger*) (1999), a mother-and-son collaboration by Mary and Regan Ryzuk; and *Yours Truly, Jack the Ripper* (1998) a musical concept by Frogg Moody. The latter, with collaborator Ian Marshall, made a CD recording, *Angels of Sorrow*, which was based on individual interpretations of the musical characteristics of the five Whitechapel victims, linked with word portraits of each woman by five Ripper authors (Begg, Evans, Fido, Odell and Rumbelow). Carl Jay Buchanan made similar interpretations in his highly original investigative book of poems, *Ripper*.

Jack's Back! was an Off–Off-Broadway production by T. Schreiber Studios which was given its world premiere in 2012. It was described as 'a madcap look at one man, sausage-stuffer Herbert Wingate, who might be able to put a stop to the bloodbath'. In both Seoul and Tokyo the same year, a Czech musical *Jack the Ripper*, written by Ivan Hejn and composed by Vaclav Patejdl opened with Lee Sung-min, one of the first members of Korea's top boy band, starring as Dr Daniel, a young doctor claiming to know the identity of the murderer. The Korean production first premiered in 2009 and was adapted from the original Czech for Korean audiences.

Two other Whitechapel productions worth mentioning are the Curtain Theatre Company's *Hunt the Ripper* (1975) in Toynbee Hall itself and *The Harlot's Curse* performed in a disused Spitalfields synagogue in 1986. The former's programme was also part song sheet and the audience were invited to participate in the 'Eine Kleine Rippermusicke':

> Oh, oh, oh what a lovely whore,
> What do we want with Frau and Dame,
> When we can rip them into jam.
> As soon as I get them alone,
> I let my fingers roam,
> And I never care if they do not laugh,
> But scream and shout and moan.
>
> Oh, oh, oh what a lovely whore,
> I will never be satisfied,
> Until the very last one has died.
> Step outside if you'd like to see,
> A ripping good time down an alley with me,
> Oh, oh, oh what a lovely,
> Oh, oh, oh what a bloody,
> Oh, oh, oh what a deathly whore.

The setting played an important part in the Operating Theatre Company's production of *The Harlot's Curse* by Rodney Archer and Powell Jones. This dramatized documentary focused on the Victorian prostitute's life as personified by Mary Kelly. Sources ranged from Dickens, Stead, Blake and Shaw to 'Walter' (not surprisingly) and Flanders and Swann (most surprisingly). Kelly's fictional life from birth (actually Oliver Twist's) to death (Nancy's from the same book) was the single link with the Whitechapel murders. In between was a curious amalgam of information on sexual perversions, child prostitution, flagellation and upper-class whoring, with digressions on such matters as how to simulate virginity by means of small sponges of blood, the insertion of fish bladders or, more painfully, but requiring less acting, the use of fragments of broken glass.

A play, *Force and Hypocrisy*, and a movie, *Murder by Decree* (1979), can both be arbitrarily described as 'political' stories. The murders are part of the class war and in both instances the instrument of revenge is the coachman John Netley. In the former he is one of the 'have-nots' of the world and the final scene shows him triumphing over Clarence, who is wrapped only in the banner of the Social Democratic Federation. Clarence later cuts his wrists, a nonentity to the end, fearing to see a throne at the end of every room. In the latter Netley is the instrument of the ruling classes, murdering to prevent the ruin of existing society by a 'radical anarchistic ideology'.

Doug Lucie's *Force and Hypocrisy* openly acknowledges that it is based on Knight's book. Contemporary parallels such as mass unemployment, riots, trade unionists fighting the police, armed struggle in Ireland, murderous attacks on women, and establishment scandals are heavily underlined. The entry of a trade unionist is treated like the Second Coming, even down to the shaft of light. The aristocracy, on the other hand, are sado-masochistic perverts. Such soft targets contribute to the play's imbalance. An unusual touch is having Gull, after his stroke, confined under the name of Thomas Mason and nursed and breast-fed by Annie Cook (this is a name change). But the evening is Netley's.

Murder by Decree treads much the same ground but, possibly for legal or copyright reasons, there are name changes again – Sir William Gull becomes Sir Thomas Spivey, John Netley becomes William Slide – and the story is rendered much more fictional by the inclusion of Sherlock Holmes. One example of the author's juggling is that Annie Crook commits suicide and is buried at the same time as Mary Kelly. Although the film is extremely atmospheric, a long explanation by Holmes is still needed to explain the illicit marriage and the masonic conspiracy.

Ripper and royalty was an equally irresistible combination for Michael Caine's centenary offering *Jack the Ripper* and fourteen years later Johnny Depp's *From Hell*. Caine played Inspector Abberline as a drunk, while Depp showed him as a drug addict dying of an overdose in 1888 rather than as a respected police pensioner in 1929. While Abberline might have had something to complain about, Sir William Gull had even more cause to do so, for making him the Ripper in all three films led to his grave being vandalized. The same thing happened to James Maybrick's grave. No doubt, someone somewhere will slash a Sickert painting believing the Cornwell nonsense. Caine's film was hyped by claims that the company had been given access to secret Home Office files naming the murderer. This farrago of nonsense was eventually blamed on an over-zealous publicity department and, despite the claims at the end of the film, there was not a shred of evidence for the company's claim that they had solved the mystery.

Class warfare was once again the dominant theme of Robert Tine's futuristic 1980s novel *Uneasy Lies the Head*. Jack the Ripper imitation murders cause suspicion to fall on the newly crowned George VII whom palace revolutionaries hope to replace by his younger brother Eddie in order to save the nation from the cloth-capped yahoos who are ruining the country. Readers interested in such alternative histories of royalty may like to go back in time with Emlyn Williams's novel *Headlong*, which is about a 25-year-old actor called Jack Green who suddenly finds himself King of England in the year 1936. He is the Duke of Clarence's son by his secret marriage and, as rightful heir, displaces Edward VIII, later Duke of Windsor, to become King. But once he starts tap dancing at the Albert Hall, it is clearly time for him to abdicate.

In early 2012, Hammer announced that it had acquired the rights to *Gaslight*, by Ian Fried, which the project said would be 'an atmospheric thriller in the vein of *From Hell* meets *Silence of the Lambs*'. 'Secretly imprisoned in a London insane asylum, the infamous Jack the Ripper helps Scotland Yard Investigators solve a series of grisly murders whose victims all share one thing in common: dual puncture wounds to the neck'. A BBC One production opened late 2012 with *Ripper Street*, shot on location in Dublin, dealing not with the Ripper, but the aftermath of the Ripper murders and how they affected Whitechapel's H Division, now in a chaotic state after trying to keep order after the tumultuous investigations of the year before. One of the more interesting interpretations of the murders was the ITV show *Whitechapel* which, in its first series (2009), was an updating of the 1888 murders to the present day with the suspects, witnesses and policemen using the same names as those involved in the original investigation. The use of an enthusiastic London tour guide steered the detectives through the complexities of the original murders and the parallels he found with the contemporary twentieth-century murders.

Futurism

In the final, futuristic category Jack the Ripper is a time-traveller, part human, part spirit. He can be found arguing with the Marquis de Sade, solving the mystery of the *Marie Celeste*, escaping from H. G. Wells, stalking his eighty-eighth victim or provoking *Star*

Trek's chief engineer to murder. In Hammer Films's *Dr Jekyll and Sister Hyde* he is not only mixed up with the Stevenson character but with the body-snatchers Burke and Hare in his search for the elixir of life. Alternatively, he can become Al Borowitz's 'Umbrella Jack', the first Ripper to commit murder *and* suicide with a poisoned umbrella.

Sometimes, the perspective is that of the victims. In Patrice Chaplin's novel *By Flower and Dean Street* Jack the Ripper meets and kills 'Long Liz' Stride; the big difference is that it is set in modern Hampstead, Jack is an advertising executive called Ken, who writes dog-food jingles, and Long Liz a modern wife called Connie. Whether we are dealing with a case of possession or not isn't clear. Connie keeps experiencing a time warp which takes her back to Victorian Whitechapel and the persona of Elizabeth Stride. The reason for the haunting is that Jack (let's stay with the name) has returned to finish the killing that he couldn't complete in 1888. In the second half of the story Ken (or is it Jack?) is incited by Jack (or was it Ken?) to hack himself to death among the tomato plants in the conservatory. No more dog jingles for him – which explains one book review headed: 'The new Ripper and his tasty morsels'.

Taking the same character of Elizabeth Stride, a more subtle approach was used by Kay Rogers for her short story, 'Love Story'. The narrator is Stride herself, now a gin-soaked creature haunted by the clean, virginal and loving girl that she once was. However much she drinks she cannot stop this other self from haunting her. She knows that she will be free of this other self only if she can find the pure love that she once dreamed of and still craves. Eventually, she does find it – in a Whitechapel courtyard where she sees in the eyes of Jack the Ripper a pure 'scarlet' love. In that instant the other self deserts her, leaving Stride alone with the man who is about to kill her.

Finally, perhaps the best of the Ripper short stories, and one that certainly grows on the reader. This is Harlan Ellison's 'The Prowler in the City at the Edge of the World'. Jack is transported forward in time to the last city in the world, a place of antiseptic aluminium cubes from which the Whitechapel slums have disappeared and where there are only metallic buildings and a metallic sky. He is glad because (here the story is following Cullen's theory) he was motivated to commit the murders to bring about social reforms. But something is wrong. Suddenly there is a time transference and he is back in Whitechapel, committing murder once more. As he does so he understands what has happened. He has been brought forward in time by a group of hedonists so that they can batten and feed on his unspoken thoughts and sensations. This leads up to the most sensational motivation ever attributed to the Ripper, and one worth ending on: 'He hates them all, every one of them, something about a girl, a venereal disease, fear of his God, Christ, the Reverend Barnett, he . . . he wants to fuck the Reverend's wife!'

9. Beyond the Grave

According to a leading forensic pyschiatrist the multiple killer is increasing. The world's worst serial killer is thought to be a British doctor, Harold Shipman, who killed more than two hundred people. In June 1993 New York police announced the capture of Joel Rifkin, a modern Jack the Ripper who had admitted to the killing of at least seventeen prostitutes while cruising the streets of Manhattan. His truck carried the bumper sticker 'Sticks and stones may break my bones but whips and chains excite me'. In November 2003, a former lorry painter, Gary Ridgway, pleaded guilty to the killing of forty-eight women to become America's most prolific serial killer. In Britain in the same month, Anthony Hardy, 'The Camden Ripper', was convicted of murdering three prostitutes. In 1994, the Russian Andrei Chikatilo, the 'Rostov Ripper', was executed, with a bullet in the neck, after having been found guilty of the killing and mutilating of fifty-two women and children. He had murdered twenty-one boys between the ages of eight and sixteen, fourteen girls between nine and seventeen, and seventeen older women. There was the Polish Jack the Ripper who was first known as 'The Red Spider of Katowice'. In America in 1978 Richard Chase, twenty-eight, of Sacramento was charged with six murders; one of his women victims had been disembowelled to remove certain internal organs. In Britain in recent years there has been the Yorkshire Ripper, Dennis Nilsen (fifteen victims) and the Stockwell Strangler. The majority of murders are still committed in the domestic situation, where victim and killer are known to each other, but why there should be this increase in apparently motiveless mass killing is not clear. Nor is it possible to draw up a profile of the typical mass killer, as the motivation for such murderers, when it is known, varies greatly. The Boston Strangler had an excessive sex drive, Nilsen said that he had not known penetration for some years and Sutcliffe, the Yorkshire Ripper, penetrated only one of his thirteen victims. The publicity is an important element but again, like the sexual motive, is not true of all mass killers.

In some cases there is a clear identification with Jack the Ripper. In November 1972 the body of a young girl, well known for her casual sex relationships, was found lying on the floor of her London flat. Her head was covered with a towel, her skirt was rumpled up and about her waist, her bra was undone and her underclothing pulled down. There was a torn stocking around her neck. Her body glistened from a quantity of yellow, lemon-smelling, domestic fluid that had been sprayed over her and was running down her legs. The room had been greatly disturbed, but on the wall was a message, written in the same yellow liquid that was on the body. There was only one word: 'Ripper'.

In 1978, a fifteen-year-old boy was acquitted at Nottingham Crown Court of a Jack the Ripper-style murder. In court he claimed that his stepfather had told him about the Ripper and had taken him to see a film about the murderer; further, that the stepfather had a thing about stabbing women and used to stab nude pictures. He claimed that he had told him to stab the teenage victim 'like Jack the Ripper'.

The National Society for the Prevention of Cruelty to Children warned that warring parents are producing a new breed of mini Rippers. Because of the violence at home innocent children are being turned into potential psychopathic killers.

The sinister undertones of the Whitechapel murders are increasing rather than diminishing. For example, some years ago a man left a message with my colleagues asking if I would go to see him as he had a Ripper collection. Naturally enough, I was sufficiently intrigued to go to his house. It was on a bright Saturday morning in early summer. My host, a short, dark-haired man with a heavy jaw, was waiting outside to greet me. We went upstairs to his first-floor flat and he shut the door. Although it was only 11 a.m. there were heavy blankets, doubling as curtains, pulled across the window to keep out the light. There was very little room to manoeuvre. Behind the door was a double bed and at the bottom, wedged in between the wall and the bed, there was a table of which only one side could be used. I sat at this table while my host pottered about, making coffee.

Sensing my unease, he eventually pulled out his collection. It could be broken down into three categories. The first consisted chiefly of photographs of himself at the various murder scenes, dramatically pointing out the 'spot' on the twentieth-century pavements. The second consisted of tracings of the *Illustrated Police News* drawings of the Ripper's victims. Each of the bodies had been slashed with red ink to simulate the mutilations and was lying in a large pool of red ink; at some point he had run out of red ink and had changed over to green. He told me that he was hoping to make models of these, beginning with Mary Kelly.

The final category was probably the most frightening of all. He knew that I was interested in the affair known as the Siege of Sidney Street and so he had made a similar tracing of the shooting of the three policemen. Underneath it were other tracings of victims of the Nazis and Japanese war crimes. Most of these had been copied from Lord Russell of Liverpool's books *Knights of the Bushido* and *Scourge of the Swastika*. I particularly remember one of a Chinese man who had been bound to a tree, his eyes gouged out. As was the case with all these tracings, the only colouring in them was to indicate the mutilations.

By the time I had leafed through them all – I just did not grasp at first what I was looking at – I was feeling decidedly uncomfortable and a little bit scared. Suddenly I realized that neither of us was talking any longer, and that my host was staring at the tracings in my hand. His eyes glazed and he pushed his heavy jaw forward.

'I've always wanted to see a dead body,' he said.

Without once turning my back on him I rose to my feet (happily I was bigger than he was), made some polite excuses and left. I have not seen him since. Some years afterwards I was told that he was working in a hospital as a mortuary attendant.

Clearly, interest in the Ripper can be unhealthy. This is a fact often overlooked by those, such as myself, who play Hunt the Ripper. On 12 March 1974, Terence Collins, aged twenty-one, was found guilty of battering a 79-year-old woman to death with a tombstone as she knelt by a grave in a Surrey churchyard. After killing her he ran into the street and screamed at a schoolteacher he bumped into: 'Don't look at me. I will cut your face. I have got the devil in me today.' He then went into an antiques shop and said that he wanted a swordstick, sharpened to a fine point, and a black cloak with a red silk lining, 'like the one that Jack the Ripper wore'. When he was arrested and questioned the next day he told the police, 'Sometimes I think I am the devil; sometimes Jack the Ripper or a vampire or something like that.' The court was told that he had been in a mental hospital three times and was suffering from a psychopathic disorder. Collins pleaded guilty to manslaughter, with diminished responsibility, and was sent to Broadmoor indefinitely.

Three months later, on 4 June, eighteen-year-old Thomas Hopkins was jailed at Manchester Crown Court for life after pleading guilty to wounding with intent a 67-year-old woman. The judge told him that there was some dispute among the doctors about just how mentally ill he was, but all of them agreed that he needed treatment of some kind in prison. The prosecution said that when detectives searched his home they found documents relating to Jack the Ripper and a tea caddy containing photographs of Hitler. One of the documents read: 'Jack the Ripper. I have returned from the dead. I will kill again – I hate women (bitches).'

In September 1980, a former actor, John 'The Preacher' Sherwood, and a 'brother Christian', Anthony Strover, stamped, kicked and punched to death a 31-year-old mentally ill woman during an attempted exorcism to drive out the Devil. Both men belonged to a religious sect known as the Invisible Church which was based in Richmond, Surrey. Sherwood, according to one witness, looked 'like a Mormon off a wagon train. His beard was long and he looked just like a preacher.' Both men violently assaulted the woman during the two thirty-minute exorcism sessions and continued to beat her even after she had lost consciousness. The exorcism, Sherwood claimed, had happened on the spur of the moment. He said: 'The spirits were contorting her face. I wasn't meaning to harm her. She was full of the evil which kept showing itself. Looking back I remember pressing down on her body and rib cage and buffeting it with my hands, elbows and knees. I don't remember kicking her.' Strover said that he didn't believe that in exorcism the actual person could be hurt, that it was just the spirits being cast out. Sherwood explained that he thought the body had been injured 'by the great force of the devils leaving her – the last one was Judas Iscariot'. The other demon which had hovered over her body told Sherwood, as he called out to Satan and asked for the name of the Devil, that his name was Jack the Ripper. Sherwood told the court: 'I wasn't hallucinating in any way, it was a different being to me. It was against the Devil that my attack was directed, I believe he went out of her.'

Echoes of the Whitechapel murders can be found in these and many other cases. Yet only two categories can be considered as genuinely Ripper-style murders. These can perhaps be defined as firstly, those where all the victims are prostitutes, and secondly, where the murderer has consciously imitated his famous predecessor and has admitted it. Even so, this definition has its drawbacks, as there have been many prostitute killers, especially in continental Europe, where the Ripper has become something of a cult figure.

Ten years after the Whitechapel murders a French Jack the Ripper was sent to the guillotine. His name was Joseph Vacher. The fifteenth child of a poor peasant family, when he was eight years old he had been attacked and bitten by a mad dog. He would later claim that the resulting mental instability was the explanation and excuse for the murders, mutilations and sexual assaults which led to him being called The Ripper. In 1890, after conscription into the army, the official reports show that he suffered from a persecution mania. He would become over-excited. He believed that he was surrounded by and being threatened by unknown enemies. In this dangerous mood he would threaten to cut the throats of his fellow-conscripts with a razor; the threats were such that some of them would keep a bayonet by their bed in case of a surprise attack.

In May 1893 he was on sick leave when he quarrelled with and tried to murder a young woman in the town of Baume-les-Dames near the Swiss frontier. He tried to kill himself with the gun that he had used on her but only succeeded in damaging his left eye; he was left horribly scarred but refused to have the bullet extracted from his face. Committed once again to a lunatic asylum, he made several escape attempts. Less than a year later, in April 1894, he was discharged as sane, and free to begin a series of wanderings, killings and mutilations along the highways of France. In the cloth bag in which he carried his clothes he also carried a butcher's cleaver, a large pair of scissors and several knives. By 1897 he was suspected of having murdered at least fourteen people, including two shepherd boys and a shepherdess.

In the circular that was issued in July 1894 to trace him he was described as being about thirty years old, of medium height with black hair, beard and eyebrows and a bony face. 'His upper lip is raised. It is twisted to the left and his mouth contorts when he speaks. A scar runs vertically from his lower lip to the right side of his upper lip. All the white of his left eye is bloodshot and the lower lid has no lashes and is slightly raw. The man's appearance makes a highly disagreeable impression.' The circular concluded: 'This is the man referred to in the press as the "Jack the Ripper of the Southeast".'

The following month he was near Tournon, in the Rhône valley, when he launched an attack on a woman gathering pine cones, not seeing that her husband was nearby. Her husband heard the attack and with the help of another man managed to overpower him. Vacher tried to explain: 'I'm an unhappy man, a cripple, a good-for-nothing. I should be in a hospital. I desire women and they spurn me. If I go into a brothel, they take my money, are disgusted with me, throw me out without giving anything in exchange. I'm accused of assaulting people. But if I do anything wrong, it's God who makes me do it – and He will protect me.'

Astonishingly, it was not realized at first that the Ripper had been arrested and Vacher was remanded on a charge of having offended against public decency. The examining magistrate ordered further enquiries to be made and only then was it realized who the authorities had in custody. There was a prolonged medical examination, lasting until the summer of the following year, into Vacher's mental condition. The doctors' conclusions were that he was sane. 'His crimes are those of an anti-social individual, a bloodthirsty sadist, who believed himself to enjoy immunity because of the fact that he was not condemned by a court and because of being a released lunatic.'

His trial took place in the Assize court of Bourg-en-Bresse in October 1898. Outside the waiting crowds shouted, 'Vacher to the guillotine'.

The verdict was not in dispute. Vacher's plea of insanity was rejected and he was sentenced to death. Enormous crowds were watching as he was part-carried, part-dragged to the guillotine on New Year's Eve 1898. Vacher had fainted from fright.

Jack the Stripper

There are obvious similarities between the London 'Nude' murders of 1964–5 and the Whitechapel killings of 1888. Neither murderer was caught and, in both cases, the police investigation was abruptly terminated, apparently for the same reason – that the murderer was thought to be dead. The victims of both men were prostitutes. Jack the Stripper's had an extra peculiarity: they were all between 5 ft. and 5 ft. 3 ins. tall. In both cases there was the same intensive manhunt. Eight senior detectives, ranging in rank from Commander to Superintendent, led the Nudes investigation; between them they had solved between seventy and a hundred murder cases.

The six murders occurred in inner London between February 1964 and February 1965, when they ended abruptly. All the women were from the Bayswater and Notting Hill areas. Initially it was thought that there might have been eight victims, murdered over a much longer period. The two victims who were discounted were Elizabeth Figg, who was murdered in June 1959, and Gwynneth Rees, murdered in November 1963. Figg's partially clothed body was found on a river walk between Chiswick Bridge and Duke's Meadow. Both women solicited in the Notting Hill area. There were many similarities between their murders and the other six, but there were also enough inconsistencies in the murderer's modus operandi (such as leaving the bodies partially clothed) to make it advisable for the police to exclude them altogether from the Nudes investigation and to concentrate on those with a defined and well-established pattern.

The first Nudes murder was that of Hannah Tailford who was last seen alive when she left her home at Thurlby Road, West Norwood on 24 January 1964. She was a former part-time waitress from Northumberland who had drifted into prostitution.

For a time she had lived with a man named Walter Lynch and they had a three-year-old daughter. She used various pseudonyms, including Teresa Bell and Anne Taylor, and generally solicited in the Bayswater Road. Her body was found on 2 February 1964 in the Thames near Hammersmith Bridge. The flame-coloured blouse, dark skirt, dark blue coat and hat which she had been last seen wearing were missing. She was still wearing stockings, which were around her ankles, and her briefs had been stuffed into her mouth, presumably to stop her from crying out. From the injuries to her head it was thought that she might have been knocked unconscious and thrown into the river somewhere along Duke's Meadow, which was about half a mile away, and which was a local spot for prostitutes and their West End clientele as well as for courting couples.

About seven hundred people were questioned in the investigation. At first there was a strong suspicion that she might have been killed because she was blackmailing a client. She had a reputation for attending 'kinky' parties, and in a flat she rented in Victoria for purposes of prostitution the police found cameras and studio lighting equipment. However, strong though these suspicions were, the coroner's jury was impelled to return an open verdict. The bruising on her face was not conclusive evidence that she had been attacked. It might just as easily have been the result of a fall. It was equally possible – though there were strong reasons for doubting it – that she had committed suicide by undressing and stuffing her briefs in her mouth to stop herself from screaming in case she lost her nerve, which frequently happens with a certain type of suicide.

The post-mortem showed that she was pregnant. So was Irene Lockwood, whose naked body was found on the Thames foreshore ten weeks later on 8 April at Duke's Meadow, about three hundred yards from where the first body had been found. She had been in the water for about twenty-four hours. She was identified by her fingerprints and the tattoo on her right arm, reading 'John in Memory'. She had been strangled. She was found to have been friendly with a girl who had been murdered a year before named Vicki Pender. They had both been car prostitutes and taken part in the 'blue films' racket. At first it was thought that, like Hannah Tailford, she might have been killed because she had tried to blackmail a client with photographs; Vicki Pender had been beaten up a number of times for precisely this reason.

While this investigation was under way a man confessed to the first murder. At his trial, this 54-year-old bachelor said that he had only confessed because he was 'fed up', but the more likely explanation was that he had done it out of loneliness and the need for some attention. The police took his confession more seriously than they do the usual imitative confession (common enough during a murder investigation) because some of his descriptions of the girl, including details of her accent and clothing, were uncannily accurate. After a six-day trial he was found not guilty and acquitted. He told reporters as he left the court: 'I was confused and depressed although I shall never really know why I said I did it.'

The main proof of his innocence was that while he was in custody the Stripper struck again. This time the victim was a convent-educated girl named Helen Barthelemy, who had run away from home to Blackpool and had there worked on the Golden Mile as a striptease artiste. She had moved to London about a year before she died. Shortly before doing so she had been sentenced to four years' imprisonment for her part in a robbery, but the sentence had been quashed on appeal. She was a prostitute in the Shepherd's Bush and Notting Hill areas. Her body was found in an alley in Brentford, sixteen days after Lockwood's body had been dragged from the river. She had been asphyxiated and, from discoloration marks on her body which had been left by her underclothes, it was certain that her clothes had been removed after death.

Another factor, which was to be found also in the later murders, was that four of her teeth were missing – one, broken off, was lodged in her throat – although there was no evidence to suggest that this was the result of a blow. Apart from being the first of the bodies to be found away from the river, she also gave the police their first and apparently their only clue. On her naked body were flakes of paint. From the analyst's reports, it emerged that the body had been kept in or near a paint spray shop, perhaps a motor repair works.

Until now, the public and press had not realized that this killer was on the prowl. New Scotland Yard, however, took the unusual step of calling a press conference and giving the widest publicity to the three previous murders. In particular, the police emphasized their fear that if they did not get the information they wanted, another woman might soon be murdered. They stressed: 'This is urgently directed to all women whose means of livelihood places them in danger of meeting the same fate.'

As a result of this appeal, quite a lot of information was given to the police, particularly by prostitutes, about known deviants. For three months there was an uneasy lull, thanks to this publicity and to the increased police patrols in north London. Then, on 14 July, the Stripper struck again.

His fourth victim was Mary Fleming. She was last seen alive in the early hours of Saturday, 11 July. Her body was found in a half-squatting-half-sitting position outside a garage in a cul-de-sac in Chiswick. When she was first spotted at 5.30 a.m. from a bedroom window opposite, the man thought that she was a discarded tailor's dummy. Moments later, a motorist had to brake sharply as a small, dark-coloured van drove out of the cul-de-sac, narrowly missing him. He was so incensed that he called the police. Minutes later they were dealing not with a dangerous-driving incident but with a murder case.

Again there were some teeth missing from the victim, although this time they were from her dentures.

This case was still being investigated when the fifth victim, Margaret McGowan, was found under some debris in a car park in Kensington on 25 November 1964. The body was badly decomposed – she had been missing since 23 October – and her hands had to be severed and taken away in plastic bags to be fingerprinted. There were tattoo marks on her arms, and the words 'Helen, Mum and Dad'.

McGowan was a Glasgow girl who had come to live in Shepherd's Bush. She had three illegitimate children and several aliases, including that of Frances Brown. This had been the name she used when she gave evidence at the Stephen Ward trial, which saw the culmination of the notorious Profumo scandal, two years before. (I can remember her pacing up and down outside the Old Bailey, puffing away on a cigarette. She was a tough, hard-faced little Scot, wobbling precariously on her stiletto heels, with those incongruous-looking tattoos on her bare arms which were poking out of tiny puff sleeves.)

The closest the police came to a lead was through a girl she had been with twenty-four hours before she disappeared. The two were picked up in the Portobello Road by two men who, so the police later thought, might have been businessmen connected with the Earls Court Motor Show. Certainly the men seemed to know each other. They drove off together with one girl in each car. McGowan's car was lost in the traffic. Probably the driver was inhibited by his social standing from coming forward later; it is highly unlikely that he was the killer, but the police would have liked to eliminate him from their inquiry.

The sixth and final victim was Bridie O'Hara, last seen alive outside the Shepherd's Bush Hotel public house after it closed at 11 p.m. on 11 January 1965. Yet her body was not found until 16 February, behind a workshop on the Heron Trading Estate only a short distance away. The man who found her saw both feet sticking out from under a bush and also thought they belonged to a tailor's dummy. The post-mortem showed that she had been asphyxiated and strangled. Some of her teeth were missing.

The same day Detective Chief Superintendent John Du Rose, known to his subordinates as Four-Day Johnny because of the speed with which he normally solved his murders, was brought back from vacation to lead the investigation.

The most remarkable thing about this last murder was that the body had been partly mummified because of the conditions in which it had been kept. Rose's problem was to find out where. Similar paint traces and dust particles to those found on Barthelemy's body were present. There were also traces of oil. The bodies must have been kept in a factory or small shop where car repairs were carried out. From the spray pattern the police knew that the bodies had been kept in a small room next to the paint shop. Every garage, factory and repair shop which used a paint-spraying process was searched. Thirty-six detectives swept through the twenty-four square miles of London west of Paddington to find it. Hundreds of samples of paints were sent away for laboratory analysis but, with one exception, there was always some slight difference.

A system of 'flagging' was introduced as a check on cars. Any that turned up more than once in the same area during the night became suspect vehicles; three times or more and they were 'red flagged' and the drivers put down for questioning. If this system had been introduced earlier the killer might perhaps have been caught.

Eventually the place where O'Hara's body had been kept was found. It was in a transformer building at the rear of a factory on the Heron Trading Estate and opposite a paint spray shop. Analysis showed that the paint used here was the same as that found on the body. However, it seemed that this major clue was only incidental to the killings. The body had certainly been stored in the transformer, but this did not lead to the identification of the killer – although he clearly had a specialized knowledge of this estate. Policemen carried out checks on cars that passed through the estate and concentrated their efforts more and more on this small area. Du Rose waged a war of nerves on the Stripper. He didn't know his identity but, in a steady stream of press releases, he let it be known that the number of suspects had dropped from twenty down to three, of which the Stripper was one.

Du Rose guessed that the man he wanted was about forty years old and of strong sexual urges. Each of his victims had died at the moment of his frenzied orgasm. One theory which has been postulated is that some of the teeth had been taken out after death in order to permit further oral sexual release. Possibly, if just one of his victims had died through this particular perversion, he might have been acquitted of any charges brought against him. Another theory was that he might have been revenging himself on these women, who had all at some time had venereal disease, and with which he had become infected. A third possibility was that he was challenging the police to catch him by flaunting his killings, which he might have committed for a grudge motive. Nothing was too bizarre to be considered.

Yet instead of the murders continuing it soon became clear that they had stopped altogether. Gradually the number of police patrols in the area were reduced, and a degree of normality begin to return to north-west London.

The Stripper had been stopped – but how? Was he dead, in prison, ill or had he fled the country? Four-Day Johnny ordered an investigation to be made of all men who had been jailed since February 1965, and asked for details of London inquests for the same period on young and middle-aged men. It was while they were checking the background of a south London suicide that certain facts suggesting that he might have been the Stripper began to emerge. This man had had the ideal cover. He was a security man. On the nights when the women had been murdered, he had always been on duty between 10 p.m. and 6 a.m. His motives for suicide were obscure. He left a note saying that he was 'unable to stand the strain any longer', but there was no obvious reason for his death. Why should he take his life? And why, if he wasn't the Stripper, had the murders stopped since his death?

In spite of intensive searches of this man's home and garage nothing turned up, such as clothing or jewellery, which might have linked him firmly with the murdered women. His bewildered family could not explain his death and there was as much of a mystery about him as before.

The remarkable similarities of this case with the Ripper case are obvious and show just how the Victorian police, working on the same lines, could have back-tracked to Druitt. At least it demonstrates that an apparently motiveless death, a note threatening suicide, and the perfect cover for murder are not such unusual phenomena.

The Düsseldorf Ripper

On Friday 23 May 1930, Frau Kürten met her husband, Peter, in the Hofgarten, in Düsseldorf. After a meal, which she didn't feel like eating, they went for a walk across the Rhine bridge. They were an oddly contrasting couple. She was a gaunt, raw-boned woman, prematurely wrinkled, and he was a short, well-dressed man, wearing a hat, as was the fashion, partly to cover his neatly pomaded hair which was parted in the middle and partly to protect the powder and rouge on his face which made him seem much younger than he was. For once in his life Kürten seemed unnaturally dejected. He was deep in the grip of an uncontrollable urge to share his terrible secrets with someone else. His wife was the only confidante he had. Until a day or two before not even she had had the slightest suspicion that he might be the Düsseldorf Ripper, as the press called him. Even now, when he told her that he was the man who had committed the series of murders and attacks that had paralysed the city for the past fifteen months, she couldn't believe what he was saying. Finally, to convince her that he was indeed the man that the police were looking for, he took her step by step through the killings, giving her such a mass of detail that she was forced to believe him.

Kürten said later that his love for his wife wasn't based on sex but 'on respect for her noble character'. Probably his infidelities and his years of imprisonment and theft as a petty criminal had drained her of emotion. Her reaction now to his tale of horror was not one of fear for his safety, as one might have expected, but of fear for her own old age, unemployment and starving alone. Her grief was inconsolable. The only advice that she could give him was that he should kill himself and that she should do the same, as there was no hope left for her in this life. Eagerly, Kürten told her that there was, that he could help them both. He pointed out that there was a large reward being offered for his capture and that, if she told the police what she knew, then she would be entitled at the very least to a large part of it. He did not find it easy convincing her that this was not a betrayal in the true sense of the word. But after extracting from her a promise that she would not kill herself, he arranged to meet her outside St Rochus church the next afternoon.

Next morning he bathed, had his hair cut, and dressed neatly for the meeting. He spent part of the morning walking up and down outside the house of a widow whom he had marked down for his next victim. He was arranging in his mind the grand finale to his terrible career, but had not yet decided whether to kill the widow only or her family as well. His wife arrived, and as they stood talking four policemen with revolvers rushed forward and seized him. He had not expected her to carry out his wishes quite so soon.

His reign as the Düsseldorf monster was at an end. But the fame which he had sought, when, as a teenager he had stood in front of some wax models of murderers and boasted that one day he would be famous like them, did not elude him.

In the past fifteen months he had carried out a series of sex murders and attacks which are almost without parallel in the annals of crime. He was a pyromaniac, a fetishist, a masochist, a sadist and a sex killer. The best brains in the Berlin Alexanderplatz, as well as Düsseldorf's own efficient police, had been engaged in running him to earth. Nearly three thousand clues had had to be followed up, and over thirteen thousand letters of help had poured in from a terrified public. Nothing, not even spiritualists, mediums and amateur graphologists had been too bizarre to be used in tracking down this sadistic killer.

Peter Kürten was born in 1883 in Mulheim on the Rhine. He was the third child in a family of thirteen. His mother's family were normal, hard-working people. But the background on his father's side was far from normal: the family was noted for its arrogance, violence and megalomania, while criminal tendencies, feeble-mindedness, paralysis and delirium tremens characterized it. His grandfather had served several prison sentences for theft, and his children, Kürten's uncles and aunts, were alcoholic psychopaths.

Kürten's father was by profession a moulder, and he forced Kürten, who wanted to be a draughtsman, to be apprenticed to the same trade. He was also a brutal, over-sexed alcoholic. For long periods his large family lived in one room. Besides the constant brutality and the drunkenness, his long-suffering wife was often forced to have intercourse with him in front of the children when he came home drunk. Kürten said that if it had not been for the marriage bond, his father's aggressive brutality to his mother would have constituted rape. Eventually, when Kürten was in his teens, she divorced him.

Kürten's sisters were also heavily over-sexed. According to his own confession, one of them actually made sexual advances towards him. In 1897 his father was sentenced to fifteen months' imprisonment for attempted incest with one of his daughters, who was then only thirteen and a half years old. (It was this incident which seems to have given his wife the grounds for divorce.) Kürten himself tried to commit incest with the same daughter, his sister.

When he was only eight years old Kürten ran away from home for several weeks, sleeping, for part of the time, in furniture vans. In the next six years, he frequently repeated this episode. Some of the time, before he reached his teens even, he lived as a street thief, snatching purses and handbags from his victims, mostly women and young girls.

After his father came out of prison the drunken brutality became even worse and on more than one occasion he attacked

Peter with a knife. He began to threaten that he would cut off his head and once, Kürten said, he was prevented from doing so only by the screams of the other children. Kürten, by now fourteen years old and already apprenticed to a moulder, decided to escape yet again. He absconded with several hundred marks belonging to his employer but was caught and sent to prison. He was ashamed at first of the humiliation of being led through the streets in handcuffs. However, during the first of the seventeen sentences that were to take up twenty-seven of the forty-seven years of his life, he was so impressed by the hardened professionalism of the criminals he met that he had himself tattooed like them.

In prison he began to think about how he could avenge himself on society. While he had been on the run he had lived with a prostitute who had submitted to his sadistic practices. Even as an adolescent Kürten's sexuality was abnormal. As a boy his family had lived in the same house as a sadistic dog catcher. Dogs picked up on the streets and not claimed by their owners were killed for meat or for their fat, which was used as a special ointment by the superstitious. The dog catcher showed Kürten how to torture the animals, and the boy derived even greater pleasure from watching them being killed. Gradually, through reading and talking about his feelings, he began to understand his own character. Instead of attempting to control his impulses he gave free rein to them. From the age of thirteen to sixteen he practised bestiality with sheep, goats and pigs. His greatest pleasure, he discovered, was having intercourse with a sheep and stabbing it simultaneously.

According to his own statement, Kürten had already committed his first murders when he was nine years old. He had gone swimming with two boys and had pushed one of them into the river. When the other one tried to rescue him, he managed to push both of them under the raft, and they had drowned.

Of his time in prison, he wrote: 'I did myself a great deal of damage through reading blood-and-thunder stories, for instance

I read the tale of *Jack the Ripper* several times. When I came to think over what I had read, when I was in prison, I thought what pleasure it would give me to do things of that kind once I got out again.' (Consciously or not, he imitated the Ripper when he began his own reign of terror. A good omen was that the sky was blood red over Düsseldorf when he returned to the city in 1925, as it was over London in the autumn of 1888.)

When he was released from prison in August 1899 he resumed his career of petty thieving. He also began living with a woman, twice his age, who, significantly for his development, was a masochist. Whereas Kürten's other mistresses had unwillingly submitted to his perversions, this woman positively demanded them, which only served to increase his sadistic leanings.

In the November after his release, when he was just sixteen, he tried to strangle a girl while he was having intercourse with her in the Grafenberger Wald. He thought that he had left her for dead, but as no body was ever found and no murders were reported in the press for that month, it is probable that she regained consciousness and staggered home without ever revealing her terrible experience.

Kürten certainly thought that he had killed her. For the first time he had discovered that he could obtain maximum sexual release in this way, and from this point on he was prepared to go to these lengths to have such orgasms. It is significant that this happened within such a short space of time of his release from a long prison sentence. As a prisoner, Kürten had frequently committed minor breaches of prison discipline so that he could be further punished by spells of solitary confinement where, in the darkness of his cell, he could weave his fantasies and dreams of revenge. While indulging in these fantasies he would have seminal discharges. This, he confessed, would happen if he had imagined that he had cut somebody's stomach or injured them in some way. It gave him final and complete satisfaction. He also invented a number of schemes for smashing bridges, poisoning reservoirs, killing whole schools of children with poisoned chocolates, each mass killing involving hundreds and thousands of victims. He made no attempt to control these perverted imaginings and steadily got more pleasure out of them. Behind them, there was a completely illogical theory of revenge which he called 'compensatory justice'. For example, if he killed somebody, such as a child, who could in no way be blamed for his (Kürten's) imagined wrongs, then society, if there was such a thing as compensatory justice, must feel it in the same way even if society did not know who had committed the crime.

Soon after his release he was given two minor sentences for fraud and petty theft, and these were followed by a more severe two-year prison term for trying to intimidate a girl by firing shots at her and, through a window, at her family. After he was released in 1904, he was conscripted into the army but soon managed to desert. He went to live with a woman who joined him in his thieving activities until he was caught and sentenced to a further seven years in prison.

In May 1912 he was released again, but a few months later was convicted of attempted bodily harm when he shot at a waiter who had tried to interrupt a conversation that Kürten was having with a woman he was trying to pick up.

So far, he had not been linked with any sexual offences. Instead he began to specialize in robbing from certain kinds of buildings, preferably those with a public house on the ground floor and rooms or flats above them.

On 25 May 1913, however, he went to the Cologne suburb of Muhlheim, where he had been born, and found a suitable house to burgle in the Wolfstrasse and between ten and eleven o'clock managed to get upstairs. In one of the bedrooms he found thirteen-year-old Christine Klein asleep. He seized her by the throat and strangled her for about a minute and a half. She struggled and then lost consciousness. Kürten slashed her throat four times and penetrated her vagina with his fingers. The whole incident lasted about three minutes. One of the tragedies of this case was that her uncle Otto was accused of the crime but acquitted for lack of evidence. He died with the stigma still attached to his name. On the evening of the murder he had quarrelled with his brother, Christine's father Peter, and in a rage had sworn to do something that his brother would remember all his life. The police found by the girl's body a handkerchief with the initials P.K. which they assumed to be the name of the girl's father – Peter Klein. It was just conceivable that Otto might have borrowed the handkerchief, and this was one of the points of evidence which led to Otto Klein's acquittal.

A few months later Kürten crept into a bedroom where there were several children and a young girl of seventeen asleep. In a rush of feelings which he was later unable to explain he fell upon the girl and tried to strangle her before escaping unobserved. The bruises on her throat testified to the seriousness of the attack. In the summer he broke into another house and was about to strangle another girl, but somebody heard him and he was forced to flee. In the same period he attacked an unknown man and an unknown woman with an axe, in both cases reaching orgasm at the sight of their blood. He also tried to strangle two women.

Soon after the axe attacks he burned haywagons and hayricks. He had committed his first arson offences in 1904, setting fire to barns and hayricks. He found great delight in the sight of the flames, but more exciting still were the attempts to put out these fires and 'the agitation of those who saw their property being destroyed'.

The next eight years he spent in prison. He boasted subsequently that he poisoned some of the patients in the prison hospital where he went to work as a volunteer nurse. After his release he went to Altenberg, where his sister lived, and told her he had been a prisoner of war. She believed him and introduced him to the woman who became his wife despite rejecting his first advances because of his obvious success with other women. Apart from being a very hard-working and frugal person, she was also a very jealous one. She had been engaged to a gardener for eight years and had been his mistress; when he had refused to marry her she had shot him and had served four years of a five-year prison sentence. When Kürten threatened to kill her if she didn't marry him, she gave in and stuck loyally by him to the end. She didn't know of his prison sentences when they were married in 1923 and later regarded their marriage as some sort of penance in expiation of her own earlier sin. He struck her only once in their married life, but the incident made her realize that there was a violent side to his character. Philosophically, she shrugged off the gossip about her husband's conquests, knowing them to be true, and stubbornly justified her behaviour by arguing that without her he would go under completely.

For the first two years of their marriage Kürten was a steady and reliable worker. He stayed at home in the evenings and joined the trade union. The only discordant note was when he left the Catholic Church, which he decided to do because of a fund-raising church tax. He had no friends and was an extremely self-contained person. He was dismissed from his job because of general unemployment, and in 1925 he returned to Düsseldorf. He was delighted to see that the sky was blood red on the night of his return. It was a good omen for him and it was to mark the beginning of Düsseldorf's reign of terror. It started slowly. The first attacks were carefully spaced over the four years until 1929, when they accelerated into truly horrific proportions. Between 1925 and the end of 1928, Kürten later confessed, he had been responsible for three cases of attempted strangulation of women, and seventeen cases of arson involving barns, hayricks, hay wagons and, on two occasions, houses.

At the beginning of 1929 he committed six more crimes of arson. Then on 3 February, a woman, Frau Kuhn, was walking home from a friend's house when she was caught by the sleeve and savagely attacked. She was stabbed twenty-four times and lay in hospital for some weeks, unable to give any information as to what had actually happened. Kürten remembered that he had been feeling particularly excited. 'On that evening, if an animal had crossed my path I would have fallen upon it and killed it,' he said. He had leapt at Frau Kuhn with a pair of scissors, which he drove into her head several times. As he hurried away he had seen her pick herself up and stagger off. Kürten found afterwards that he had broken off the point of his scissors.

He had them ground down to a point again.

Ten days later, on the Tuesday of Carnival Week, he bumped into a 45-year-old mechanic, Rudolf Scheer, who was helplessly drunk. Kürten stabbed him twenty times with his scissors. On 8 March he had a different pair with him when he killed eight-year-old Rose Ohliger. He took her to a building plot and strangled her before he stabbed her thirteen times. Later the same evening he went back and tried to burn the body. This attempt was unsuccessful, and so was another when he went back to the spot for the third time early the next morning. Because of the damp the clothes would only char.

The local press, when they picked up these stories, also began to publish stories about London's Jack the Ripper with whose activities there were obvious parallels. In time they would refer to Kürten as the Düsseldorf Ripper. Some newspapers, as the savagery of the attacks increased, also referred to him as the Vampire and the Werewolf. The police were puzzled by the apparent inconsistencies of the attacks. It was clear that this was the work of no ordinary sex maniac. The victims, so far, had been a man, a woman and a child. Yet the stabbings in the temples, and the similarity of the cuts, all pointed to the attacks being the work of one man. In spite of hundreds of interrogations and plain-clothes police observations, there were no real leads.

In July Kürten tried in the space of twenty-four hours to strangle two more women. A sixteen-year-old-girl was lassoed from behind and dragged backwards to a hedge where her attacker knelt by her head and tried to strangle her with his hands. She caught hold of his nose and fought him off until she could get to her feet. Twenty-four hours later he attacked another woman in an identical manner. She remembered afterwards that he had knelt down by her head and listened to hear if she was still breathing. Because of the tightness of the lasso she couldn't open her mouth or scream. As he dragged her over the ground by the rope still around her throat, a couple out walking saw him and, although they couldn't make out what he was dragging along, except that it was large and heavy, they went to investigate and Kürten was forced to flee.

From their description the police arrested a 21-year-old epileptic named Hans Strausberg, who was living in a home on the outskirts of Düsseldorf. He couldn't read or write and had a cleft palate and a hare lip. When he was questioned he confessed not only to the attacks but to the killings as well. The discrepancies in his statements and vagueness of response to some of the questions that he was asked were put down to the loss of memory which is a frequent condition of epileptics, and he was committed to a lunatic asylum for life.

Only a few weeks later the reign of terror began again.

On 30 July a prostitute named Emma Gross was found lying naked in her room. She had been strangled. Kürten was not, as it happened, the murderer, but the killing set off a new wave of panic. On 21 August three people were stabbed from behind, at different times during the day, by an unknown assailant. Two of the victims were women. One was only slightly wounded but the other was more seriously hurt by a thrust through her liver and stomach. The third victim, a man, was stabbed in the small of the back; but fortunately the injury was lessened to some extent by the heavy leather braces (which were cut through) he was wearing.

There was an immediate outburst of press and public comment criticizing the police. Some people were already saying that the police had got hold of the wrong man and there were demands for Strausberg's immediate release. Faced with such a barrage of hostile criticism, the police intensified their efforts to catch the Düsseldorf Ripper. A special watch was kept on the fairs where intended victims might be picked up.

On 24 August the bodies of two foster sisters, one aged fourteen and the other five, were found on an allotment not far from their home. The youngest one had been strangled and stabbed and the older had been stabbed. Kürten later described how he had persuaded the older girl to go and buy him some cigarettes from the fair. While she was away he had killed her sister and, when she came back he took her to the same spot and stabbed her. She had run away screaming but he had chased after her and killed her by stabbing her in the back four times. On the Sunday when the bodies were discovered Kürten, still feeling sexually excited, picked up a servant girl named Schulte and introduced himself to her as Fritz Baugmart. In a wood he tried to have sexual intercourse with her but she told him that she would rather die first. 'Well die then,' he said, and stabbed her several times. The last savage thrust broke off the point of his knife which lodged in her back. Fortunately some young men nearby had heard her screams for help and came to her rescue. Kürten ran away. The woman could give only a confused description of her attacker. The only thing it seemed she could remember about him was that he had a tooth missing from his upper jaw.

The police conviction that there was more than one maniac at work was now strengthened. It seemed inconceivable that the same man would kill two children on a Saturday and, just over twelve hours later, try to commit a third murder.

Nearly a month later Kürten struck again. A domestic servant named Ida Reuter went to Düsseldorf to spend the afternoon and evening there. When she was found on the Monday morning it was apparent that she had been dragged from a footpath into some nearby woods and battered to death with a hammer. Kürten's later explanation for using the hammer was that he thought that he might get more enjoyment out of it. Her handbag and knickers were missing.

Ten days later Elisabeth Dorrier was killed in the same way. She was still breathing when she was found but she died before she regained consciousness. Her hat was missing, as were some fragments of her coat, which had been torn to ribbons.

On 25 October a 34-year-old woman, Frau Meurer, was accosted by a man in a lonely street in Flingern. 'Aren't you frightened? So much has happened here!' he said. Before she could turn her head, Kürten battered her unconscious with his hammer. She knew nothing more for an hour or two until she woke up in hospital. The force of the blows had broken the skin and exposed, but not broken, the bone. This attack had not given Kürten quite the satisfaction he wanted; later the same evening he attacked a woman in a park in the centre of town. He hit her four times, knocking her unconscious with the first blow, but when his hammer broke he left her alone.

On 7 November, five-year-old Gertrude Albermann was reported missing from her home. Her body was discovered, two days later, lying in some brick rubble and nettles, close to a factory wall. She had been strangled and stabbed thirty-six times with a pair of scissors.

Still more horrific was the news that the killer had sent a letter to a communist newspaper telling them exactly where they could find the body of a child *as well as the body of another victim*. There can be no doubt that at this point Kürten was imitating the Ripper's tactics. Kürten forwarded a sketch map showing where the body was; he drew it on some greyish-white wrapping paper and marked it: 'Murder at Pappendelle. In the place with a cross a corpse lies buried.' The police began to dig at once in the lonely meadows indicated on the map. A farmer handed in a bunch of keys and a battered straw hat which he had found some weeks before and these were soon identified as belonging to a domestic housekeeper, Maria Hahn, who had been missing since 14 August. There was a further storm of criticism about police failure to catch the Düsseldorf murderer, and the story of Jack the Ripper (which had been a newspaper standby almost since the murders had begun) now took a new turn as stress was laid on the fact that the Düsseldorf Ripper had copied him to the extent of writing to the police in exactly the same way. Kürten said that writing the letter had given him a sadistic satisfaction. On 14 November the body of the missing woman was found in a shallow grave. She was naked and had been stabbed twenty times in the temples, throat and breast.

All the resources of the Alexanderplatz, Berlin's equivalent of Scotland Yard, were now thrown into the biggest manhunt that had ever been launched. Nine thousand people were questioned in Düsseldorf alone, and in the fifteen months covering these attacks more than 900,000 people were denounced as possible suspects in different parts of the country. Only three out of these denunciations were made against Kürten. One was made by a fellow prisoner who had once heard him talking about sadistic practices. The second was by a woman who had known Kürten when she was a girl. From the descriptions of the stranglings she thought she recognized his habit of playfully strangling his girlfriends as they went walking in the woods. At his trial quite a number of women gave evidence about this. The woman was told, when she reported it, that nobody of Kürten's name existed at his address! The third informant was Christine Heerstrasse whom Kürten had half strangled and thrown into the river. When she reported this incident to the police she was laughed at and fined for her 'gross nonsense' and only escaped payment of it on appeal.

The police still thought that there were several maniacs at work – namely, the strangler, the killer with a knife, the hammer-wielding fanatic and a fourth who was using a weapon which they had not been able to identify but which with hindsight they knew to be the scissors. Kürten had gone out of his way to blur his tracks and to create this sort of confusion. He later admitted: 'I hoped by changing the methods to bring about the theory that there were several murderers at work.' More importantly, he thought that these variations would give him still greater sexual satisfaction. The police carried out intensive raids on the underworld to find him. They even dressed a tailor's dummy in the clothes of one of his victims and took it around the dance halls, cinemas and theatres in the hope that somebody might be able to identify her mysterious escort.

Soon afterwards, Kürten made the mistake that led to his capture.

On 14 May 1929, twenty-year-old Maria Budlick travelled to Düsseldorf to look for a new job. A friend who had arranged to meet her did not turn up, but a man who spoke to her on the station told her that he would show her the way to a girls' hostel. He took her through the main streets of Düsseldorf but when he turned into the Volksgarten, a public park, she became alarmed. She hung back, and refused to go any further with him, remembering the stories of the Düsseldorf monster. Fortunately a second man came along at this point and offered his help. It was Peter Kürten. Gratefully the girl explained what had happened and, as the first man scuttled away, she thankfully accepted Kürten's offer of a temporary rest and some food at his flat in the Mettmannerstrasse. She was disappointed to see how poorly furnished his attic rooms were, but after some milk, bread and ham she insisted on leaving as it was now after eleven o'clock and she had to find lodgings. They went the last part of the journey by tram. But instead of going towards the centre of Düsseldorf they were going, in fact, towards the Grafenberg woods, to a dell which was locally known as the Wolf's Glen. After they got off the tram and had been walking for only a little way Kürten suddenly stopped and tried to kiss her. He told her that she could scream as nobody would hear. She struggled violently and Kürten tried to have intercourse with her standing up. Suddenly he let go of her throat and asked her if she remembered where he lived. She said no. The lie saved her life, and trapped Kürten.

He showed her the way out of the woods and let her go. Instead of going to the police, the girl said nothing at all about the incident to anyone. It was only when she wrote about it in a letter to a friend that it came to light. Fate took a hand: the letter was wrongly addressed and the woman who opened it immediately realized its probable significance and handed it to the police. The police just as quickly contacted the girl and asked her to identify Kürten's house. She remembered the name of the street, as she had seen it by the light of a lamp, but she hadn't seen the number of the house. She walked up and down the street several times before picking one house out. Only when she was at the top of the four flights of stairs did she feel almost certain that she had picked the right house. When she was shown into Kürten's flat she immediately recognized it as the one that she had been brought to. As she came out onto the landing she saw, coming upstairs, the fair-haired man who had picked her up and attacked her. He started when he saw her and hurried downstairs again, walking briskly away. The landlady wrote his name down on a piece of paper: Peter Kürten.

That same evening Kürten went to call for his wife, who normally worked until 4.30 a.m., and told her that he would have to leave the flat for a while because of this girl. It was only an assault case, he explained, but with his record it would mean a fifteen-year sentence. He walked about the streets all Wednesday night, and hid in a room which he rented close by until the Friday morning when he met his wife as arranged. She told him that the police had searched their flat and that he wasn't to go back there as she didn't want him to be arrested at home. It was then that he told her he was wanted for the other attacks and persuaded her to go to the police. The next day they had their fateful meeting outside St Rochus church and he was arrested.

His wife could never understand what other girls saw in him. She never suspected his perversions and Kürten had been obliged to fantasize acts of sadistic violence in order to go through with their irregular bouts of marital intercourse. However, she was used to his infidelities. Soon after they were married she had had to talk a girl into dropping an assault charge. Less than a year before she had publicly slapped a girl's face when she saw her give her husband a rose in the street. (Kürten had playfully brushed it against her cheek as he had turned on his heel and walked away. At the time he had a pair of scissors in his pocket, with which he was planning to stab the young girl if the opportunity arose.) Later that same afternoon he half strangled a girl he picked up, and she later gave evidence that for days afterwards the marks of his fingernails were clearly visible on her neck.

The women who came forward and testified against him clearly enjoyed being treated brutally. Brutality, Kürten had told them, 'belongs to love'. His charm and fascination were undeniable. He boasted once to a fellow workman, 'Come with me to the Rhine meadows and I'll show you, on a Sunday afternoon, I can count them – ten to each hand.' Sometimes, to demonstrate that the blame wasn't always his, he would arrange a rendezvous with a girl and take his wife with him as his sister so that she could see how the women ran after him. Occasionally his outings were likely to end in a scene as the love-making wasn't always one way. On one occasion she had come home unexpectedly and caught him in bed with a girl, but he had as gracefully as ever extricated himself from this compromising situation with a facile explanation which she had docilely accepted.

His trial opened on 13 April 1931, nearly a year after his arrest. In accordance with German custom, it was presided over by three judges. The courtroom was the drill hall of Düsseldorf police headquarters, specially converted for the occasion, and the dock was a hastily improvised wooden construction resembling a cage. In a room behind the court was a veritable museum of exhibits. In *The Monster of Düsseldorf: the life and trial of Peter Kürten*, Margaret Seaton Wagner writes: 'Here were the prepared skulls of his victims showing the various injuries inflicted by scissors or hammer blows, the weapons themselves, articles of clothing belonging to the dead women and children, and the spade used to bury Maria Hahn.'

He was indicted for nine murders and seven attempted murders. No less than forty cases of arson were omitted. There was some speculation that he might retract his confession, as he had done once before while awaiting trail, but now that the spotlight was on him he didn't hesitate to play to the hilt the role of monster.

Among the women who testified against him was one referred to as Charlotte U. Unwittingly she testified to the ease with which Kürten could persuade women to go with him to a lonely spot, even at the height of the terror. Margaret Seaton Wagner quotes his statement in court:

I met a girl, and we had a glass of beer together and then went to the Grafenberg woods. I was able to calm away her fears of the dark and the murderer; I said there were always couples about the woods. At the spot called Beautiful View I gave her a blow with my hammer on the right temple. She dropped with a scream; I left her lying there after hitting her several times. The hammer was as big as those I had been using before. I saw the blood flowing.

She had seen him take something out of his pocket and when he hit her she felt the blood running down her face like water from a tap. She was able to save her life by protecting her head with her hands. Afterwards she bandaged it up with her underskirt and hid for a fortnight until the wounds healed. She didn't dare go to the police. If she had done so, she might have brought about Kürten's arrest much sooner.

An interesting point that came out at the trial is that killing was not always necessary to Kürten's sexual relief. This explained why again and again his victims were allowed to recover consciousness, or even why, when they were battered and stabbed, they were still allowed to get up and stagger away while Kürten still had them in view and could have quite safely killed them. The question that the court had to decide was whether he acted with premeditation before or after these attacks. Professor Karl Berg, who examined him, said that with the exception of the Klein case in 1913, they were not the acts of irresistible impulse. Kürten was always fully in command of the situation. Occasional lapses of memory in some of the details he recalled were attributable to sexual excitation. Neither insanity nor irresistible impulse could be put forward as a defence for these murders.

Some of the details Kürten revealed were quite horrifying. Once, when he could not find a victim, he cut the head off a sleeping swan and drank the blood. In a dream he pictured himself as saving the city from the Düsseldorf murderer, a torchlight procession being given in his honour, and himself being nominated as a commissioner of police. Margaret Seaton Wagner says: 'He pictured himself being badly wounded in a fight with the vanquished mass-murderer, lying ill in a hospital with the populace storming the building to do honour to Kürten, whose recovery was hampered by their attentions. At the time of his arrest he had probably reached the climacteric of his sexual life.'

In the prosecution's address it was revealed that twelve thousand individual clues were followed up; that two hundred people gave themselves up for the murders; and that about two hundred and fifty accusations were received by the police on average each day.

The case ended on 23 April. The jury deliberated for one and a half hours and when they returned Kürten was sentenced to death nine times for murder. The judge, giving detailed reasons for the verdict, underlined the point that Kürten had always acted with premeditation. He always armed himself with a weapon, he was always capable of leaving off an attack and there was always a carefully thought-out plan of flight and concealment of evidence. Throughout the trial he had 'created the impression of cleverness, calmness, and considered deliberation. Kürten is normal,' he said.

There was such a storm of controversy about the execution, which would have been the first since 1928, that for a time it seemed as if the sentence would not be carried out. Kürten, meanwhile, was being bombarded with letters, most of them anonymous, including love letters, poems and requests for autographs; he also received letters in equal numbers elaborating on the most horrible ways that he could be made to die.

He appealed against his sentence but on 30 June the Prussian Ministry of Justice, in secret session, turned it down. The information was leaked to the press that he was to be executed at 6 a.m. on 2 July.

Kürten was not told of the decision until twelve hours before his execution. He received the news quite calmly and spent the time he had left writing to the families of thirteen of his victims asking for their pardon. He claimed that since his arrest his sleep had not been disturbed by any more sado-erotic fantasies. His last meal, the Henkers-Mahlzeit, or hangman's meal, consisted of Wienerschnitzel, fried potatoes and white wine. He enjoyed it so much that he had a double helping.

At 6 a.m. as the 'poor sinners' bell' began to toll, he was led into the inner courtyard of Klingelputz prison in Cologne where the Magdeburg executioner was waiting for him, and walked briskly to the guillotine. His hands were tied behind his back and he was asked if he had any last request to make. He said 'No' in a quiet, firm voice. A few seconds later his head tumbled into the canvas bag.

He had told his psychiatrist that his last wish would be that he might have the pleasure of hearing his own blood running into the bag.

The Yorkshire Ripper

The trial of Peter Sutcliffe, dubbed by the press the Yorkshire Ripper because some of his victims were prostitutes and because of the way in which he mutilated some of the bodies, opened in London's Old Bailey, the Central Criminal Court, on 29 April 1981. He was charged with thirteen murders and seven attempted murders. Initially, the prosecution was prepared to accept a plea of diminished responsibility since the psychiatrists to be called were unanimous in their diagnosis of paranoid schizophrenia and it was unlikely that Sutcliffe would ever be released. The judge, however, having expressed some anxieties about such a plea, ruled against acceptance and ordered that the case be heard by a jury.

Opening the prosecution's case several days later, the Attorney-General said that what the jury had to decide was whether Sutcliffe, as 'a clever, callous murderer, deliberately set out to create a cock and bull story to avoid a conviction for murder'. There was a marked difference between the stories that Sutcliffe had told the police and the doctors.

Sutcliffe's defence would be that he had killed the women as part of a divine mission given to him by God to kill prostitutes. He had told the doctors when examined that his mission was only partially fulfilled and that the urge to kill could return (although there was no outside evidence for this). What the jury had to decide was whether this story was an attempt to fool the doctors and escape the mandatory life sentence which a murder conviction carries; or, alternatively, whether he really was suffering from diminished responsibility at the time of the killings. If the latter, then there was a possibility of a lighter sentence and an early release, although the balance of probabilities was against this. In prison he had been overheard to tell his wife Sonia that he expected to get thirty years but that if he could convince people that he was mad he would only get ten years in a 'loony bin'.

Sutcliffe's reign of terror in north-east England lasted for five years. More than £4,000,000 was spent in the hunt for him, but when he was eventually caught it was only as the result of a chance stop in the street by two uniformed policemen. There had been near-misses. Once he had nearly been caught when a man heard his girlfriend's screams and ran to her rescue. Another victim, Maureen Long, who had miraculously survived his murderous attack with a hammer, had passed by him in Bradford city centre only two weeks before he was captured, giving him a nasty turn as he recognized her, although she had not recognized him. Three times he went back to bodies when they had not been discovered, once after eight days and another time after a month, to mutilate or move them, each time risking capture. He was interviewed nine times by police, once when he was wearing his murder boots and the detective questioning him was holding a photograph of his boot sole. As the manhunt intensified, his car was repeatedly logged in the red-light districts of Leeds and Bradford; but each time he was interviewed he would explain it away by saying that he lived and worked in the area and was just passing through.

Undoubtedly, his biggest stroke of luck concerned three letters and a mocking cassette tape sent to the police in 1978–9 from someone claiming to be the killer, and appearing to have a detailed knowledge of the crimes, signing and identifying himself as Jack the Ripper. The letters all came from Sunderland; the margins were cut off where the writer might have left his finger-prints. The voice on tape had a flat, unemotional Geordie accent.

Although subsequently shown to be fake, the hoaxer seems to have implied direct comparisons with the 1888 murders, including the taunting suggestion that he might kill in September or October, consciously or not suggesting that almost a century later he might create a second autumn of terror. He mocked the police, as did the writer of the letter to Dr Openshaw in 1888, saying that the only time they had come near to catching him was when they had disturbed him a few months previously in the Chapeltown district of Leeds. Because of a theory that the letters and tape displayed similarities to the letters sent to the police in 1888, libraries in the north were checked to see if anything could be found out about readers who had borrowed books on the Whitechapel murders (I'm told that an earlier edition of this present book disappeared from the shelves completely). Although fake, the tape and letters were enough to send the police on what has been described as one of the wildest goose chases of all time. Twenty-four hours after they had been made public the police were inundated with more than three thousand calls from persons claiming that they could identify the man. Nobody ever did. But the trail had been so effectively blurred that even people who had had their doubts about Sutcliffe now shrugged off their suspicions and mentally struck him from the list of suspects.

Sutcliffe was described by a friend as a quiet, unaggressive man. He was one of a family of six and had left school when he was fifteen years old. The eleven jobs that followed included factory work, labouring and two spells as a gravedigger. Nine times out of ten, a workmate recalled, he would open up the coffins and rob the bodies of rings and other pieces of jewellery, sometimes forcing open the mouth to see if there were any gold teeth to be had. Even more macabre, he would sometimes use the body like a ventriloquist's doll or peer under bandages or into the plastic-bagged remains of road accident victims sometimes found in the coffins. As a mortuary attendant he enjoyed washing up the post-mortem instruments. It was during his second spell as a gravedigger that he claimed to have heard the voice of God speaking to him from the top of a cross.

After being sacked for bad timekeeping he qualified as a heavy goods driver. Prints from his moulded rubber boots, with the twist in the centre of the right sole which told police that the murderer was continually pressing some sort of pedal, were found at two of the murder scenes.

Sutcliffe courted his future wife Sonia for seven or eight years and eventually they were married in August 1974 when he was twenty-eight and she was twenty-four; they lived with her parents until they bought a house of their own in Bradford. They had no children. Sonia's regular job was as a supply teacher but one night a week she worked as a nursing auxiliary.

That was the night Sutcliffe usually chose for the killings.

Ten of his twenty attacks were on either the Friday or Saturday night when his wife was working. Cross-examined by Mr Ognall QC for the Crown, one of the consultant psychiatrists, Dr Milne, was asked: 'Why did God only direct him on Friday and Saturday nights?' Milne answered that he didn't think God did only direct him on those nights. 'Paranoid schizophrenics are extraordinarily cunning,' he explained, 'extremely involved in premeditation and determined not to be found.'

'That isn't the hallmark of a schizophrenic. It is the hallmark of the normal criminal,' was the crushing retort.

One of the explanations for his behaviour given by Sutcliffe was that in 1969, before they were married, in an attempt to get even with Sonia whom he suspected of seeing someone else, he had gone with a prostitute and been duped, not only out of the 'business', but also of the £10 that he paid her. Significantly, it was in September that same year, while being driven through Bradford's red-light district, that he asked his friend Trevor Birdsall to stop the car while he got out. He came back a little later, looking excited and as if he had been running. He told Birdsall that he had followed a woman and hit her on the head. He pulled a sock from his pocket and threw away the small brick or stone that it had been holding. Both men were subsequently interviewed by police but the matter was dropped as the woman did not press charges.

Later that same month Sutcliffe was arrested and charged with going equipped for theft. He was in possession of a hammer. It was in his mind to kill prostitutes.

Birdsall was with him again six years later when he brutally attacked 51-year-old Olive Smelt in Boothtown Road, Halifax on 15 August 1975. Sutcliffe again stopped the car on the pretext that he was going to see somebody. He seemed to reach down for something by the side of his seat as he got out. He was gone about twenty minutes and unusually quiet when he got back. Next day Birdsall read about the murderous attack on Olive Smelt the previous evening and it crossed his mind then that the two incidents might be linked. Smelt was walking home down an alleyway when she was hit about the head with a hammer fracturing the skull in two places. She remembered nothing until she woke up in hospital. On her back were two slash marks, twelve and four inches long respectively. Her attacker had been disturbed by a motorist who had driven up to the spot with his headlights full on.

Although Birdsall was suspicious he did nothing and, four years later, when he heard the Ripper tape, those suspicions disappeared completely only to reappear in 1980, after the final killing, when he thought that Sutcliffe's dark red Rover might belong to the Ripper. He was worried enough to send an anonymous note of his suspicions to the police before finally going to them in person.

Police subsequently linked the attack on Olive Smelt with one that Sutcliffe had carried out the previous month, on 4 July, on a 37-year-old divorcée named Anna Rogulsky. Sutcliffe attacked her as she tried to waken her boyfriend at his home near Keighley town centre. When there was no answer she took off a shoe and broke the ground floor window. Sutcliffe attacked her as she tried to get into the house. He had already seen her and spoken to her but when he asked her if she 'fancied it' he was rebuffed. Rogulsky was found in a nearby alleyway. Sutcliffe had hit her three times with a hammer and, lifting her clothes, had slashed her stomach with his knife. He was disturbed before he could finish her off and had to escape.

Later, when questioned about his compulsion to kill, he blamed it on a motorbike accident in which, he alleged, he had run into a telegraph pole and struck his head, telling some friends that it had caused him to lose consciousness for several hours and others for only half an hour. Since then, he said, he had suffered severe bouts of morbid depression and hallucinations. At his trial the Attorney-General commented that the jury should note that he made no mention of any directions from God but only of hallucinations and depressions.

Sutcliffe killed Wilma McCann on 30 October 1975. A milkman found her partly clothed body lying on a grass embankment about one hundred yards from her home in Leeds. Sutcliffe had intercepted her in the early hours of the morning and offered her a lift. She was separated from her husband, sexually promiscuous, drank too much and neglected her home and three children. Sutcliffe gave her the impression that he wanted to have sex. In reality, he wanted to kill a prostitute. As she got out of the car he hit her twice with the hammer, one of the blows being so hard that it penetrated the full thickness of the skull. She made a lot of noise after the first blow and so he hit her again. This did not silence her and so he stabbed her fourteen times in the chest and abdomen and once in the neck. None of the stabbings would have been fatal if they had occurred singly. It was the cumulative effect which killed her.

Asked why he disarranged her clothes after the murder Sutcliffe explained: 'When they find them [the prostitutes] they will look as cheap as they are.'

According to her husband, 42-year-old Emily Jackson had an insatiable sexual appetite and had numerous affairs. The Jacksons were in monetary difficulties and so, about four weeks before she was murdered and with her husband's agreement, she went to work as a prostitute. He would drive her to the Chapeltown Road area of Leeds and park while she solicited for business. If the client did not have a vehicle of his own she would take him back to the van. Her body was found in a works yard on 21 January 1976. Her head had been battered with a hammer and she had died of multiple stab wounds, those in the back being inflicted by a Phillips-type screwdriver. Altogether there was a total of fifty-two wounds in five groups. On her thigh and in some sand nearby was a bootmark which eventually matched a pair of Wellington boots found in Sutcliffe's Bradford home.

Four months later, he bungled a killing when on 9 May he picked up a twenty-year-old West Indian girl named Marcella Claxton on the Chapeltown Road. She had been to a party and had had a bit too much to drink. She suggested that they go to the Soldier's Field where he told her to strip off. Sutcliffe dropped his hammer as they got out of the car but attacked her with a knife until her screams forced him to run. Incredibly he stumbled across his hammer in the dark and so was able to retrieve it while the girl crawled to a telephone box and dialled for help. In hospital over fifty stitches were needed for the injuries to her head. She was able to give the police an accurate description of both her attacker and his car but, because of the change of weapon, they did not immediately make the connection with the other attacks and she was only added later as a 'possible'.

It was almost a year before Sutcliffe killed again. When asked why it was so long, he answered that it was because of his state of mind. 'I was having a battle in my mind. My mind was in a turmoil whether I should kill people.'

Almost as though seeking to wipe out the memory of the previous failure, Sutcliffe went back to Soldier's Field and chose a spot not far from where he had attempted to kill Marcella Claxton the previous year. The body of 28-year-old Irene Richardson was found on Sunday, 6 February 1977. She was out of work, separated and living in a bedsitter in Leeds. The cause of death was massive fractures to the skull – one of the blows had driven the skull three-quarters of an inch into the brain – and stab wounds to the throat and stomach.

Ten weeks later he murdered again. Like the 1888 murders, this was the only crime committed indoors. Patricia Atkinson, aged thirty-two, was last seen alive on Saturday, 23 April 1977 as, drunk and staggering, she made her way back to her flat in Oak Avenue, Bradford. Sutcliffe later commented: 'It was obvious why I picked her up. No decent woman would have been using language like that at the top of her voice.' Separated from her husband and three children, she lived alone, had convictions for prostitution and was probably alcoholic. Sutcliffe hit her from behind and, when he had killed her, hoisted her body onto the bed. He left his bootmark on the bottom sheet and this was identified as being possibly of the same size as that found at the scene of Emily Jackson's murder.

Now there was barely a pause between killings. Sixteen-year-old Jayne Macdonald was murdered on Saturday, 25 June 1977. She was a totally respectable young girl and her death was described by the Attorney-General as 'typically tragic'. She had been out for the evening and was quite prepared to walk home. The way home took her through the vice area of Chapeltown. Next morning her body was found by two small children in an adventure playground. She had been hit three times with a hammer, and stabbed some twenty times.

Two weeks later Sutcliffe attacked 42-year-old Maureen Long as, unsteadily, she left the Mecca ballroom in Bradford. Instead of a taxi she accepted a lift in Sutcliffe's car. Next morning, about 8.30 a.m., two women heard her cries for help coming from some waste ground not far from her husband's home. She had been attacked about five hours before and suffered a fractured skull and stab wounds to her back and abdomen. Not only was she able to describe Sutcliffe but a night watchman had seen his car driving away shortly after the attack. On a piece of broken kitchen sink the police found part of a bloodstained palmprint.

Slowly the police were building up details of the man they wanted – boot size, car makes, physical description and tyre treads. They came closer still following the murder of 21-year-old Jean Jordan. She was unemployed and had two cautions for soliciting. It was a disturbing story, said the Attorney-General; 'because she was not reported missing, no search was mounted for her'. She was last seen alive on Saturday, 1 October 1977. Her body was not found until Monday 10 October; it was lying on a disused allotment site at Chorley in Manchester – a favourite spot for prostitutes. Sometime during the previous twenty-four hours the murderer had gone back to the scene and dragged it out of hiding, stripped it and mutilated it. The reason for this was in the prostitute's green handbag, which was also found by the allotment holder. Inside was a brand new £5 note which had been given to Sutcliffe in his wage packet. There was a chance that it could be traced back to him, so he had gone back to search for the note, and in sheer frustration at not finding it had tried to cut off the victim's head.

At this point in the trial the judge intervened and asked if there was any particular reason why he had tried to do that?

'Yes,' Sutcliffe had answered, 'because she was in league with the Devil and between them they had hidden the £5, and I was going to do the same thing with her head. I felt great anger.'

'You are saying that she and her colleague, the Devil, had beaten you and your God.'

'It seemed very much so.'

The note was actually hidden in a small concealed compartment on the front of the handbag. Strenuous efforts were made to trace the note. Six thousand people were interviewed by the police. One of them was Sutcliffe. Like the others he denied ever having been paid it.

Just before Christmas, on 14 December, Sutcliffe attacked 25-year-old Marilyn Moore. She had been a prostitute for six years and was soliciting in the Chapeltown area when she was picked up by Sutcliffe who was cruising for business. They agreed on a price of £5 and drove away to some spare ground about a mile and a half away. Sutcliffe suggested that they get on the back seat. As she got out and tried the back door he came up behind her and hit her a savage blow on the head. She screamed in pain and put her hands on her head for protection as he beat her to the ground. The last thing she remembered before losing consciousness was trying to catch hold of his trousers. Fortunately her screams were heard by someone nearby and Sutcliffe was forced to run for cover. The hospital operated to release the pressure on her brain caused by a depressed fracture behind the left ear. She was able to give the police a good description of her attacker, including the fact that he wore a beard and had a drooping moustache like the television character Jason King.

Nineteen seventy-eight began with two fresh killings, although this was not realized right away. The body of the first victim lay hidden for two months. She was murdered in January. In February Sutcliffe murdered a pretty, eighteen-year-old Jamaican half-caste named Helen Rytka. She worked the streets in Huddersfield with her twin sister Rita. Both had been in care for most of their lives. Working together they evolved a safety routine. Punters were allowed no more than twenty minutes. If one went away in a car the other took down its number. On 3 February they missed each other by five minutes: while Rita was waiting for her sister, Sutcliffe was killing her in a timber yard close by. A police dog found the body two days later under some timber and corrugated asbestos, naked except for a jumper and bra pushed up above the breasts in the Ripper's familiar modus operandi. Sutcliffe later confessed that after she had got him aroused he persuaded her to get out of the car to have sex in the back. He mistimed his swing with the first blow of the hammer, catching it on the door; when she asked what it was, he said, 'Just a small sample of one of these,' and hit her again. Seeing that two taxi drivers had come into the yard and were talking nearby he dragged her by the hair to the other end, jumped on top of her and covered her mouth with his hand, telling her that she would be all right if she kept quiet. As she had already got him aroused he had sex with her. 'She didn't put much into it,' was his incredible comment. As she staggered to her feet, he attacked her again with the hammer before finishing her off with the kitchen knife that he had taken from the car.

The Attorney-General asked him, 'How did you manage, with your hatred of prostitutes, seething with rage, to bring yourself to have sexual contact with them?'

'I didn't have sexual hatred for them,' Sutcliffe explained.

He was reminded that he had been taunted and embarrassed by prostitutes, then came God's intervention and his deadly mission began. But 'Surprise, surprise, pretty little Helen Rytka, you went and had sex with her. Why?'

'I didn't have sex. I entered her, but there was no action. It was to persuade her everything would be all right.'

'God didn't tell you to put your penis into that girl's vagina. You had a choice.'

Reverting back to January 1976, the Attorney-General then asked why he had placed a piece of wood against Emily Jackson's vagina, which led in turn to the suggestion that he had stabbed his victims against their genital areas to obtain sexual gratification. Sutcliffe denied this.

On Sunday, 26 March, two months after she had been murdered, the body of 22-year-old Yvonne Pearson was found on a piece of waste ground in Bradford. She had last been seen alive on 21 January when she had left the Flying Dutchman pub to see if she could get some business. She was reported missing two days later. Her body was found underneath some debris, including an upturned settee; her right arm was entangled in the springs which showed that it had been put there after rigor mortis had set in. Sutcliffe had shattered her head with a walling hammer and then dragged her over to the settee from which he had stuffed filling down her throat to keep her quiet.

Sutcliffe murdered again on Tuesday, 16 May 1978, behind the Manchester Royal Infirmary. A man taking his son to Casualty thought he heard Vera Milward's dying screams as Sutcliffe battered her with his hammer. Next morning she was found lying in a compound behind the hospital, legs straight, fully clothed, and with her shoes on top of her body. She had one savage slash in her abdomen, so deep that her intestines had spilled out; she had then been rolled over and stabbed in the back before her killer had straightened her clothes. The combination of tyre tracks found nearby showed that the same car had been used for the murder of Irene Richardson and the attack on Marilyn Moore in 1977.

Sutcliffe's last six victims have a special significance. None of them were prostitutes, all were respectable women. This brought a change in the modus operandi employed. None of them could be picked up in the red-light districts and taken away to a deserted spot as had happened with the other victims. As the Attorney-General said: 'You can't pick them up and it is rather difficult to drive them to a quiet spot and it is unlikely, if you succeeded in that, that you could get them into the back of the car.'

Josephine Whitaker, nineteen, a building society clerk, had visited her grandparents' home in Halifax about a mile away from her own on Wednesday, 4 April 1979. One of the reasons for this impromptu visit was to show them the new watch that she had bought from a mail order club. At about 11.30 p.m. she said goodnight and left. Her way home took her through Savile Park in a well-lit residential area. A man walking his dog saw a man and a young woman walking side by side towards the park. Sutcliffe was chatting to her. Shortly before killing her he said, 'You can't trust anyone these days.'

Cross-examining, the Attorney-General asked: 'Can you think of a more horrible and cynical thing to say to someone you were just about to murder?'

'No.'

'Why did you say it?'

'Because I couldn't trust myself.'

'You were trying to convince her she was safe with you?'

'Yes, in a sense.'

'Did God tell you to do that?'

'No.'

'It was a bit of private enterprise on your part?'

'It was what I thought.'

Sutcliffe had stopped and, feigning poor eyesight, had asked her to look at the church clock to get her to stand still while he jockeyed her into position.

'Did God tell you to tell that poor girl to look at the church clock?'

'Yes.'

'Are you just standing there telling us deliberate lies?'

'No.'

Sutcliffe hit her twice, fracturing the skull from ear to ear, before dragging her back into the park. He had specially sharpened a giant Phillips screwdriver before coming out. He stabbed her twenty-five times. A man walking in the park heard a noise, the type of noise that makes your hair stand on end.

The same terrible weapon was used to murder Barbara Leach, a twenty-year-old student living in Bradford. On Saturday, 1 September 1979 she had been to a pub party and when it broke up decided to go for a short walk to clear her head. She was wearing a pair of jeans with a 'Best rump' patch on the back pocket. Her body was not found until the Monday afternoon. It had been squashed into a dustbin recess and was covered with a carpet weighted down by bricks. As with two of the other victims her cheesecloth shirt and bra had been pushed up to expose her breasts. She had been hit with the hammer once and stabbed with the Phillips eight times.

The murder precipitated an unprecedented million-pound police publicity campaign to swamp the public with information. There were mobile exhibitions, continuous broadcasts of the Ripper tape, newspaper challenges ('The Ripper is a Coward'), two million copies of a four-page newspaper devoted solely to the killer, freefone telephone lines to hear the mocking tape and police Project R, 'Help us Catch the Ripper'. A quarter of a million people were interviewed, there were 17,000 suspects, 26,000 homes were visited, 175,000 vehicles were checked, and reward money offered totalling £30,000.

The Ripper went to ground. It was nearly a year before he killed again, with a temporary change in method.

He was driving through Farsley, a district of Pudsey between Leeds and Bradford, when he saw walking towards him Miss Marguerite Walls, a 47-year-old executive officer at the local Department of Education and Science. She was going on holiday and had been working late. It was late in the evening, about 10.45 p.m., on 20 August 1980. Sutcliffe was already in a rage, heading for Liverpool with the intention of killing a prostitute. Miss Walls happened to be in the wrong place at the wrong time. Sutcliffe parked the car, went after her and struck her on the head. As he did so he shouted out, 'You filthy prostitute.' Bloodstains were found by the gateway of the house where she was attacked. Sutcliffe dragged her into the driveway, across a rockery and into a wooded area where he strangled her. He stripped her body naked except for her tights and hid it under some grass cuttings where it was discovered the next day after her shoes were found by the driveway and, near the rockery, her skirt, shopping bag and cheque book. It was his twelfth killing.

The change of method caused the police to rule out any connection between this and the other murders. Not until Sutcliffe confessed to it some five months later were they aware of the link. Even then he was reluctant to admit to it, fearing that it could open up completely new lines of inquiry on other murders which he hadn't done, including one at Preston that had already been wrongly attributed to him.

Asked why he had changed his method of killing, Sutcliffe said that it was because of the stigma that had been attached to him. He added that he did not like strangulation because that way his victim took too long to die. Clearly he did not abandon it, however, since a length of cord was found in his pocket when he was arrested.

Just over a month elapsed before he struck again. Dr Uphadya Bandara was on a year's scholarship at Leeds University's Nuffield Centre. On 24 September 1980 she was walking home when she heard footsteps behind her and she moved to one side to let the person pass. Next thing she knew, a bearded man had slipped a rope about her neck and she was struggling to prise it free. She lost consciousness. When she regained her senses a policeman was standing over her. Sutcliffe hadn't had time to finish her off.

Although a link was established between this attack and the murder of Marguerite Walls, neither was seen as part of the Ripper attacks. Nor was the next one, this time on bonfire night, 5 November, when he attacked sixteen-year-old Theresa Sykes only thirty yards from her home in Huddersfield. She had gone to buy some cigarettes and was on her way back when Sutcliffe struck. Asked why he had picked her Sutcliffe could only reply, 'I think something clicked because she had on a straight skirt with a slit in it. She crossed the road in front of me.' As the girl fell screaming to the ground Sutcliffe struck again at her unprotected head. She tried to grab at the weapon but already her screams had been heard by her boyfriend who came racing out into the street. Fast as he was, Sutcliffe was faster. It was the nearest he came to being caught. He escaped by hiding in a front garden until the boyfriend went back to the injured girl.

He murdered his last victim, number thirteen, on 17 November 1980. Jacqueline Hill was a trainee probation officer planning to become a full-time one when she left Leeds University. She was walking back to her hall of residence in Headingley, having been to a seminar, when Sutcliffe, who had just got off a bus, saw her at about 9.30 p.m. He attacked her with his ball pin hammer just as a car appeared. He threw himself to the ground as it passed by, and surprisingly was not seen. Jacqueline Hill was still alive and moving about so he struck her again before dragging her fifty yards onto some waste ground, tearing off her clothes and stabbing her in the lungs with a screwdriver.

'Her eyes were open and she seemed to be looking at me with an accusing stare. This shook me up a bit, so I stabbed her in the eye.' (In court the Attorney-General held up the yellow-handled screwdriver, bent at the tip, and demonstrated how it was placed on the eyeball and then banged down with the palm of the hand.) The murder coincided with the formation of a 'think tank' of experienced police officers drawn from different forces to bring fresh minds to the problem of how to secure the Ripper's capture. In 1978 there had been a Prostitute Murder Squad of a dozen men; the squad had been named thus to avoid using the press label of 'The Ripper', although the Ripper Squad is what they were immediately called. Later on, there were references to Ripper Task Force officers. The clumsy and inaccurate name Prostitute Murder Squad was an attempt to avoid glorifying the killer by the more famous nomenclature. Failure to capture him led to increasing criticism. At a press conference the West Yorkshire police were asked if they were going to call in the Yard to help them catch the Ripper. There was a pause before one of the investigating officers witheringly replied: 'Why should we? They haven't caught theirs yet.'

To have brought in the Yard might have seriously shaken morale as well as betrayed a lack of confidence in the investigating officers. Fortunately there was no need.

Sutcliffe was caught on Friday, 3 January 1981, not by any super squad but by two policemen on a normal patrol who saw him parked with a 24-year-old prostitute named Olive Reivers. A fee of £10 had been agreed, but Sutcliffe didn't really want sex. He just wanted to talk about his domestic problems. He had come away from home because of his wife's constant nagging, he said; and then the girl herself had put him off by telling him that she had just been with a big fat taxi driver who smelled. When questioned, Sutcliffe told the policemen that Reivers was his girlfriend, but that story disintegrated when he could not tell them her name. This alerted them that all was perhaps not as it should be. A call on their radio revealed that his Rover licence plates were false. Both of them were arrested. But Sutcliffe, saying that he needed to urinate, was allowed to go behind a nearby storage tank, where he got rid of his ball pin hammer and knife. At the police station he managed to drop a second knife into a lavatory cistern. All three weapons were subsequently recovered. In his pockets was found the length of cord he had wound about Dr Bandara's neck.

Reivers would have been his fourteenth victim. Reviewing the range of weapons he was carrying, the Attorney-General said that 'All the options were covered.'

After his first police interview it was a further twenty-four hours before Sutcliffe was questioned again. This time lapse was crucial to the inquiry as it was then that one of the arresting officers went back to the oil tank and found the hammer and knife. In Sutcliffe's pocket they had already found the cord used on Dr Bandara. In his garage they found the yellow-handled screwdriver and hacksaw. When interviewed for a second time Sutcliffe was challenged by Detective Inspector John Boyle on his reason for going behind the oil tank: 'I think you went there for another purpose.'

When he didn't reply, Boyle asked: 'Do you understand what I am saying? I think you are in serious trouble.'

Sutcliffe answered: 'I think you have been leading up to it.'

'Leading up to what?'

'The Yorkshire Ripper?'

'What about the Yorkshire Ripper?'

'Well, it's me.'

After this admission Sutcliffe felt the need to talk. He unburdened himself in a statement that took nearly sixteen hours to take down. Asked if he knew the names of his victims, he replied: 'Yes. They are all in my brain, reminding me of the beast that I am.'

In Armley Gaol, Leeds, Sutcliffe was interviewed eleven times by a consultant forensic psychiatrist, Dr Hugo Milne. Milne was one of three psychiatrists who gave evidence at the trial. Although presented by the prosecution their evidence was also the basis of the defence. Milne began his interviews with the suspicion that Sutcliffe might try to feign madness but by the time of the third he was sure that he was ill, extremely dangerous, and that he had been a paranoid schizophrenic for the past fifteen years. In Sutcliffe's past there was already the model of a schizophrenic; this was his wife Sonia, who had suffered from the same delusions of grandeur in 1972. She had had a delusion that she was the second Christ. Sutcliffe's symptoms were similar to those displayed by his wife. She had been treated for her illness and it was subsequently suggested that he could have learned in this way how to simulate mental illness. The most that Milne would concede was that Sutcliffe could have learned 'ideas of reference' but not schizophrenic thinking. His ability to detach himself from his crimes was one of the symptoms of paranoid schizophrenia. Other symptoms were uncontrollable impulses, paranoia concerning prostitutes, over-controlled behaviour, misidentification ('his confusion at times to identify absolutely and with certainty who were and who were not his victims – that is, prostitutes'), religious delusion (ideas of grandeur and special powers), mind control, thought argument (between his mind and a voice) and psychotic detachment (his ability to divorce himself from the enormity of what he had done). A schizophrenic could be in and out of touch with reality. In layman's terms schizophrenia was a madness but it was Dr Milne's opinion that 'because people might be clinically mad they are not necessarily out of contact with reality'.

On the third day of cross-examination Dr Milne was reminded that prison officers had given evidence that Sutcliffe expected to go to prison for a long time unless he could convince the doctors that he was mad. Asked what he made of that in the context of the evidence, Dr Milne replied: 'Either he is a competent actor or I am an inefficient psychiatrist . . . Perhaps I have been duped.' There were only three matters that could confirm Sutcliffe's account of his illness: photographs of Bingley cemetery where Sutcliffe said he had heard the voice (the judge commented in his summing-up that this was like being told that someone had swum the English Channel and, in response to a request for proof, being shown the Channel); Sutcliffe's evidence; and forensic evidence relating to Yvonne Pearson, one of his murder victims.

Sutcliffe consistently denied that his attacks had given him sexual excitement. The psychiatrist said that there was no suggestion that he had sexual sadistic deviation. He was convinced that the killings were not sexual and that the stabbings had no sexual components. In one of the eleven interviews Sutcliffe had related how he had heard a voice coming from a Polish grave: 'It was an echoing voice, vague and distant . . . and it was direct from the stone itself.' He had decided that it was some kind of message from God. He had been encouraged to kill 'scum'. Sutcliffe denied trying to mutilate his victims. There was no reason to do so. He exposed them, pushing the clothes up above the breasts or below the pubic region to show them for what they were. 'It's only a matter of killing them,' he said.

Milne could find no definite reason for Sutcliffe stabbing his victims through the same wound hole on repeated occasions. He did not believe that the action contained any significant sexual symbolism. Sutcliffe had wondered if the killings had been part of God's purpose to get him back into the faith. He had been brought up a Catholic and was regularly attending mass in prison. God was in the dock with him. Sutcliffe added, 'I surprised myself I had to confess so little. God shares the killings with me.'

Milne's conclusion was that Sutcliffe believed he had a mission to kill prostitutes and that it was at the direction of God, with whom he was in constant communication. Sutcliffe had been mentally ill at the time of his attacks on all twenty women and this had substantially diminished his responsibility for them.

One contradiction was immediately apparent. He now believed that all of his victims were prostitutes, which contradicted an earlier statement that some of them were not.

The Attorney-General analysed the dates of the interviews with Dr Milne. It was not until the seventh, two months after his arrest, that Sutcliffe had spoken of his mission. The voice from the Polish grave was not mentioned until the eighth. This posed the question why had it taken him so long to tell the doctors of this compelling reason for the attacks. Dr Milne had described Sutcliffe as being of higher than average intelligence. That would be the requirement for sustaining a lie; it would be very difficult to do so with a poor IQ.

Cross-examined, Dr Milne agreed that if Sutcliffe knew that the last six women he attacked were not prostitutes then the divine mission theory was in smithereens. Milne explained to Mr Ognall, who was cross-examining, that Sutcliffe never wanted to be seen as a sexual killer. Mr Ognall dealt with this by retorting that the reason why Sutcliffe didn't want to be seen as a sexual killer was that if he put himself forward as that then the divine mission went out of the window. The greater number of instances of sexual molestation there were the more the validity of the diagnosis was undermined. Mr Ognall then reminded the jury of certain components of some of the attacks which were quite clearly sexual. It had been a sexual act to insert the screwdriver three times into Josephine Whitaker's vagina; to stab Jacqueline Hill through the breast; to push a piece of wood against Emily Jackson's vagina; to scratch Olive Smelt's buttocks with a piece of hacksaw blade; and to leave fingernail scratches on the entrance to Marguerite Walls's vagina. Although agreeing that there were obvious sexual components in the attacks, Dr Milne would not agree with Mr Ognall's assertion that 'This isn't a missionary of God, it is a man who gets a sexual pleasure out of killing these women.'

Dr Terence Kay, a consultant forensic scientist, agreed with his colleagues that Sutcliffe was a paranoid schizophrenic. He did not believe that Sutcliffe was a sadist-killer. Had he been so, he would have expected the sexual aspect to have been present in all except the first one or two cases and to spread, so that in the final killings there would have been greater mutilations than in the first. Nor did the use of a hammer, because of its speed, suggest a sadistic killer. Multiple knifings could be explained by a sadistic killer but the usual emphasis was on the slowness of death and the agony of the victim.

A third psychiatrist said that it had taken him only thirty minutes to diagnose paranoid schizophrenia.

Mr Ognall's devastating cross-examination of the psychiatrists, and the judge's decision to have committed the case for trial, led to a thorough investigation of the medical diagnosis which the psychiatrists had not expected to have to defend publicly. But as the judge said when summing up, the psychiatrists were not on trial.

In the prosecution's final address the Attorney-General said that what the jury had to decide was whether Sutcliffe was 'mad or just plain bad'. He reminded them that the doctors had based their views on the statement of just one man – Sutcliffe. His hatred of prostitutes was nothing to do with a message from God: 'How convenient after that for the mission to appear.'

Summing-up, the judge said that the question that had to be answered was whether Sutcliffe believed that he was directed or instructed by God to kill prostitutes. 'Put it another way: did he, though deluded, believe that he was acting under a divine mission to kill prostitutes?'

It took the jury just under six hours to reach their verdict. By a majority of 10–2 they found Peter Sutcliffe guilty of murder. They rejected the divine mission; in their view he was sane.

Sentencing Sutcliffe to life imprisonment, the judge said that he hoped that the sentence would mean precisely that, but added a recommendation that he should serve a minimum of thirty years. The judge further added that the psychiatrists were of the opinion that he should be locked up for life. (It was estimated that, at the current rate of inflation, the cost of keeping him in prison for that length of time would be likely to reach about £3,000,000.)

Asked by his brother why he had done the murders, Sutcliffe smiled and said: 'I were just cleaning up the streets, our kid. Just cleaning up the streets.'

10. Conclusion

I have tried throughout this book to take a long, hard look at what is known about Jack the Ripper, and attempted to clear away some of the many obscurities that bedevil researchers. My modest objective has been to return to basics and to encourage others to do the same, while we are still close enough to the Ripper's time to add – with luck – just a few more facts to the precious few that we do know about him. Nobody can stop the 'legend' of Jack the Ripper from finally triumphing over these facts. Indeed, it can be argued that it has already done so. Jack the Ripper, over a hundred years of his crimes, is already part folk hero, part myth.

There is one thing, however, of which we can be sure. Children once used to chant it in skipping games in the East End of London.

> 'Jack the Ripper's dead,
> And lying on his bed.
> He cut this throat
> With Sunlight soap.
> Jack the Ripper's dead.'

Bibliography

BEGG, PAUL, FIDO, MARTIN and SKINNER, KEITH, *The Complete Jack the Ripper A to Z* (John Blake Publishing Ltd, 2010).

CORFE, TOM, *The Phoenix Park Murders* (Hodder & Stoughton, 1968).

EVANS, S.P. and RUMBELOW, DONALD, *Jack the Ripper: Scotland Yard Investigates* (Sutton Publishing Ltd, 2006).

EVANS, S.P. and SKINNER, KEITH, *The Ultimate Jack the Ripper Source Book* (Robinson, 2000).

HOUSE, ROBERT, *Jack the Ripper and the Case for Scotland Yard's Prime Suspect* (Wiley, 2011).

ODELL, ROBIN, *Written & Red: The Jack the Ripper Lectures* (Timezone Publishing, 2009).

RULE, FIONA, *The Worst Street in London* (Ian Allan Publishing, 2008).

TROW, M.J., *Jack the Ripper: Quest for a Killer* (Wharncliffe True Crime, 2009).

TROW, M.J., *Ripper Hunter: Abberline and the Whitechapel Murders* (Wharncliffe True Crime, 2012).

Whitechapel Society, *Jack the Ripper: The Suspects* (History Press, 2011).

Index